WORLD CLASS SELLING

WORLD CLASS SELLING

The Crossroads of Customer, Sales, Marketing and Technology

JIM HOLDEN

John Wiley & Sons, Inc.

NEW YORK • CHICHESTER • WEINHEIM • BRISBANE • SINGAPORE • TORONTO

This book is printed on acid-free paper. ♾

Published by John Wiley & Sons, Inc.
Published simultaneously in Canada.

Library of Congress Cataloging-in-Publication Data:

Holden, Jim, 1948–
World class selling : the crossroads of customer, sales, marketing and technology / Jim Holden.
p. cm.
Includes bibliographical references and index.
ISBN 0-471-32605-4 (cloth : alk. paper). — ISBN 0-471-32877-4 (pbk. : alk. paper)
1. Selling. 2. Sales personnel. I. Title.
HF5438.25.H637 1999
658.85—dc21 98-48341

Printed in the United States of America.

10 9 8 7 6 5 4 3 2 1

Let the wise listen and add to their learning, and let the discerning get guidance

Proverbs 1:5

Foreword

JOACHEM KEMPIN
Senior Vice President, OEM Division
Microsoft Corporation
Redmond, Washington

World Class Selling builds on Jim Holden's first book, *Power Base Selling,* which was published in 1990. In this new book, Holden advances his proven sales and marketing methodology by redefining the sales and marketing process as "value management." It is written for a much larger audience than just the sales and marketing executive. Holden demonstrates that a company constantly striving to improve value for its customers might ultimately have to change how it does business. Therefore, this book contains critical food for thought for CEOs, COOs, and CFOs in addition to extremely helpful sales and marketing strategies, tactics, and implementation tools. The integration of all corporate entities with the single goal of improving customer value and, therefore, shareholder value, is applicable to a majority of companies today. In describing the changes a company might be required to undertake to achieve improved customer value and outshine the competition, the author honestly points out how painful this might be and how much political in-fighting it could generate in companies that still operate with less than optimal customer focus in mind.

In a change from the more professorial style of *Power Base Selling,* this book is presented in a rather unusual "personal dimensioning" style of writing. As a business topic, it is real life, engaging the reader immediately, as it tells the compelling story of a younger sales executive who faces an incredible challenge in order to deliver the right value to her customers. The company for which she is working, and some of its key executives, are still operating in the past while she is trying to energize all forces to change their future way of doing business. This dilemma, which becomes a serious challenge for her, weaves a thread through all chapters, making the reader eager to follow along. While doing so, he will probably side with her and look for the desired outcome. As the story unfolds, the reader learns how to align sales, marketing, and technology, formulate competitive strategies, and how to map out political infrastructures within and outside a company. This book also teaches how to outmaneuver the opposition.

The question, "will the good guys win?" is left open as in any good story—until the end. However, the answer becomes less important as readers at all business levels become engaged with learning how to develop methods to improve their own situation, and the competitive advantage of their company.

The Holden Corporation and its value concept teachings are not new to the Microsoft OEM division. For the past three years, we have worked with them, immersing ourselves in their value management methodology, applying it to a variety of scenarios in our business, with excellent results. During that time, we have seen a steady fine-tuning of this method by Holden, without deviating from its original message. For us, *World Class Selling* is another great extension of what we have been practicing for some time. I am sure it will make us an even better organization to reckon with.

Reading and understanding the advanced ideas presented here, and their implications, will be challenging for readers not yet familiar with this subject. For technology leadership companies, where self-centered product concepts sometimes cloud executive thinking, this reading might serve as a real wake-up call. Customer intimacy often is not the strength of these companies, but in order to excel in our fast-changing environment, the lessons being taught here might be the only way to succeed in the future.

I hope all readers will find *World Class Selling* as compelling as I did, and will use it to make great strides toward the dream of increased competitive immunity, by implementing the key "value management" concepts they learn from it.

Acknowledgments

In business, the true origin of innovation resides with a company's customers. The marketplace influences our thinking and creativity in many ways, providing direction and guidance to the discerning company. The concept of value chain management grew out of such guidance. And so, I would like to thank Holden Corporation's many customers for the inspiration they have provided.

Discernment also is a human quality. Over the years, Holden Corporation has built one of the strongest and most caring staffs in our industry. The value-centric company orientation that has resulted spurs our business forward on a foundation of customer loyalty, supported by a staff of dedicated, talented, and loyal employees. They make the concept work, which created the opportunity for sharing the results in *World Class Selling*. For that I am most grateful.

This book has been a labor of love. Sharing the adventure with me, providing world class editing and support, has been Carol Jose. Writer, author, and editor extraordinaire, she is my friend, and for several years now she has been my writing mentor. *World Class Selling* and its new concept of *personal dimensioning* are a result of the countless hours we have spent together developing plot lines, characters, and intellectualizing the process of applying a virtual business fictional overlay to the objective and practical business content of the book.

Also contributing is a new friend and advisor, who has provided me with guidance and direction in the area of fiction. Robert A. Mitchell, when reviewing my new novel, an international thriller, pointed me to a writing process that has become the fictional backbone to *World Class Selling*.

My thanks also to Professional Examining Service, an authority in validation and reliability testing of assessment and diagnostic tools like those found in *World Class Selling*, for their review and validation guidance.

And I want to thank my publisher, John Wiley & Sons. Few authors are privileged to have the kind of close working relationship that I enjoy with my publisher, most particularly executive editor Henning Gutmann. When I first developed the concept of *personal dimensioning* for business writing, Henning listened, provided encouragement, and ultimately made *World Class Selling* a reality.

J.H.

CONTENTS

INTRODUCTION

Selling at the Forefront of Change

Today's marketplace is no longer an extension of the past, where becoming highly proficient in yesterday's sales methods and practices would win the day. Optimizing legacy practices will not work in the face of today's business trends and challenges. They require new, nontraditional thinking and a value-centric focus, one that has strong organizational as well as personal selling implications. Add to that significant cross-functional considerations involving the role of technology, sales and marketing integration, sales and human resource integration, training, and development, and you have a completely new role for sales professionals and executives at every level of every company, right up to the CEO.

Every sales and marketing professional and every company executive committed to world class superiority must consider these new market issues, explore them, and position themselves to take advantage of the opportunities, meet the challenges, and avoid the pitfalls associated with today's changing marketplace. For many, it will be survival of the fittest, requiring that we sell differently, and that our companies organize themselves to operate differently.

The purpose of *World Class Selling* is to examine in depth the significant personal and organizational implications of selling in today's marketplace and to illustrate how best to deal with those implications to ensure your personal success and that of your company.

This book is in a different format from standard business writing. It is written in a manner that I call *personal dimensioning*. Fictional characters, cast in a virtual business setting, deal with how industry trends victimize a salesperson of fifteen years' experience, launching her and her company on a quest to climb the value chain ahead of their competitors.

Blueprinting the integration of sales, marketing, human resources, and technology must deal with not only the challenges of creating a more value-centric organization, but must also confront internal company politics, the ever-present informal dimension to any significant change management effort.

Sales professionals have always lived under competitive threat, but today that threat profile has changed. Sales effectiveness requires new, organizational cross-functional support which, when not formally present, thrusts salespeople into an internal and informal change management role, one that quickly introduces career enhancing opportunities, or conversely, limiting consequences.

Value Chain Management

To characterize this new role, we interpret market trends from a strategic point of view and translate them into new, nontraditional approaches to selling that will drive competitive advantage and profitably increase sales. We will look at:

- Identifying and shaping new, nontraditional customer buying patterns.
- Segmenting markets according to new buying patterns, in addition to traditional factors like account size, geography, or industry classification.
- Assessing your personal competitive sales ability and the competitiveness of your company.

- The organizational implications of selling in today's marketplace, integrating sales, marketing, and human resources to create a robust business front end that is correctly aligned to specific market segments.
- The emerging and critical role of technology in selling.
- The personal success and career implications for you if your company has not fully integrated sales, marketing, and human resources in a manner that is properly aligned to the marketplace.

This strategic perspective is based on trends that are currently changing the competitive landscape, requiring that new, best-of-breed, world class practices be put in place—trends that include:

- Globalization, particularly as it relates to team selling.
- Consolidation, creating fewer, but larger sales opportunities.
- Commodification of products and services, driving prices, and margins downward.
- Value redefinition, developing new nontraditional forms of customer value, in order to protect margins and create increased competitive differentiation.
- Growing turbulence, where internal organizational change destabilizes sales efforts.
- Technology, as e-commerce introduces new sales and distribution opportunities and challenges.
- Outsourcing, where you can quickly become subordinated to a competitor.

These and other trends are changing the face of competition and require changing the very nature of how we sell. For the first time in many industries the "we" in "how we sell" goes beyond our personal efforts as sales professionals, and even beyond team selling. The new nature of selling requires the direct involvement of marketing, human resources, executive company management, and often, customers. Anything less sub-optimizes the performance of the sales organization.

Never before has company structure played such an important role in driving the success of individual sales professionals. If that structure is not right, it will not only sub-optimize the salesforce, but will also pressure it to coordinate sales and sales-related functions informally in order to remain competitive. When this happens, the result is always the same—increased internal focus at the expense of face-to-face selling time.

Integrating Sales and Marketing

At the individual level sales professionals, particularly high performers, often become compelled to do "in-field marketing," that is, create an informal approach to sales-marketing integration that not only consumes selling time, but is difficult to leverage within the sales organization. Rarely are these types of initiatives packaged for replication. Examples of these in-field marketing efforts include:

- Developing industry-oriented, high-level customer presentations.
- Creating example value statements and propositions that go beyond the feature-benefit expressions of yesterday's marketplace.
- Formulating product and service strategies that position offerings against competitive alternatives.

Actually, there are eleven such marketing efforts, or *outputs to sales*, that are addressed. They characterize the sales/marketing interface, significantly impacting the effectiveness of the salesforce. Building this interface properly, however, requires three critical elements:

1. Top-down senior management commitment and support.
2. The willing spirit of sales and marketing to make it work.
3. Front-end organizational alignment with your customers.

Not all customers are created equal: Some you invest in, others you avoid, and some you do nearly anything for because losing even one of them to a competitor is not an option. Recognizing this leads us to a discussion of approach-to-market, in terms of packaging products and services to best address specific market sectors, and creating a front-end organizational company structure that puts the right salespeople in the right roles, implementing the right practices with the right sales coaching and marketing support—all under the right compensation system that should also be approach-to-market specific. It is not uncommon for the most successful companies today to have several approaches-to-market, where in the past they may have had only one, represented by a single, direct salesforce, operating under a single compensation system. This book illustrates specific examples of this new approach-to-market.

Integrating Sales and Human Resources

While the interface between sales and marketing can be characterized by eleven distinctive and cooperative activities that reflect successful sales/marketing integration, the interface between sales and human resources is based on something very different: Competency Profiling and Mapping.

Assume that your company has four lines of business, each with its own approach-to-market. The first is your Consumer Products Group, with an approach-to-market that focuses on selling through catalogs and distributors. The second, your Commercial Group, relies primarily on telemarketing. The third line of business, the Commercial Systems Group, is represented by a direct salesforce and the fourth, the Commercial Business Group, utilizes sales teams to penetrate and develop accounts. Each of these approaches provides your company with access to specific and different market sectors characterized by differing customer needs, buying patterns, pricing, and service requirements. Similarly, the sales interface will differ. For example, in the Commercial Group, salespeople are selling products over the telephone while in Commercial Systems the salespeople are calling on accounts, selling yield improvement through the use of their products. Here the focus has shifted away from the product to the business value associated with properly employing the product. Perhaps in some cases, your company even bases its pricing, in part, on the amount of yield improvement achieved. Going even further up the customer value chain, the Commercial Business Group has gone beyond yield improvement, and is selling yield itself. That is, they go into accounts and build a business justification to completely take over an aspect or function of the company's business. It may be the Information Technology function, a manufacturing department or even the training and development of a sales organization. Here, the focus has shifted even further away from the product, to center on the business value, not in employing your *products,* but in employing your *company,* to directly manage a specific operation.

What all this means is that the sale's role within each approach-to-market will differ, requiring different types of selling, different types of marketing support, and most importantly, different sales skills and knowledge. The business acumen required in the Commercial Business Group is far greater than that of the Commercial Group. Yet, the opposite is often true when it comes to closing skills. Expressed simply, different approaches-to-market require different competencies (skills and knowledge) to be successful, which can be expressed in the form of Competency Maps.

Competency Maps, unlike the standard position description, clearly articulate what is required to be successful in a sales role, as determined by the marketplace, and express this in terms of observable behaviors.

These same competencies can also be used to describe an individual's capabilities, in the form of a Competency Profile. Comparing the two, Competency Profile to Map, can answer several extremely important questions:

- What competencies are required for me to be successful in a particular sales position?
- What do I specifically need in terms of training?
- What type of coaching assistance do I need from my sales manager and what does his or her own Competency Profile illustrate, in terms of having the ability to assist me?
- What other sales positions would I be suited for, or could I aspire to, in terms of career growth?
- Is my compensation consistent with my capabilities and the value I provide my company as a salesperson?

From a management point of view, a Competency Profile-to-Map comparison enables human resource practices—such as recruiting and selection, performance management, and compensation—to operate on an approach-to-market specific basis. It allows the recruiting process, coaching and development, and compensation systems to be driven by the marketplace, creating a true customer-centric, front-end organizational structure. Additionally, it creates a strategic role for the human resources department as they become a nontraditional source of competitive advantage for the company, manifested in the sales organization.

One way to put all this into perspective is to look at business today. Most companies have significantly streamlined operations, pulling out costs wherever possible. The challenge now is to profitably increase revenues, which means, in part:

- Creating new, nontraditional sources of competitive advantage internally, like that of our human resources example, and externally, with new value-centric offerings.
- Creating increased sales leverage and effectiveness through sales and marketing integration.
- Rapid expansion into new markets, organically and through acquisition, with the right alignment between a company's front-end and its new markets.

Your Personal Challenge

The sales, marketing, and human resource professionals of today's marketplace must be adventurers—mountain climbers able to read the most complicated topological map, innovators confident enough to challenge legacy sales methods—who think nontraditionally and can move ahead, accepting the challenges of the higher peaks and deeper gorges that will define the business landscape and ultimate success.

It will not be easy, as those individuals must become the vanguard for change within companies that are all too often not yet ready for change. In many cases, they will be plagued by internal politics, always running the risk of becoming too internally focused, or of stepping on a political landmine.

To illustrate this complex new landscape in a more comprehensible way, *World Class Selling* uses personal dimensioning to create a virtual experience for you, taking you along as we negotiate this hazardous terrain in a real world business situation.

Mary Gagan, a successful sales professional, is at a decision point in her career, after fifteen years of successful selling with her company. She sees the challenges and opportunities ahead and wants to capitalize on them for her company's benefit. A high-level individual in her company does not share her vision, and he is probably not alone. The way of the past still dictates their thinking, despite the company's eroding market share and diminishing margins.

Mary is not one to give up easily. She also is wise enough to know that the grass is probably not any greener at another company. Still, the chances that she could play a significant role in driving change are very questionable.

As you read *World Class Selling*, you will learn to navigate, along with Mary, the intimidating white-water shoals of company politics—an area that Mary has always avoided, but which she must be willing to raft through and break past, in order to progress and succeed in today's marketplace.

You will come in contact with corporate FOXES, people of high integrity, very powerful, who are not necessarily found at the top of their organizations. You'll learn how to identify them, to your advantage. You will also experience working with individuals at the other end of the spectrum, those who would advance themselves at your expense or that of their company.

World Class Selling: The Crossroads of Customer, Sales, Marketing, and Technology builds on the Power Base® theory introduced in my earlier book, *Power Base Selling: Secrets of an Ivy League Street Fighter* (John Wiley & Sons, 1990). *World Class Selling* covers present and future marketplace requirements and the personal and professional tools necessary to deal with them. It also addresses the implications and the internal employee perspective of company politics.

You will meet Mary Gagan's sales manager, Mark Avery, along with Jim Watkins, vice president of sales, and Sally Loxner, manager of marketing. Also present are Danilo Salenger, Chief Information Officer, and Dick Chainy, the Chief Operating Officer, who emerges as a powerful internal political threat to change. At the senior executive level, you will meet Dr. Robert Tullis, the Chief Executive Officer, who is amenable to change, but must also protect the company's strategic interests in the fluid and volatile environment of acquisitions and mergers, answering to the stockholders and the Board of Directors.

You will be there as Mary, her colleagues, and her superiors interact and position themselves to assess opportunities, avoid pitfalls, accept responsibility and accountability, identify and manage strategic risks, work to initiate positive change to remain competitive, win and lose allies, and finally reach the ultimate outcome, which, as in any game, is positive for some players, negative for others.

This virtual business experience will advance your understanding and your sales leadership ability, enabling you to take an active role at the forefront of change, through enhanced comprehension and performance ability, like the master who can both understand and perform.

A college professor may be an expert in art appreciation, yet not be able to paint. A gifted artist may astound people with his work, yet not be able to explain how he is able to understand the science behind that performance.

In *World Class Selling*, we examine market trends and their sales significance, and we also dive into the practical implications of how we need to sell differently in today's marketplace, using specific tools to guide us. Every master either builds, or is handed down, such tools. *World Class Selling* gives them to you.[1]

Note

1. As a reader of *World Class Selling*, you are invited to visit the *www.efox.com/wcs* performance learning web site.

CHAPTER

1

The Competitive Landscape

In the early 1980s, when Mary Gagan joined St. George Pharmaceuticals, selling was a lot simpler and more discretely defined. There were customers, competitors, and suppliers. Mary's customers then, as now, were hospitals, doctors, and pharmacies in the greater Chicago area. Her competitors were most of the major players in the pharmaceutical supply world.

At that time, everyone knew who everyone else was and what role they played, giving clarity and definition to what was otherwise a growing, vibrant marketplace. It was a great environment for a new salesperson learning to sell, and Mary had grown and thrived in it.

Then, just a few weeks ago, as she was anticipating another banner year of sales and commissions, Mary hit a wall that not only shocked her confidence, but brought her to an unexpected crossroads in her career.

Mary is the single mother of two children, who were aged two and four when she first joined St. George Pharmaceuticals in 1984, shortly after her graduation from the University of Chicago with a bachelors degree in business administration. Her major was in marketing, and one of her professors had recommended that she move into sales upon graduation, where she'd be most likely to make enough money to support herself and her two children. Mary had followed the professor's advice, joining St. George in Chicago as a young sales representative.

She was dynamic and dedicated, and her sales career with the company had taken off and had progressed well ever since. Her children were now almost grown. Harry, the oldest, was in his first year of college, and her daughter Arlene was going into her senior year of high school. Mary had been confident that she would be able to handle their college expenses while maintaining her own upper middle class lifestyle. She had been a consistent producer for her sales manager, Mark Avery, and was well-respected by Jim Watkins, the vice president of sales at St. George Pharmaceuticals, who early on had become her mentor. In truth, none of them, least of all Mary, was prepared for what happened with the Consolidated account.

Mary had been selling to a company named Consolidated Hospitals, waging a sales campaign for more than six months. Consolidated had recently acquired seventeen hospitals, which made this sale equivalent to seventeen sales. It was one that Mary and St. George Pharmaceuticals could ill afford to lose. It was also a very tough campaign, since her competitors were equally committed to winning the business, as evidenced by their willingness to lower pricing and to offer preferred terms.

Mary found herself spending an inordinate amount of time dealing with internal issues at St. George, issues that had to be managed and resolved in order for her to get the support she needed to make her company competitive in this campaign. Even so, she was doing well with Consolidated. She had elected a sales strategy that was Indirect, one of the four classes of sales strategy (Direct, Indirect, Divisional, and Containment) she had learned at a sales seminar presented by Holden Corporation two years before.[1] Under the principles of Indirect strategy, Mary was planning to change the ground rules in the eleventh hour, just as the sales situation would peak.

Her primary competitors had elected to go Direct, depending on product and pricing superiority to win, which initially propelled them into the lead. Mary had ruled out from the start the possibility of going Direct. She knew that the top management at St. George would not be amenable to making the business concessions that might be necessary for her to win by that strategy. Therefore, she had to find a way to pull the rug out from under the competition, late enough in the sales cycle that they would not have time to recover.

All her efforts had gone into figuring out how to accomplish that, but it was not until a few weeks into the campaign, when she'd met with Consolidated's vice president of operations, Bill Stensland, that the strategy had become crystal clear to her. Mary had also learned about FOX-hunting within a customer's organization from the sales seminar she had attended, and she knew that Bill Stensland was a FOX at Consolidated: a politically astute and powerful individual who was very close to Consolidated's CEO. Bill was a force within Consolidated, even though he was rarely seen as being directly involved in decisions outside the purview of his own organization. Bill knew how to work behind the scenes. Mary recognized Bill as a FOX and built a relationship with him. She became a resource for him to help drive a number of initiatives that would advance Consolidated's business. One of those initiatives was the key to her Indirect strategy, and she intended to change her proposal at the eleventh hour to incorporate the new initiative, catching the competition off guard. Everything was in place. Mary and her boss Mark Avery were certain that the Consolidated account would be not only a win, but a big win. It was a highly visible sales campaign within St. George because of all the internal involvement. Winning it would give Mary, and Mark Avery, recognition value that promised to offer considerable impetus to both their careers. It was an exciting feeling.

The First Reality

The time came for action and, following her Indirect strategy, Mary unveiled her initiative, changing the ground rules and thrusting herself into the lead just when her competitors were feeling overconfident. She felt sure she had knocked them down for the count. Her counterpart at Consolidated was pleased and all but guaranteed her the contract. Mary was euphoric. Then came the shocking call from Bill Stensland.

"Sorry, Mary, the order has been put on hold. That word came down today from on high."

Mary could not believe her ears when the customer explained that Consolidated had just *acquired her main competitor!* It was a move to advance a health care diversification strategy that would create a continuum of care and resources, differentiating Consolidated from other hospital organizations. Mary was at first angry, then confused. By the end of the day, she was demoralized. All the months of work and internal lobbying that had gone into the campaign were down the drain, not to mention the financial significance of losing the business. The frustration of losing to a competitor she thought she had handily beaten was devastating to her morale, and she felt she'd let her superiors down.

Later that night, after her daughter was asleep, Mary thought a lot about the Consolidated campaign and its totally unexpected outcome.

Selling has radically changed, she was forced to acknowledge. *Winning deals this big is no longer a battle fought by an individual sales person like me, or even a sales team. It's an all-out war that has to be fought by whole organizations. Where does that leave St. George? They're not ready for this kind of selling. More to the point, where does it leave me?* Mary got very little sleep that night.

The next day, she began the constructive process of figuring out what had gone wrong, from her point of attack, on the Consolidated campaign. Losing it appeared to have been beyond her control, yet she could not accept that. She knew that when you lose a qualified sales opportunity, it's for one reason and one reason only—you were outsold by the competition.

But how? What did I not do? What could I have done differently? The answer came a few days later, in a win/loss review with Mark Avery.

"We covered all the bases except one, Mary—the CEO of Consolidated, who was the only person who could have divulged their acquisition plans. Maybe they'd have considered St. George as a candidate for acquisition, who knows?"

"I know," Mary agreed. "Had we been aware of those plans, we could have decided not to continue to pursue the opportunity, or maybe developed a different strategy to deal with it."

But going direct to the CEO would not have been a feasible option for me, thought Mary. *Whom might I have approached to get that information in time to use it?* The answer was obvious. Mary might have gotten a hint, an indication that something was going on, from Stensland, a company FOX. Perhaps if she had been focusing on higher-level corporate issues, like diversification, earlier in the sales cycle—before a decision had been made and they entered the "silent period" of the acquisition—she'd have picked up signals that might have tipped her off that something else was going on. This was a lesson learned.

The reality of today's competitive marketplace was really sinking in for Mary. *We are all eating from the same plate,* she realized. *Today, a company can be your customer, your competitor, and a partner in some areas of your business, all at the same time. It's definitely a strange new marketing world out there.*

Building Wisdom

In selling, we win or lose by our mistakes. But a mistake is not a failure, it is a lesson learned. Mary knew that if you didn't learn from mistakes, you would not build wisdom, and without wisdom, there is no future. She knew she had to take ownership of the loss of the Consolidated account in order to learn from it.

Many salespeople, like Mary, struggle with how to stay competitive in today's marketplace, not because they lack motivation or desire, but because the game has changed and moved out beyond their ability to play it. These are bright people who have sales experience, many years of experience, gained one year at a time. They may believe they lost a properly qualified sale because of the product, or price, or something else, never recognizing that when they, as competitive salespeople, don't take ownership of a loss, they cannot learn from it—and therefore they never build wisdom.

The lesson for Mary was more than recognizing the need to call at higher levels—after all, trying to set up a meeting with a customer CEO is not always appropriate. She knew that she should instead have climbed to the highest level on the *value chain* at Consolidated. Different from getting to the highest level in the customer's organization, this meant that she would find the most significant expression of value that her company could represent to the customer.

If St. George had resident expertise of any kind that could enhance a customer solution, thus moving them higher up on the customer's value chain, Mary was determined to find it, package it, and sell it from now on. After her stinging loss of the Consolidated sale, Mary Gagan was a woman with some questions about herself and the direction in which her career was going, but now she was a saleswoman with a mission. She wanted to sell, and she wanted to win. It would be difficult in this volatile new marketplace, and maybe she would fail, but she wasn't confused any more about the direction she needed to take. The Consolidated loss had proved she needed to sell Value to her customers.

Building and Evaluating Value

The next day, Mary returned to Mark's office, and after the customary pleasantries, she came straight to the point.

"You've been in sales a lot longer than I have, Mark. I need to know more about value—how to discover or build value, articulate it, position it within a customer's organization, and measure it. I'm beginning to realize that's where St. George needs to focus its sales efforts in today's marketplace. What can you tell me?"

Mark smiled. "Well, I don't know if St. George is ready for this, but as you probably already know, there are two types of customer value: Personal and business. The personal side of value centers on an individual's personal agenda; that is, whatever a powerful person wants to accomplish from an organizational or professional point of view. Now, that's really a discussion about organizational politics, which I'll be happy to have with you at some point, but for now let's just focus on business value."

Mark identified for Mary two forms of business value: Value Statements and Value Propositions.

"A Value Statement is a qualitative expression, based upon your customer's business objectives and their assessment of risk in pursuing those objectives. A Value Proposition goes further: It quantifies a Value Statement in such a way that it becomes compelling and measurable. Both show how a company can advance a customer's ability to achieve specific business objectives, or how to assist them in mitigating risk.

"We'll talk more about Value Statements and Propositions, Mary, but you should recognize that your problem at Consolidated was not in the value you were providing them. I reviewed your proposal when you changed the ground rules, and it was very clear and very good. The problem, which I believe you have now recognized, was that we were working too low on the value chain as it related to Consolidated's business."

"How could I have seen that?" asked Mary. "I really went by the book on this one. That acquisition thing came out of nowhere. It was never in the equation."

"Yes, you did go by the book. In the past, you'd have won, hands down, but not today. Consolidated wanted to diversify, choosing to acquire one of our competitors, but who knows if a well-structured partnership with us would have done the job for them? Or for us? Perhaps an investment in us, or maybe a joint venture between our companies, would have been a feasible option. The point is, we should have identified the highest appropriate level of the value chain at Consolidated, and operated at that level within the customer's organization.

"In this case, it would have meant setting up a high-level line of communication between the companies. Note that I said 'appropriate' level of the value chain. I used to believe that in every competitive sales situation you should work to reach the highest appropriate level in the customer's organization, in terms of management penetration. This no longer applies as a guiding principle in today's marketplace. Today, we must go up the value chain, landing on whatever organizational level supports the right kind of value."

"But, how do I know when I've landed at the right level?" asked Mary. "I thought I was at the right level within Consolidated, but was I ever wrong!"

"The answer isn't easy, Mary. The best way I can phrase it is like this. You know that you're at the right level only by knowing when you have gone too far."

Mark went into an in-depth explanation of the value chain (Figure 1.1) for Mary, and how to quantitatively determine if you're at the right level. It begins with exploring for value, producing Value Statements or Propositions that map into the three general levels of a customer's organization:

1. At the Operations level—here, expressions of value are generally short-term, operationally oriented expressions, tightly focused to a particular area of the customer's business.

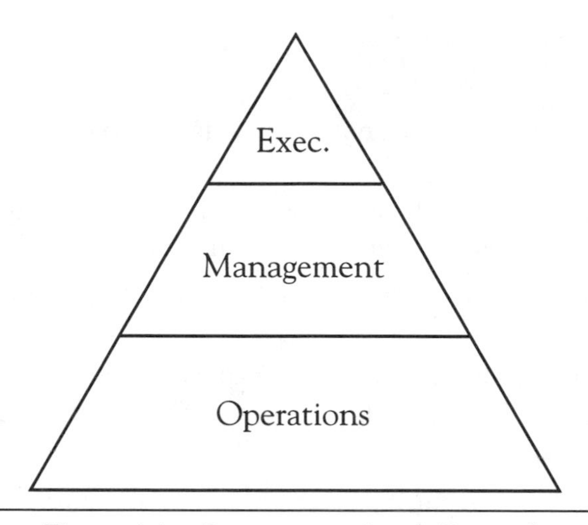

Figure 1.1 Organization Levels Pyramid.

2. At the Management level—Value Statements and Propositions reflect a broader organizational focus, perhaps interdepartmental, with more of a business orientation.
3. At the Executive level—the value perspective, or field of view, gets considerably wider, including the customer's industry, their customers, and competitors. It's a high-level business orientation that is both short- and long-term in nature.

"Now, in evaluating each of these levels," said Mark, "you will know that you have gone too far when you 'run out of gas.' You start at the operations level and move up. 'Out of gas' means that when you apply four specific criteria to an account, you get a point score that is too low, indicating that you have either gone too high in the organization, or that you are focused on the wrong Value Statement or Proposition. The four criteria take the guesswork out of determining how high you must call in an account, from the standpoint of value positioning.

"Let's look at the criteria, and the types of questions that give us insight into how to rate them." Mark went to the white board on his office wall, and began listing the questions.

1. Degree of Customer Interest
   - Is the customer window-shopping?
   - Are internal or external business factors putting pressure on the customer?
   - In general, does the customer recognize your company's resident expertise in terms of providing value?
   - Is the customer pushing your company to move the process ahead?
2. Customer Involvement in Value Exploration
   - Is the customer knowledgeable enough to make a meaningful contribution?
   - Does the customer expect to have the answer handed to them?
   - Can you create roles for specific individuals in the customer's organization, leading them in the process of defining and establishing value?
   - Has the customer organized a task force or committee, or has the customer in any way dedicated resources to the effort?
3. Business Significance of Value
   - Is there a connection to mission-critical business initiatives?
   - Is there a connection to an emerging business threat: For example, a new competitor, a new industry trend, or a move toward government regulation or deregulation?
   - Will the customer become more competitive within its marketplace, and is there a way to measure that increased competitiveness—perhaps in terms of market share, an ability to increase pricing, or enhanced competitive differentiation?
   - If the customer is a public company, could its image, in the eyes of the analysts, be improved, or could its image, within the marketplace in general, be enhanced?
4. Measurability of Value
   - Will the customer accept the accountability that comes with measuring value?
   - Do the necessary metrics exist to measure and quantify value? If not, is the customer willing to work with you to build the necessary metrics?

- Do you or your company have the expertise to assist the customer in building metrics?
- Will the customer allow your company to use the metric results data as a case study, to support future Value Statements or Propositions, as you compete for future sales opportunities with other companies?

"The answers to these questions," said Mark, "will help give you the background information and insight necessary to objectively assess value potential at each general level of a customer's organization: Operations, Management, and Executive. To do this, you can use a scoring system as a guide and sales tool. It will need to be calibrated, as you would any instrument, but once that is done, it will be a valuable aid."

Mark described the Value Potential Evaluator to Mary and presented the illustration in Figure 1.2 showing how to use it.

"I don't know . . ." Mary looked dubious. "It's complicated. Does it really work? How do I calibrate it?"

"Calibration comes with practice. You use the tool, and where you know the right outcomes, say a High Value Potential, you run it and adjust the point range to in fact read High. Doing this several times for known situations will calibrate the tool for you. As for selling today, you're absolutely right, it *is* complicated. We both remember when value expressions were set by the suppliers, and most often were product oriented. *Today, the customer defines the value, not the supplier.* It is customer-determined value, now, which forces suppliers like us into the solutions business, big time.

"Let's look at how this affects St. George Pharmaceuticals. We are no longer a pharmaceutical company alone, and neither can we stay just a notch higher, in the disease management business. To be competitive as a company, we need to move even farther up the value chain within the industry we serve. That will put us into the health care solutions business with some of our customers, disease management with others, and for a few, we will always be a pharmaceutical supplier.

"In addition, we must recognize that we are not dealing with a static situation. Our customers are also working to move up their industry's value chain, as was the case with Consolidated. *If we fall out of phase or alignment with a customer's position on the value chain,*

Value Criteria	Scale		Rating
1. Degree of Customer Interest	Passive	–3	
	Receptive	0	
	Embrace	+3	______
2. Customer Involvement in Value Exploration	Weak	–4	
	Adequate	0	
	Strong	+4	______
3. Business Significance of Value	Low	–4	
	Promising	0	
	High	+4	______
4. Measurability of Value	Low	–3	
	Workable	0	
	High	+3	______

Value Potential	
High	10 to 14
Reasonable	4 to 9
Emerging	–3 to 3
Weak	–14 to –4

Total ______

Figure 1.2 Value Potential Evaluator.

months of work and significant sales opportunities are immediately placed at risk."

"So the major challenge for us is to make this business as simple as possible by becoming very good at what we do. That means, in part, becoming accomplished in the adaptation, calibration, and use of sales tools, like the Value Potential Evaluator, in order to take some of the frustrating complexity out of it. Those of us who learn the lessons of value chain management ahead of our competitors are likely to be the most successful."

"I know that's true, Mark, but I don't see St. George organized to capitalize on these market trends."

"You're right, we have a long way to go, but management is working on it, and there may be a role for you to play in that effort,

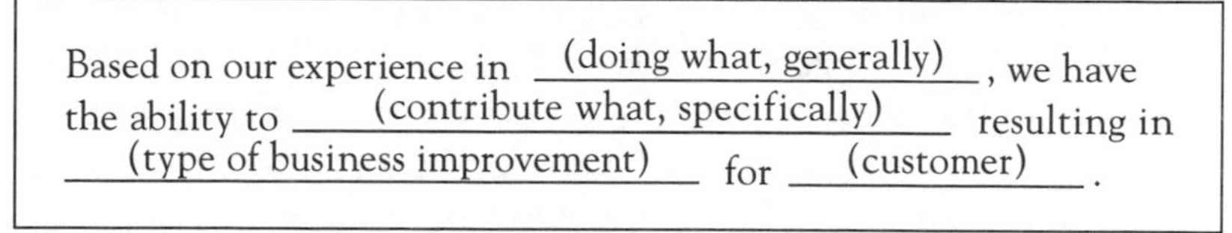
Based on our experience in (doing what, generally), we have the ability to (contribute what, specifically) resulting in (type of business improvement) for (customer).

Figure 1.3 Value Statement Template.

Mary. We'll talk more about that later. For now, let's stay on the subject of value. There's a lot that we can do at the sales level, particularly in building customer Value Statements and Propositions."

Mark then introduced Mary to a series of additional sales tools that could help in the building and implementation of Value Statements and Propositions, beginning with a brief Value Statement Template (Figure 1.3).

After discussing the template, they worked together, applying it to the Operations, Management, and Executive levels of Consolidated Hospitals. The result is shown in Figure 1.4.

"Now," said Mark, "let's take the discussion a bit further and look at Value Propositions, which are designed to be not only measurable but compelling, articulating clear value for the customer. However, the sales value doesn't end there. Because Value Propositions are

Fill-In Section	Operations	Management	Executive
(Doing what, generally)	Vaccine distribution	Disease management	Diversified health care services
(Contribute what, specifically)	Prevent the spread of disease	Improve patient care while expanding your operational capacity	Enhance the business synergy between your hospital, clinical laboratory, vaccine, and pharmaceutical operations to increase patient volume and profitability
(Type of business improvement)	Incremental revenue	An increase in market share	An increased ability to compete for government contracts
(Customer)	Consolidated Hospitals	Consolidated Hospitals	Consolidated Hospitals

Figure 1.4 Consolidated's Multilevel Value Statement.

quantitative in nature, they provide us with the opportunity to operationalize a very exciting sales approach—Performance Bonding—a powerful source of competitive advantage used to advance either a Direct or an Indirect sales strategy. Value Propositions can also serve us well from a marketing point of view, creating a barrier to entry for competitors."

Performance Bonding

"Being able to quantify customer value is extremely important. It differentiates a salesperson from the competition, enables him or her to better justify higher pricing and better margins, and it can also shorten sales cycles, by creating customer awareness of the significance of realizing value sooner as opposed to later. But what is even better is what's behind the ability to produce value propositions—business performance expertise.

"As you build experience with Value Propositions, you'll begin to see how and where you provide value, in very precise terms, and how to accurately measure that value. You will notice customer factors, quite removed from your role in an account, that influence the same business parameters that are used to measure your own success. They are the key to Performance Bonding."

It was a little strange, Mary thought. She had worked for Mark for nearly two years and had never heard him this enthusiastic about a subject before. There was so much to absorb, and he was giving her so much information, that Mary felt inundated, as if she were drinking from a fire hydrant. Also, she was a bit perturbed, especially in light of the recent Consolidated loss, that Mark had never mentioned these theories to her before. She decided to speak up.

"Mark, I really appreciate your letting me in on your thinking on this, but I have to wonder why I have never heard it from you before today."

Mark looked away, then turned back, and leaned toward her. "Look, Mary, when I first joined St. George, I was vocal about these issues. In fact, I believed that my views on this issue of value were somewhat instrumental in getting me hired. Jim Watkins and I used to talk about this for hours, back in those days, but it didn't go anywhere. That was when St. George was flying high, and could do no wrong. It was the golden age of pharmaceutical sales. Our business was thriving, producing so much cash that the company had to begin investing in real estate, even foreign countries, to keep the money working and largely 'out of sight.' The investors were thrilled, but if the general public knew how much profit we in the industry were making, they would have gone nuts.

"It's hard to drive change in that kind of an environment, even though it would have given us a big lead on the competition, in terms of being more prepared for what we are experiencing today. Well, I tried to drive change anyway, tried to get people to listen to me, and a few actually did. The problem came when our chief operations officer, Dick Chainy, brought the hammer down on me. I nearly lost my job in a very heated discussion that he later swore never took place. Jim Watkins is a wonderful guy, but I never understood why he didn't back me up when I told him about Dick Chainy quashing the new initiatives we wanted to put in place.

"I've avoided company politics ever since, and have followed, rather than challenged, the thinking of upper management. You, and this loss to Consolidated, opened my eyes again. I can see now that playing blind was the wrong thing for me to do. What I clearly recognize now, that I did not see before, is that we have to practice what we preach. We cannot work so hard to go up the customer's value chain and not do the same in our own company. We can't work the political issues within the customer's organization and pretend that they don't exist on our home turf.

"Since we've both been here, Mary, St. George has been restructured four times. God only knows how much money has been spent on re-engineering projects to cut time-to-market and improve manufacturing. What we need now is to refocus the business from a sales point of view, then reshape the company again, becoming value chain-centric. I decided last night that I'm going to use our miserable experience at Consolidated Hospitals to begin the process. Maybe we can make it happen. What do you think?"

"Well, in theory I agree with you, Mark," said Mary, "but I don't know if I'm ready for that. Getting involved in internal company politics is something that I avoid like the plague, too. I promise I'll give it some careful thought, though." She paused. "Why don't we take a break for now, then I'd like get back in more detail to our earlier discussion on value."

Mary shut down all discussion of internal change rather abruptly, which was not her usual style. But her instincts were telling her that aligning with Mark to drive new, internal changes within St. George might be right for the company and for the marketplace, but possibly wrong for her personally—for her own interests and career.

When Mark and Mary met again, nothing more was said about internal change. They moved back into their discussion of Value Propositions, with Mark taking the lead.

"If you are measuring the impact your company will have on the customer's bottom line—profitability, earnings per share or their market share—you are going to put yourself in a high risk position. Too many other factors influence those business parameters. You could do a great job at whatever you're going to do, only to find that some other aspect of the customer's business could not perform, thus negatively impacting the measurement parameters like bottom line. These are factors out of your control. Maybe the customer hires the wrong people to manage a new operation or they have equipment problems. Perhaps they are not year–2000 ready. Who knows? It could be anything."

"So, how can a salesperson deal with that?"

Mark answered Mary's question by focusing on two points.

"First, keep in mind what Performance Bonding actually is. As opposed to proposing a particular solution for a customer at a specific price, you are making a part of the price a variable, a function of how well St. George performs. That performance is based upon specific criteria to which you and the customer agree, before the order is placed. The business parameters we have been discussing make up that criteria, but if they are too general, like measuring changes in sales revenue or profitability, you will get into trouble. So, you define impact parameters that are 'close' to the intervention.

"Suppose we develop a Value Proposition for a chain of clinics that involves our jointly promoting certain drugs through an advertising campaign—a kind of pull-through marketing effort. The major parameter we might use to measure success could be drug sales over and above what the customer would have forecast without the promotional campaign. That gives us a good indication of our impact on their sales. Further suppose, however, that we are not looking at incremental changes in sales of the specific drugs that are being promoted alone, but are also measuring changes in the profitability of sales. Since other considerations might impact profitability, like increases in customer overhead that are beyond our control, we expose ourselves to the risk of doing a good job, but not having it recognized in the profit numbers.

"That brings me to my second point, Sensitivity Analysis, which is a way of determining how much impact we are creating in an account, relative to a specific measurement parameter. We begin by identifying all the significant customer factors that could impact results. In our example, that would be changes in customer overhead. If sales of specific drugs that we are jointly promoting increase, the increase in profit from those sales can be normalized against increases or decreases in overhead. Basically, we track with the customer how much overhead costs have changed, then subtract out the change to calculate or normalize the impact we would have had if overhead had not changed. Sensitivity Analysis is simply adjusting for customer factors beyond our control, ones that impact our measurement parameters. That enables us to determine if the Performance Bond is earned.

"If I can get management support, I would like to apply that concept at St. George, as it can stop competitors in their tracks. They not only have to get high on the value chain, they have to guarantee, to some extent, concrete results. That's one of the major benefits to Performance Bonding; it makes a statement of commitment that engenders customer confidence."

Mary was intrigued. "What about Consolidated, would this have worked there?"

Mark thought about it for a moment. "No, I don't think so, Mary. Performance Bonding is not for every account, nor for every sales situation."

"Well, then, how do we know when to use it in a sales campaign?" she asked.

"I'd use it when the Value Potential Evaluator score is 'off the charts' for both the management and executive levels, and the Sensitivity Analysis is clear and complete."

Mary and Mark discussed the details and internal implications of proposing a Performance Bond. She realized that if she and

Mark were talking about this, her competitors were probably talking about it, too.

First, they would have to figure how to build an actual Performance Bond, then determine how to sell it internally. Mary could see the potential as Mark had described it, but they both knew that diving into the company's internal politics to secure upper level management support was not high on Mary's list of exciting things to do with her time.

In fact, the more she learned from Mark, the more doubts she had about her own future at St. George. If the company wasn't prepared to get a handle on how these new market trends of consolidation, diversification, and value redefinition were impacting its business, Mary would soon just be spinning her wheels. She'd spend an inordinate amount of time and effort trying to move sales situations, and her resistant company, forward in a marketplace that not only demanded new thinking, but was becoming increasingly intolerant of thinking in the old way.

Building Value Propositions

The next day, Mary switched her focus away from Consolidated and onto one of her other important accounts, Alexander Drugs—a chain of drug stores known for their progressive nature. Building on what she had just learned from Mark, *Mary began to think about creating demand, as opposed to servicing demand.*

Alexander Drugs was the perfect account to approach with the concept of moving higher up on the value chain. Their business was now seventy percent third-party prescriptions, meaning that many of their customers were not their customers. For the most part, insurance companies were paying for prescriptions, making organizations like Health Maintenance Organizations (HMOs) Alexander's new customers—a notch above retail selling on the value chain.

St. George was a leader in the area of prescription and over-the-counter (OTC) drugs and remedies to treat depression. Perhaps, with the expertise and industry recognition St. George enjoyed in that field, Mary could help Alexander construct a disease management program in the area of depression. It would require that Alexander provide certain nontraditional services to their customers, like seminars and other programs, which would be supported by St. George. Depressive disorders were on the rise, and St. George knew that drugs were being prescribed as an expedient, without careful forethought. They also knew that, in the case of children, parents were generally not well educated about the problem of childhood or teen depression, nor were they familiar with how to deal with it. The same could be said for men, or husbands. Statistics showed women to be the primary risk group, diagnosed with depression at least twice as often as men.[2]

This could be a great opportunity to build a compelling Value Proposition and drive additional business at Alexander Drugs, thought Mary. The prospect excited her.

Mary met again with Mark, and told him what she had in mind. To her relief, he was very receptive to working with her to build her first Value Proposition. Mark introduced Mary to another sales tool, the Value Proposition Template (Figure 1.5), and described each of its components.

"Let's try to apply this to Alexander Drugs," Mark suggested. "What customer level should we focus on first: Operations, Management, or Executive?"

Mary thought for a moment. "Executive, I think. If we can get that right, and if the Value Potential Evaluator gives us a green light, I can build the Management and Operations expressions of value myself."

"Good enough. When do you think the project might begin?"

"Let's say June 1," suggested Mary.

"Okay. Now, how about if we refer to our 'product/service/capability' as our range of prescription and nonprescription drugs and

Beginning ___(implementation date)___ as a result of our ___(product/service/capability)___, ___(customer)___ will be able to ___(do what)___ resulting in ___(quantified business improvement)___ for ___(total investment cost)___, with economic payback achieved within or by ___(time)___. We will document our delivered value by measuring ___(results tracking parameters)___.

Figure 1.5 Value Proposition Template.

remedies, and our current research in the field of depressive disorders—something like that?"

"Sounds fine to me."

Mark began filling in the Value Proposition Template. "Hmmm. What about the 'do what' piece?"

"I have a thought on that. I feel that Alexander, with our help, could better position itself as a solutions provider, helping people to understand depression, and perhaps even prevent, detect, and treat it. Particularly since more and more of their customers are interested in alternative methods."

"Good. Then our Value Proposition reads like this: 'Beginning June 1, availing itself of our range of prescription and OTC drugs and remedies, and drawing upon our research and formidable expertise in the field of depressive disorders, Alexander Drugs will be able to better position itself as a solutions provider, with both retail customers and insurance customers, helping people to understand depression, and perhaps even prevent, detect, and treat it, particularly as more and more customers are looking for alternative methods.' Does that capture it?"

"Sounds good to me," said Mary. "Let's go with it for now."

"Now, what about quantifying the business improvement that we're suggesting for Alexander Drugs?" asked Mark.

"Well," said Mary, "based on my knowledge of their business, I would like to approach Alexander with an initial three percent increase in sales and a two percent decrease in costs of depression and depression-related products. Then allow them to react, telling us what they feel is reasonable, given what we have in mind.

"For example, we'll suggest a project where they set up a series of community seminars, with our assistance, or maybe a high school and college program focused on teachers. Perhaps even a series of clinics with physician support. Let's estimate a budget of $250,000 for this first project. The idea is to help transition Alexander from being a product or drug provider to also being a *health* provider, bringing knowledge and guidance to the communities they serve. It places them in a community leadership position, which will bring in new retail and insurance customers, like the HMOs, and new respect and name recognition, giving them more value than Alexander's competitors provide. In fact, people might attend a short seminar on depression, and while they are there, pick up other, nonrelated OTC items, like health and beauty aids, and the like.

The return at even a half percent increase in sales will more than justify the cost of the project. In any case, we need to open a dialogue to run the Value Potential Evaluator, to be certain this makes sense for Alexander." Mary felt her confidence begin to rise.

Together, Mary and Mark worked out a first-draft Value Proposition, which they knew probably would be revised again and again in the future as they worked together with senior officials at Alexander Drugs and with their own internal management.

When their meeting ended that day, the Value Proposition looked like this:

"Beginning June 1, availing itself of our range of prescription and nonprescription drugs and remedies, and drawing upon our current research and formidable expertise in the field of depressive disorders, Alexander Drugs will be able to better position itself as a solutions provider, helping people to understand depression, and perhaps even prevent, detect, and treat it, particularly as more and more customers are looking for alternative methods of treatment; resulting in a three percent increase in sales and a two percent decrease in costs of depression and depression-related products for an investment of approximately $250K, with economic payback achieved within one year of the project's commencement. St. George will document its delivered value by measuring specific parameters associated with the project, such as seminar attendance levels, along with tracking sales volume, product mix, revenues, and cost of sales."

Mary was pumped, anxious to proceed with the Alexander Drugs Value Proposition. Like most high-performing sales professionals, she had learned her lesson well, and was now better equipped to compete, capitalizing on the same industry trends that earlier had victimized her at Consolidated.

It was not long, however, before her enthusiasm began to wane. She thought about Mark's earlier comments about their COO, Dick Chainy. Mark had failed in trying to drive new thinking in the company, and Mary knew she might meet the same fate on this attempt to drive broader change within the company, even if she worked it so that she wasn't perceived by Chainy to be overtly aligned with Mark Avery.

To succeed on the Alexander Drugs proposition, she would need an internal strategy that would advance her position within her accounts and secure the necessary high-level support at St. George. Mary felt she could not afford at this time to become internally focused. The only way to swing it was a line-of-sight strategy, one that would enable her to remain focused on her customers.

Value-Based Relationships

While attending the Holden Corporation sales practices seminar earlier, Mary had learned about a diagnostic that had been developed by Holden to measure the quality of a relationship between a supplier and customer, based on value.

St. George routinely ran customer satisfaction surveys, but everyone knew that there was no correlation between survey results and increases or decreases in St. George's market share. The results were important, certainly, but good service and responsiveness were expected in today's marketplace. They were necessary to compete, but were not a source of competitive advantage. After her sessions with Mark, Mary knew that the real key was value chain management, and to her that meant determining:

- Value potential at the three general levels of the customer's organization: Operations, Management, and Executive.
- How to build Value Statements and Propositions.
- How to assess the appropriateness of Performance Bonding.
- How to build a Performance Bond.

What they had not discussed was how to evaluate the current value being provided, as perceived by the customer. *Mary knew that the credibility of any Value Statement or Proposition would be influenced by the customer's perception of value provided by the supplier, prior to the submission of the Value Statement or Proposition*. Measuring that perception was therefore an important first step. In addition, comparing the perception of St. George to the perception of the customer could be very interesting.

Mary decided that her line-of-sight strategy would focus on involving St. George management in a value survey, called the Valu-Driver®,[3] which consisted of two questionnaires: One to be completed by selected St. George sales and management personnel, and the second one to be completed by people at multiple organizational levels within Alexander Drugs. The results of the two would then be compared and analyzed.

She knew that she could get support from Mark, and from the sales vice president, Jim Watkins. The real question was whether or not Dick Chainy, the COO, would participate, but more importantly, whether or not he would back her idea. She'd run it by Jim Watkins first.

Two days later, after organizing her thoughts, Mary requested a meeting with Jim. She briefed him about her meetings with Mark Avery, and then presented the idea and the Value Proposition for Alexander Drugs. Jim's reaction to her idea was very positive and encouraging. He offered to approach Chainy with Mary's request. Actually, Jim did not need Dick's approval to proceed with the initiative, but he agreed with Mary that they needed to have Chainy on board and involved in this. If Jim could get senior management participation and buy-in to the process of running the value diagnostic, and then in creating the final Value Proposition for Alexander Drugs, it might open the door to leading St. George Pharmaceuticals down the path to becoming a value-centric organization. That would enable them to venture into the world of Performance Bonding. Jim thought it would be a great example of winning the battle (developing new business at Alexander) while growing in strength (beginning the process of changing how St. George does business).

Jim was able to set up the meeting with the chief operations officer, scheduled in two weeks' time. To Mary's great surprise, Jim asked her to attend the meeting with him and present the approach she and Mark had worked out for Alexander Drugs. Interestingly, he didn't ask Mark to attend. The dreaded specter of internal company politics raised itself in Mary's consciousness as Jim briefed her on the plan, and asked that she coordinate the presentation with Mark. "But let's keep Mark's name out of it in the meeting with Dick Chainy, okay?"

Mary knew this presentation to the COO was going to be very difficult for her. She didn't like Chainy, nor did she trust him, but she couldn't say why. It went back farther than just learning about Mark's negative experience with him.

Two weeks later the moment of the meeting arrived. Mary had dressed carefully, investing in a new business suit, and she knew she looked polished and professional, which elevated her confidence. Still, she was very nervous. Jim Watkins gave her an encouraging smile. Chainy wasn't smiling, she noted. In fact, he sat with his arms folded across his chest. He was showing classic negative body language.

Mary stood, taking command of the meeting. She began with an overview of the Consolidated Hospitals loss, reviewing what had happened and what she had learned from it. She did not mention Mark Avery's name at any point in the presentation. She and Mark had agreed that it would not be wise to raise any red flags with Chainy, lest they end up where Mark had earlier on this very point.

Seeing a glint of interest in Chainy's eyes, and a slight move forward that suggested she'd caught his attention, Mary moved into the value chain concept and how to map into it. With growing confidence, she set the stage to introduce the Valu-Driver, and what they would require from management in the process of implementing it. Mary paused at each stage to allow Dick Chainy to question her. His questions were appropriate to the subject, and carried constructive intent. Mary began to relax a little more. It was going well. She talked about the output of the Valu-Driver, which would compare St. George's view of value provided to Alexander with Alexander's own view, all expressed according to a Four-Stage Model. She explained to the COO the four areas upon which it would focus:

- Intent—the perceived intent of St. George in working with Alexander; for example, to get orders or create mutual value for both companies.
- Focus—where St. George's sales efforts are concentrated; focusing, for example, on product or business issues.
- Relationship—developed to the extent necessary to win a deal or achieve "insider status," building an informal partnership with Alexander.
- Value—providing business and political value at all levels of Alexander's organization, or simply product value.

Dick listened closely as Mary presented the general model of the four stages of intent, focus, relationship, and value with a customer, explaining that each Stage builds on the ones before it, in cumulative fashion, moving higher up on the value chain (Figure 1.6).

"The Valu-Driver uses questionnaires, one type for the customer and one for St. George, in order to determine:

- How well our Intent lines up with that of Alexander Drugs.
- Whether our Focus is together or divergent.
- If our Relationship is what it needs to be in order to build and maintain a Stage III relationship, and perhaps a Stage IV relationship in the longer term.
- The nature and extent to which we are delivering Value, as perceived by Alexander Drugs.

"These results will then be graphically displayed, allowing comparisons of the respective views of St. George and Alexander Drugs. More importantly, they will tell us what we need to do, together, to build the kind of relationship that will provide Alexander with excellent value, while giving us higher levels of more profitable business, in addition to increased competitive immunity."

"Who will actually participate in this assessment?" Dick wanted to know.

Quality	Stage I	Stage II	Stage III	Stage IV
Customer's Intent	Solve a problem	Acquire a solution	Capitalize on a business opportunity	Create a new business opportunity
Buying Focus	Product or service features	Product or service benefits	Supplier expertise and resources	Supplier strategic ability and commitment
Relationship	Vendor on demand	Characterized by trust and commitment	Strong mutual dependency	Business partners and advisors to each other
Customer Value	Low cost, quick fix	Able to purchase reliable solutions	Able to co-develop and create custom offerings to solve complex problems	Receives insight into business issues and creativity in addressing them

Figure 1.6 Four-Stage Customer Model.

"On our side, I would recommend that you, Jim Watkins, myself, and our service manager complete the supplier questionnaires," replied Mary. "At Alexander, my feeling is that we should approach the appropriate people in operations, middle and senior management. In fact, I see this as an opportunity to make contact with some high level individuals at Alexander Drugs that we have not yet met."

"How, exactly, would you approach them?" asked Jim.

"Well, after having reviewed the diagnostic with the lower level operations and management people at Alexander, I would call the senior executives individually, and explain that we are working on a plan to increase the value that we can provide to their organization, and would like their participation in filling out a brief questionnaire that will be instrumental in helping us become a better resource, perhaps a strategic resource to their business. If given an opportunity to elaborate, I would talk about how we want to understand their perception of the value we are currently providing, and map it against their expectations and our assessment of value. All, of course, in order to provide more value to Alexander Drugs."

Mary concluded that part of the presentation by saying, "This could be a great opportunity for St. George to gain more exposure in the account and increase our support base, from the process alone."

Dick Chainy did not ask why she had excluded her boss, Mark Avery, from the evaluation process, which she took as a good sign. Nevertheless, Mary would have liked to have Mark on the team. After all, most of the information she had used in her presentation today had come from her meetings with him. Still, she knew that in the world of company politics, a brilliant idea can be discounted, depending upon the person presenting it. Conversely, unoriginal thinking channeled properly through an organization might be well received and acted upon quickly.

Mary certainly did not want to take credit for someone else's thinking, but she did want to get the job done, and besides, it was Mark and Jim who had decreed this was the way to go. She would later find a way to involve Mark, if she got the green light on this.

At the conclusion of the meeting, Dick nodded his approval. "Okay, let's do it."

Mary breathed an inward sigh of relief. Jim asked her to write up a requisition request for the Valu-Driver. It would go though a quick approval process and they would be on their way. Mary left the room feeling very pleased, but at the same time, a bit uncomfortable. She felt it had gone well, perhaps a little too well. Why did she still feel such negative vibes about Chainy? He had been attentive, polite, engaged, and approving. She couldn't have asked for more. What was it about the COO that made her so uneasy?

Notes

1. See Chapter 2, "Formulating Strategy," pp. 55–62. See also *Power Base Selling: Secrets of an Ivy League Street Fighter,* New York: John Wiley & Sons, Inc., 1990, Chapters 5–8.
2. "DEPRESSION: Questions you have . . . Answers you need," by Sandra Salmans. People's Medical Society® Publication, 1994, p. 31.
3. Valu-Driver® is a registered trademark of Holden Corporation.

CHAPTER

2

Customer Relationships

Mary's plan was to use the results of the Valu-Driver as the basis for a jointly developed account plan with Alexander Drugs. She knew that if the customer became directly involved in the process of building a closer company-to-company relationship, the chances of creating the right Value Proposition for the right level on the value chain, and perhaps moving up to a Performance Bond, were going to be excellent.

However, Mary also recognized that this joint initiative approach was a departure from the norm at St. George. The few major account plans that had been developed in the past had been constructed internally in their entirety, without any customer involvement. Even in Mary's account plan there would be pieces of the plan, particularly those areas that might address internal politics at Alexander Drugs, that would be built privately. But for the most part, it would be a team effort, involving both companies.

Mary knew that the very process of building the plan, particularly the teamwork involved, would set the stage for the type of relationship they might enjoy with this customer in the future. The attention that the customer would receive from St. George, in the absence of a short-term sales opportunity, was a positive element in itself.

Mary was reminded of an e-mail that Mark had sent her a month or so ago citing the results of a management study of car buyers. The study reported six major reasons a salesperson loses a customer supporter, ranging from factors over which a salesperson has no control to factors directly influenced by a salesperson. The study results in Figure 2.1 show the percentage of time each factor is the main cause.

Mary knew that using value as the foundation for a joint planning effort with Alexander Drugs would signal to them that Mary and St. George cared about them, as well as for the account itself. She was learning that in today's marketplace, the supplier organization had to personify all that is involved in the selling effort. Mary needed to show the customer that she as an individual cared, and that her company also cared.

But how does an organization communicate a caring attitude, she wondered? *And did St. George actually care about Alexander Drugs?* Certainly they cared about the business they were deriving from Alexander, and wanted the relationship maintained, to the extent that it ensured future business. But what about caring for them in general, as a company? This was something that an organization could not fake.

Good salespeople always care; in fact, they often over-identify with certain customers. It is an attribute which companies generally value in the recruiting process, but how can they assess or develop it at the organizational level?

In thinking about how to handle the Alexander Drugs proposition internally, Mary recalled a sales situation where she had

1. The customer dies.	1%
2. The customer moves.	3%
3. A friend of the customer emerges as a competitor.	5%
4. The competition converts the customer to become their supporter.	9%
5. The customer becomes dissatisfied.	14%
6. The customer believes that the salesperson doesn't care.	68%

Figure 2.1 Causes for Loss of Customer Support.

brought Dr. Robert Tullis, the chief executive officer of St. George, into an important account that had just provided them with a letter of intent for a very large purchase. The meeting was intended to cement the relationship between the companies, with the purchase order to follow. Midway through the discussions, the customer suggested that it might be necessary to alter a few of the terms covered in the original letter of intent, including a discussion of price. Dr. Tullis was not prepared for a renegotiation, particularly not one that involved price. He and Mary were both good negotiators, but for some reason, the CEO at that moment had elected to stand pat on the terms of the original letter of intent. When the customer demurred, Dr. Tullis had remarked that at St. George, they honored their commitments, an implication that the customer was reneging.

Mary's heart had fallen to her shoes as the customer politely but quickly brought the meeting to a close, his anger evident. Challenging the credibility and intent of the customer had not only communicated indifference to the customer's business, it had shown disrespect, even a degree of contempt, for the customer. At the time, Mary had viewed the loss as an anomaly, but now she wondered if it was symptomatic of a more fundamental problem—an inward focus at St. George that was out of step with the realities of selling into this new marketplace.

She could not help wondering, too, if she would be successful in bringing the top executives of St. George into the negotiating process with Alexander Drugs. More to the point, if she succeeded, how effective might they be with the customer? Given her own previous experience with Dr. Tullis, and Mark's experience with the COO, Dick Chainy, she wondered if it were a good idea to include high level executives at St. George after all.

Thinking about that, Mary became even more disheartened, and wondered if she would do better to leave St. George Pharmaceuticals and look for a position with a more forward-thinking company. However, at heart she was not the type of person to run from adversity, so she decided to stick it out a while longer at St. George, and at least give the new process with Alexander Drugs a fair try.

The Valu-Driver requisition was still in the approval process when Mary decided to begin planning its implementation. She had already identified herself, Jim Watkins, Dick Chainy, and Paul Toomey, the service manager, as the team from St. George, but she was thinking about how she might involve Mark Avery, too. Finally, Mary concluded that it was an issue best left for Jim Watkins to address, as she knew Mark could make substantial positive contributions to the effort, but she did not want to be perceived by Dick Chainy as being aligned with Mark.

On the other side, she needed to determine which people at Alexander she should select to fill out the questionnaires. Taking the same approach she had presented in her recent meeting with Jim Watkins and Dick Chainy, Mary contacted Alexander Drugs, secured their support and organized the necessary logistics. They indicated they were ready to proceed with the proposed project.

A few days later, the requisition was approved, and everything seemed to be coming together nicely. Jim informed Mary that Mark would, in fact, be involved, but that Dick Chainy would not be able to participate, due to a very busy schedule. Mary hoped that was the real reason. She shifted into high gear, distributing and explaining the questionnaires.

It took three weeks to get everyone's completed questionnaires, and another week to process the results. St. George had been working with Alexander Drugs for nearly three years, with good Customer Satisfaction Survey results each year. Therefore, they were expecting to see a strong value rating of St. George by Alexander when the questionnaires were completed by the Alexander Drugs participants. The results, however, had something quite different to say.

Value Expectations

The overall assessment by the customer indicated a Stage II business relationship, while the assessment by the St. George team had been high Stage III. More significantly, Alexander Drugs had rated their satisfaction with the Stage II business relationship with St. George at thirty percent. The rating scale suggests that a rating of fifty percent is minimum to meet a customer's basic expectations. This was illustrated using the same Four-Stage Customer Model (Figure 2.2) that Mary had presented in the meeting with Dick Chainy.

The final results of the questionnaire tabulation were scheduled to be presented to the customer shortly, but first the St. George

Quality	Stage I	Stage II	Stage III	Stage IV
Customer's Intent	Solve a problem	Acquire a solution	Capitalize on a business opportunity	Create a new business opportunity
Buying Focus	Product or service features	Product or service benefits	Supplier expertise and resources	Supplier strategic ability and commitment
Relationship	Vendor on demand	Characterized by trust and commitment	Strong mutual dependency	Business partners and advisors to each other
Customer Value	Low cost, quick fix	Able to purchase reliable solutions	Able to co-develop and create custom offerings to solve complex problems	Receives insight into business issues and creativity in addressing them

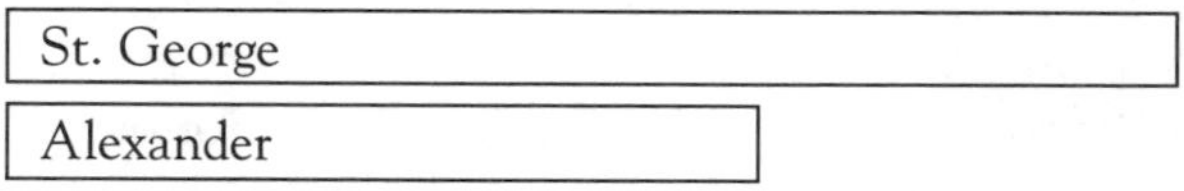

St. George

Alexander

Figure 2.2 Four-Stage Customer Model with Results.

team needed to meet, in order to fully analyze and understand the report, and determine how best to present it. During that meeting, it became clear that a number of factors characterized the situation, as they worked to interpret the results:

- In reviewing the four areas of diagnostic emphasis—Intent, Focus, Relationship and Value—St. George came out at a high Stage III on Intent, indicating that they were really trying to provide value, much of it undoubtedly the result of Mary's individual efforts.
- The low Stage III score in the area of Focus and the low Stage II score on Relationship suggested that St. George was in fact providing value, but was not getting credit for it from the top management levels at Alexander Drugs.
- The scores further indicated that St. George was too low on the value chain, contributing not just too little value, but also not the right *kind* of value to the customer.

- The gap between St. George's perception of value provided to Alexander, and that held by management at Alexander Drugs, combined with the low satisfaction rating from the customer, meant that the risk of being displaced by a competitor was very real. *The marketplace had educated Alexander Drugs about how much and what kind of value they should be receiving*. Now, they were educating St. George.

Mary knew that in the old days, a customer would most often become dissatisfied with the value a supplier was providing if a competitor came in and was able to offer them more. Now, customers work to go up their own value chains, and they do not need someone to tell them—they know. A supplier is either in sync with them on their value chain, or is not.

Using that measure, the bad news was that St. George was not properly aligned on the value chain with Alexander Drugs. The good news was that they knew what had to be done to create value alignment, which would become a key goal in the process of building an account plan. Correcting the alignment problem was how St. George, as a company, would show Alexander Drugs that they truly cared about them and their business. It put value contribution ahead of financial returns.

Mary dismissed for the present any thoughts of Performance Bonding. She knew that correct value alignment must precede such shared-risk ventures, but the concept would remain in the back of her mind. She sensed the power of Performance Bonding, but recognized that the environment had to be exactly right in order for it to work.

The next day, Mary asked for an appointment to meet with Sally Loxner, the director of marketing at St. George. Sally had not been involved in the Valu-Driver process, but Mary knew that she had always believed that sales and marketing should work more closely together, and Sally also was skilled in strategic planning. She was a possible resource and ally for Mary. On a larger scale, Mary felt that value chain management should be driven by marketing and implemented by sales. This meeting would be an opportunity to explore that concept. She was pleased when Sally readily agreed to an informal get-together to discuss the idea.

Mary briefed Sally on the situation with the Alexander account, and the Valu-Driver process and outcomes. Mary had not yet set a date with Alexander Drugs to present the results, because she wanted to use that opportunity to introduce her recommendations to create value chain alignment, centered on a joint planning process. Mary felt she needed Sally's experience and expertise to help her better understand that process.

"People tend to think that planning is about organizing an effort to accomplish something and, as such, they quickly focus on the process of building a plan," Sally explained. "This is not to say that a focus on process is bad, but process is not planning. People think of planning as a way of determining what is required to achieve some objective or goal, perhaps even to formulate those objectives or goals. And it is that, but at a strategic level, it's much more. You used the word 'alignment' earlier. Basically, alignment is one word that describes strategic planning. Most successful planning efforts require some form of alignment. It may be between the objectives you want to accomplish and the resources required to accomplish them, or it may be aligning people and roles, or aligning management support with the strategy to achieve specific objectives. In your case, with Alexander, it's a bit more complex. First you have to create alignment in four key areas in order to take it a step further, and align the companies on the right level of the value chain. Those areas are:

- Reward.
- Risk.
- Accountability.
- Philosophy."

Mary scribbled a few quick notes.

Sally continued, "Earlier in my career, I believed that joint planning was based upon sharing reward, risk, accountability, and philosophy. But that only implies a common interest. In business today, both companies need to achieve *congruence* between their individual rewards, risk, accountability, and philosophy. That makes it a two-dimensional challenge."

Mary paid close attention as Sally focused in on the essential elements of strategic planning. Mary had been involved in planning before and had built several account plans, but now she realized that while she had done a good job of organizing these sales efforts, it was not the kind of carefully orchestrated strategic planning

Sally was describing. Maybe that was why her account plans were never really updated or used as 'living' or working documents. True, they had helped her to think through what she wanted to accomplish, but they were never 'strategic' in the true sense of the term. She could see that planning was a one-dimensional effort, while strategic planning was clearly two-dimensional in nature.

"If you get the alignment right," Sally was saying, "you will achieve more than you hoped. Two organizations properly aligned for a well-defined purpose will create new value for both."

"Can we explore the four areas of alignment in more detail?" asked Mary. "I can see I have a lot to learn. Do you have the time?"

"Certainly. Now that you have described to me what you are trying to do with Alexander Drugs, I'm really interested in the project. This is important to St. George for the development and retention of an important account, but it's also important to me, personally—not just from a marketing standpoint, but because it might also move us along toward some goals and objectives I've had for a long time. I have always believed that marketing and sales can, and should, work in an integrated fashion on these things."

Sally picked up the phone and spent a few minutes reworking her schedule with her administrative assistant. When she replaced the receiver, she was smiling. "There now. I've just cleared my afternoon so we can work on this project together."

Mary was pleased. She knew she had gained an ally in Sally Loxner.

Sally went over to the white board in her office and wrote the word:

REWARD

REWARD

"The best way to begin is to examine your goals. Sketch out qualitative expressions of value, similar to Value Statements. These can be long-term in nature, or broad in their scope. Characterizing these goals brings us to our objectives. Objectives are the *measurable* reflection of a goal, or set of goals.

"For example, in marketing we may have the goal of becoming the leader in a particular market. But what does that actually mean? How do we know if we are achieving it? The answer is we must characterize that goal in terms of accomplishing specific measurable objectives, such as:

- Increasing our current market share from 42 percent to 55 percent in the first year;
- Introducing the next-generation product in the fourth quarter of the first year; and
- Increasing market share another 10 percent, from 55 to 65 percent, by the end of the second year.

"Goals and measurable objectives are the first dimension of reward," remarked Sally. "The second is congruence. Now we must examine how compatible our goal is with those of other departments upon whom we must depend in order to achieve it. Take Research and Development (R&D), for example. Marketing will require their help to meet the second and third objectives. R&D will have to design the next generation product, if we are to further increase market share in the second year. But, suppose that R&D's goal is to establish technological leadership for St. George in its field, pushing state-of-the-art to the 'bleeding edge,' ahead of other companies. Therefore, there is no way they can have the next generation product ready in the fourth quarter of the first year. To accomplish their goal, they will need another two quarters to complete the design work. To bring the two goals into alignment requires taking a strategic perspective on both, making the right compromises or tradeoffs to accomplish both goals, or negotiating which goal is more critical to the company's success and should take precedence.

"Creating alignment between or among divergent goals becomes a strategic process, which requires strategic thinking.

"Now let's look at Risk."

RISK

"Just as reward can be expressed in terms of two components—goals and objectives—risk can be described in terms of magnitude and manageability, often referred to as a risk profile. Determining the amount of risk requires that you identify and examine a number of considerations, along with their associated consequences. Considerations in assessing risk magnitude include:

- Investment costs.
- Opportunity costs, in terms of what could have been achieved if the resources had been allocated differently.
- Relationship quality. Resource allocation, and commitment of resources, are only as good as your relationship with the people who control those resources.
- External factors, such as competitive counter-responses, new market trends or changes in technology.

"Assessing risk manageability to complete the risk profile involves a careful analysis of each risk element in terms of other considerations, such as *operational control,* which suggests that you look at:

- Authority sufficiency, remembering the governing principle, 'responsibility minus authority equals risk.'
- Political compatibility: The unspoken considerations within and between organizations that may support or conflict with your plan, or with you personally.
- Philosophical compatibility; divergent values or operating principles between you and other individuals involved in the formation and/or implementation of the strategic plan will reduce your operational control.
- Assessing the potential for the emergence of a significant new risk factor, such as the loss of a key individual, or a key resource, or perhaps an unanticipated change in funding or in management commitment.

"*With a well-constructed risk profile, you're ready to test congruence with the customer's profile, which is mainly a question of balance.* It is a matter of reviewing the nature and extent of risk on both sides, in terms of magnitude and manageability, to determine if they are in proper proportion. Viewed in this sense, 'balance' does not mean that each company assumes an equal amount of risk. Balance here is two-dimensional. On one axis, you are looking at the relationship of risk to reward within your own company. If St. George is going to receive the lion's share of the return in a joint initiative, the amount of risk it assumes should be proportional to its potential gain, assuming that its risk is adequately manageable. On the other axis, we consider the risk-to-dependency

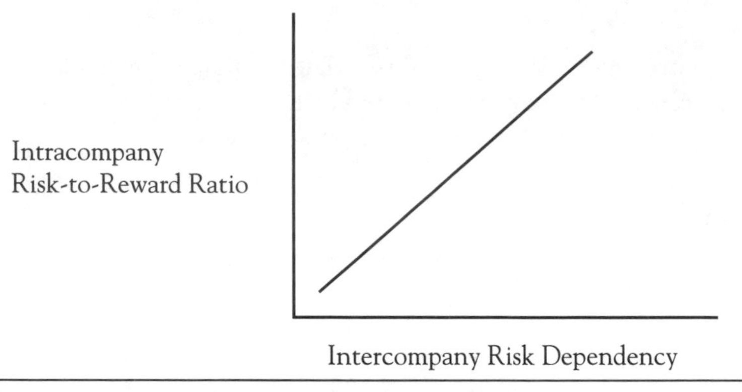

Figure 2.3 Balancing Risk.

relationship, which concerns manageability across company lines. An illustration of the concept looks like Figure 2.3.

"Let's say Alexander has the smallest amount of risk, consistent with reward, but the risk Alexander has could be significantly increased if St. George fails to perform, perhaps due to a change in company control. Without additional safeguards in place, the risk is out of balance for Alexander Drugs."

Sally emphasized that these four key factors must play together in concert to form a strong foundation for a good strategic plan. In reality, Sally was providing Mary with a great deal more than a strategic planning process format. Mary was receiving wisdom, which is the most important asset of an organization, but is helpful only if it is shared within the organization. Sally then addressed the issue of accountability.

ACCOUNTABILITY

"Again, two dimensions prevail," she commented, sketching on the board. "First, accountability of the plan to itself, and second, the accountability of the people involved to the appropriate plan authorities within each company."

The sPlan™

"*A plan is an organized effort to accomplish something,*" *said Sally.* "*A strategic plan, what I call an sPlan,*[1] *is like a contract between all the individuals involved in its formation and implementation*. It incorporates all the legal requirements of offer, acceptance, and consideration, just as a purchase order does, yet it is not binding. Fully committed participants should, however, treat it as though it were a legal document, which establishes the seriousness of the effort and the significance of achieving the identified goals and objectives. This will show anyone whose attitude is 'it's nice if it works out, but I'm not going out of my way' how seriously everyone else expects the sPlan to be taken. A 'whatever' type attitude might be all right for a plan, but it won't work with an sPlan.

"This higher level of accountability begins and ends with measurements. Unless every significant aspect of an sPlan is measurable, the project is not real. Without measurable results, you cannot hold people accountable, even if they appear fully committed to the sPlan's success. That's why well-defined objectives are critical to an sPlan. Without them, there is no way to define success for the project, much less any ability to assess the rate of progress, or to calculate risk.

"At the individual level, accountability is also crucial, because the achievement of specific, tactical responsibilities are what will drive the sPlan. We can characterize that accountability as having two components:

1. *Logistical accountability:* The commitment to do something at or before some point in time.
2. *Results accountability:* The commitment to effectiveness or quality, relative to a specific responsibility."

"I can relate to that," Mary nodded. "Last week, I asked an individual in our accounts receivable department to help us get payment from a customer who is long overdue, where I was not having any success. The next day, the accounts receivable manager left me a voice mail saying that they had put in a call to the customer and left a message requesting payment. I could tell that he thought receivables had done their job, and were in fact being very responsive. But—bottom line—they were no help to me at all. I had already left countless messages with the customer, requesting payment, which didn't work. I expected receivables to come up with something different, something stronger. Needless to say, we have not yet been paid by that customer."

"That's not uncommon, I'm afraid," said Sally. "It only serves to highlight the importance of being very clear in the communication of what actions or results are expected from each participant, and then measuring performance by those results. It applies to both the formation of objectives and the specific tactics assigned to people. Without it, you can't exercise operational control beyond the purview of your personal influence. You'll note that I use the word influence here, and not authority. Politically, in any organization, an individual may have authority without influence, and conversely, influence without authority. In any event, politically speaking, influence rules in many instances, not authority. That's a subject on which we really should try to get Jim Watkins to talk to us. He is one of the most politically astute people I know."

"I agree with you on that, Sally," said Mary. "Jim and Mark Avery have both been very helpful to me in that area, but my own policy has always been to avoid internal politics as much as possible. I've seen too many people hurt by it when they decide to get into company politics. But maybe Jim would be willing to come into the sPlan process on this, and help us with the politics of it. He'd be a good person to evaluate the risks and accountability, and advise us on the internal politics side."

"You're right. Jim should be involved. I'll be happy to talk to him, and let him know I'm voluntarily working with you on it," said Sally. "By the way, Mary, I don't necessarily agree with your position about not wanting to get involved in internal politics, since there's almost no way you can avoid it, especially when getting into something like this Alexander Drugs project. But for now, let's review the fourth element, which sort of plays to what I'm saying."

PHILOSOPHY

"A plan will identify what has to be done to achieve its goals and objectives, but it will generally not articulate what is important in terms of the governing values, or principles, that will influence what is done. These values and principles operate at three levels, and may or may not be expressed formally:

1. *Company values.* Every organization has certain values and principles, embodied in its senior management team, that shape its culture and operating style.

2. *Individual values and principles.* Every person lives and works by a specific personal philosophy, or ethic, often developed at an early age.

"As an example of this, you've just expressed one of your principles, Mary, which is to avoid getting involved in company politics."

3. *sPlan values.* A set of defined operating principles, to which both companies formally agree, in advance, and which are stated in the sPlan, for example, "neither company will advance itself at the other's expense" or "both companies will put product quality first," are another big difference between a plan and an sPlan.

"These statements of principle may sound trite, but they do have operational significance, as they are what will govern in specific situations. In the latter example, the principle focusing on quality could give one of the companies permission to slip a shipping date in order to achieve a higher level of product quality, as they know that quality is a core value of the project.

"*Principles, then, are fundamental truths that transcend short-term considerations.* They give birth to guidelines, which operationalize the principles. It would not be practical to live by principles alone. We need guidelines that are specific to the situations that will challenge us. For example, the principle, 'neither company will advance itself at the other's expense' could be expressed as the following guideline, for purposes of an sPlan: 'Neither company will hire away the other's personnel, except by mutual agreement.' You may have seen something similar to this in one of our work-for-hire contracts, Mary. It's a standard provision that can be found in a lot of agreements, but it is often expressed without the inclusion of the principle from which it was derived. Company attorneys don't like stating principles in legal documents because they are open to too many different interpretations. However, since an sPlan is not a legal or binding document, even though we think of it as such in terms of our commitment, we don't have that same interpretive problem.

"In most companies, guidelines exist under the name of Policies and Procedures. They are shaped, but not necessarily articulated, by the few people who have enough power to break or work in exception to them, when necessary, and those people are the FOXES in a company.

"In our federal government, our principles are stated in the Constitution, and the guidelines for interpreting and implementing those principles are stated in the form of laws, established by Congress and our courts. For example, as a principle we have the right to bear arms, yet gun control laws may vary from state to state. Those state laws are valid, as long as they do not impinge upon, or violate, the intent of the principle stated in the U.S. Constitution. The difficult task of interpreting the intent of that principle, when challenged, lies ultimately with the Supreme Court.

"Dealing with the principles of an sPlan is simpler. When you build an sPlan, the wisest course of action is to shape and define, up front, the joint initiative philosophy, in order to ensure compatibility and manageability, and to avoid misunderstanding and misinterpretation later. When two organizations are not compatible, they will tend to:

- Not understand each other very well. Not recognizing an underlying principle, one side will begin to look for a hidden agenda.
- Discount each other, not seeing the significance or wisdom of a particular position.

"In both cases, lack of compatibility starts you down a path that you don't want to go down. It begins with the *irritation* of not working effectively with each other, followed by *avoidance* of certain issues. That leads to *mistrust*, then *contempt* and finally to *animosity*. In other words, incompatibility creates a downward spiral, leading to the unnatural *death* of the partner relationship. It's called the Death Spiral (Figure 2.4)."

"In addition to avoiding the Death Spiral, there is another reason for you to take the lead in shaping the joint initiative philosophy, Mary. Interestingly, it has to do with a basic, yet very important principle: 'The person who articulates the principles gets to write the guidelines.' For your project to succeed, you'll need to take command up front and establish yourself as its leader, setting the direction of the project and organizing the effort in both companies. The better you articulate St. George's philosophy, incorporating it into the sPlan as it is created, the more control you will have, which will enable you to better manage the project."

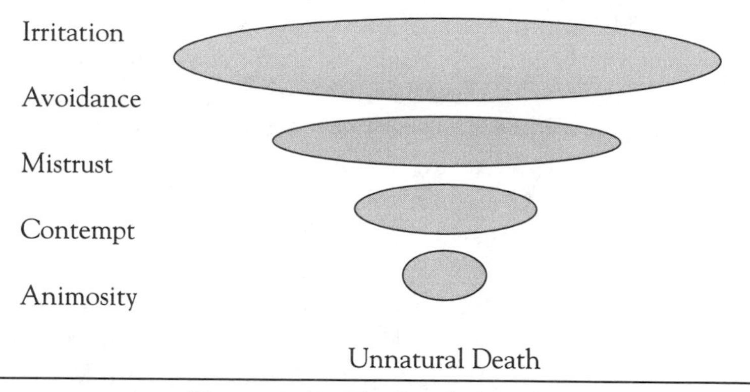

Figure 2.4 The Death Spiral.

Sally paused for a moment to look through a few call notes. "Let's take a break and have lunch. I'll grab a bite here at my desk, and take care of some of the calls I've put off. I imagine you'll want to do the same. When we come back in an hour, we'll move into the process of building the Alexander Drugs account sPlan, keeping in mind the four key areas as we go."

Mary needed the break, but she wasn't thinking of lunch. Her mind was churning with all the new information Sally had given her. When she'd devised the Alexander Drugs joint initiative idea, Mary had no idea of the depth of planning that would be required to make such a venture work. Now she realized how much work, and advance preparation, it would require. But rather than discouraging her, the idea of constructing her first strategic plan, with Sally's help, and maybe Jim's, too, intrigued and energized her. She was eager to learn more, and was prompt and attentive when she returned to Sally's office.

"I really appreciate all the help you're giving me, Sally," said Mary. "And the time you're taking out of your own schedule. I do need your guidance in constructing my sPlan, since I've never done one before."

Sally smiled. "Well, it gets easier after you've done one. The first thing you'll need to do is determine who from St. George, and who from Alexander Drugs, should be involved in the building and implementation of the sPlan. They will be people you feel are necessary and critical to the ultimate success of the project, people who will provide expertise, resources, personal involvement, and management commitment—the resources you'll require to get the job done. In addition to helping you create and operationalize the sPlan, they should be individuals who can assist you in managing the four key areas we discussed earlier—reward, risk, accountability, and philosophy. That means we'll need a FOX on each company team. Without a FOX-to-FOX connection, no significant intercompany joint initiative—whether an sPlan, a Value Proposition, or a Performance Bond—has much chance of succeeding. As you know, *FOXES are the only people in an organization who have the power and influence to operate across all four key areas.* Remember, they don't have to have official authority, but they do have to have the internal power or influence to get things done. Think of this as creating a political and cultural merger between the companies, as it relates to the sPlan."

"I understand," said Mary, "but, I'm not sure I can identify who the FOX is at Alexander Drugs. On our side, I'd say Jim Watkins."

FOX Hunting

"That may be," Sally replied. "Jim is certainly a politically savvy individual, one that we'd want on the St. George team." Sally knew that Jim had some FOX-like abilities, but that at St. George he was not a FOX. At the same time, she felt it inappropriate to say that to Mary. Instead she said, "Let's use a sales tool that I developed for my own use when I was in the field selling medical products. It should enable you to pick out the FOX we want at Alexander Drugs. It's called the FOX Evaluator."[2]

Sally flipped through a notebook and removed some papers. "The FOX Evaluator (Figure 2.5) is really simple. It consists of ten questions that will help you objectively determine who is a FOX in any organization. Like the Value Potential Evaluator that you and Mark have discussed, it's a tool wherein you simply answer each of the questions about a person you're considering, selecting responses on a point range from −2 to +2. Then, just add up the points. A person in the range +14 to +20 is most likely a FOX, a score of +7 to +13 indicates that the individual is probably in the Power Base® and −20 to +6 suggests that the person is most likely not in the Power Base.[3] Keep in mind that as Mark explained with the Value Potential Evaluator, the ranges will have to be calibrated by the user beforehand, to create accuracy.

Score	Definition
+2	I am confident that this is true.
+1	This is most likely true.
0	I don't know.
–1	I doubt that this is true.
–2	I am confident that this is not true.

Fox Evaluator Questions	Score –2 to +2
1. (the individual) has exerted influence outside of his/her organizational authority.	________
2. ____________ has knowledge of his/her company's mission and business goals, as evidenced in his/her working—directly or indirectly—to advance them.	________
3. ____________ is an effective risk taker, showing an ability to assess and manage risk.	________
4. ____________ demonstrates integrity, in being unwilling to compromise his/her company or individuals within the Power Base to advance his/her own aspirations.	________
5. ____________ is a good listener.	________
6. ____________ can appropriately and successfully work in exception to company policy.	________
7. ____________ influences important decisions before they are made formal.	________
8. ____________ has a close relationship with others who posses expertise that he/she personally does not have, but that can be important.	________
9. ____________ is not arrogant about his/her knowledge or accomplishments, as evidenced by his/her willingness to have others receive the credit for accomplishments.	________
10. ____________ is diplomatic in how he/she operates, as evidenced by rarely taking people on in a confrontational manner.	________
Total Your Score	________

Score	Probable Results
+14 to +20	Congratulations, you have found a FOX.
+7 to +13	He/she is not a FOX, but is in the Power Base.
–20 to +6	He/she is outside the Power Base.

Figure 2.5 The FOX Evaluator.

"Here are some copies of the FOX Evaluator. Why don't you go through your list from Alexander Drugs, and rate each individual in question?"

Using Sally's FOX Evaluator model, Mary set to work, and before long, she had identified her FOX. It was Liz Gordon, the Chief Financial Officer at Alexander Drugs. Initially, Mary was concerned that Liz would not have much interest in helping them to develop the sPlan, but then, as she thought about the business, and specifically the financial impact this project could have on Alexander Drugs, she knew that Liz Gordon would be interested, especially since Mary was planning to introduce a Value Proposition that would produce measurable results.

Her only regret was that she had not identified Liz in time to include her in the Valu-Driver process. But bringing her on board now, and including her in the development of the sPlan, would rectify that oversight. Mary was grateful to Sally Loxner for giving her a tool that would help her identify a FOX when she needed to do that. Sally seemed to know a lot about FOXES.

Mary and Sally continued their discussion, and soon they had completed the exercise of identifying the two company teams best suited to helping Mary develop a comprehensive sPlan. Next, they needed to review the sPlan methodology itself.

"The process is really rather straightforward," Sally explained. "It begins with the two teams presenting an overview of their individual businesses, what they do, market trends, competition, and a summary of their business plans. That is followed by a discussion of the opportunities and challenges that each company is currently facing. In the case of Alexander, we would insure relevance by discussing these issues as they relate to St. George's business. You should plan on about three hours for that when you actually conduct the sPlan session. With that foundation built, you're ready to begin defining goals, which, as we discussed earlier, are qualitative in nature. You might want to look at a three-year time frame for those goals, which could be expressed in terms of revenue or non-revenue aspirations. For example, we might want to be able to publish a case study describing the positive impact we have had on Alexander's business. From a marketing point of view, that can lend a tremendous amount of credibility to Value Statements and Propositions presented to new accounts in the future.

"Next, you'll want to introduce the Valu-Driver results, so that the goals of both companies become a backdrop for the report—a context within which it can be viewed. If I am not mistaken, you'll find the opportunity to build jointly-owned goals, focusing on helping Alexander move higher on the value chain which should, by definition, draft St. George along, as well. This should take around two hours of the session.

"Now it becomes even more interesting. On the St. George side, characterizing goals in terms of specific objectives can be challenging in one sense and straightforward in another. Make certain that each objective is clear, concise, and time-bounded. Begin by listing them. *Then, move into a critical path analysis—that is, prioritizing the objectives, starting with the most important ones first.* Make certain that there is a defined way to measure progress toward each objective. If that is not possible, it is not a meaningful objective.

"For us, the process of defining objectives is not so straightforward. A number of St. George objectives will of course be sales-oriented, which you need to address without having the process sound too self-serving. The way we do that is to identify our sales objectives in terms of their contribution to Alexander's business. For example, let's say our sales objective, expressed internally, is to secure a particular order within four months for a defined price. Here, we would express that same objective as meeting a particular Alexander need, within four months, with an Alexander investment amount of whatever the price is.

"Be careful to understand that the issue is not one of word smithing, but rather an attitudinal consideration, keeping the win-win perspective out in front of the process."

Formulating Strategy

"With the objectives in priority order, you will want to build an Objective-Strategy-Tactics (OST) plan behind each one. As you know, there are four classes of strategy from which to select in formulating the right strategies for the right objectives:

- Direct.
- Indirect.

- Divisional.
- Containment.

DIRECT

"This is the strategy employed most often. It requires clear superiority to be successful and as a result is very resource-intensive. In addition, it's a highly visible strategy, in that competition can see what you are doing and extrapolate on it, pinpointing your next move with the precision of a Global Positioning System. The market trend toward consolidation is an example of companies implementing a Direct strategy. When one has acquired one's seventh clinical lab in a row, it's not rocket science to figure out what type of company will be next on the acquisition list."

INDIRECT

"From a sales perspective, this type of strategy will look as if it is Direct, until the ground rules are changed at the eleventh hour. You're not depending on superiority to win; what you're leveraging here is time, or the lack thereof. By introducing new issues into a competitive sales situation just when it's about to close, and a decision is about to be made, you throw the competition off guard, giving them no time to catch up. The market trend of diversification is an example of firms employing an Indirect strategy. When a company acquires other companies in related fields in order to move up the value chain by being able to provide the marketplace with more complete and better quality solutions, they are changing the ground rules on the competition."

"I know. That's what happened to me with Consolidated Hospitals," said Mary. "Although at the time I thought I was the one implementing the Indirect strategy."

"You were," said Sally. "You were changing the ground rules very effectively at the level of the value chain that you were on, but your competitor, either by chance or design, was able to reposition himself at a higher level on Consolidated's value chain. *An up-shift on the value chain is the most powerful way to change the ground rules on a competitor. When it occurs, they, or in this case you, have no time to react."*

DIVISIONAL

"This class of strategy is similar to that of the Direct type, except that it is not designed to confront the competition head on, but rather to complement them. From a sales perspective, you simply partition the business, carving off a piece for yourself where your company's involvement actually enhances the success of the competitive offering. Why would you ever do that, you might ask? When you do not have the support base to go Direct or Indirect, the best option is to scale down your aspirations and go after a piece of the business. Some is better than none. It also gives you the opportunity to strengthen your support base, in order to compete more effectively in the future."

"What exactly do you mean by 'my support base?'" asked Mary.

"Well, first you use the FOX Evaluator to determine who has the power within the customer's organization. Figure out who is in the Power Base and who are the FOXES. Then run the FOXES and Power Base people through a process, using a sales tool called the Contact Evaluator,[4] to establish who is an opponent, a supporter, a nonsupporter or an ally. Superimpose the two Evaluators, and you will see who supports you, and how much influence they have. That's your support base. Do the same for your competition, and often, on the spot, you can determine who will most likely be the one to win.

"To put it very simply, Mary, if the FOX you identify is an ally of the competition, most likely you'll lose. Conversely, if the FOX is your ally, most likely you'll win. *You can often determine who is most likely to win in a particular sales situation just by looking at the relative support bases."*

"All right, now I'm really interested in that Contact Evaluator. Can you explain it to me, so I can apply it to my contacts at Alexander Drugs?"

Sally showed Mary a copy of the Contact Evaluator (Figure 2.6): "It is really a very simple device. Once calibrated, it allows you to determine objectively the nature and extent of your support within an account. Just as we did with the FOX Evaluator, you begin by

Score	Definition
+2	Almost always
+1	Often
0	Sometimes
–1	Rarely
–2	Almost never

Contact Evaluator Questions	Score –2 to +2
1. My discussions with (the individual) touch upon potential opportunities beyond the current business opportunity.	_______
2. _______________ utilizes me or my company as a nontraditional resource through which value can be derived.	_______
3. _______________ makes an extra effort to assist me in cost-justifying the value that we can contribute.	_______
4. _______________ introduces or refers me to influential people within the account.	_______
5. _______________ has a clear strategy for establishing us as the preferred supplier.	_______
6. _______________ utilizes internal contacts to provide me with business insights and information of a privileged nature.	_______
7. _______________ openly discusses his/her company's plans, projects, and personnel with me.	_______
8. _______________ can articulate my own personal or my company's long-term strategy for building a relationship with his/her company, and how the current opportunity contributes to its advancement.	_______
9. _______________ takes the initiative in assisting me in the current business development opportunity.	_______
10. I feel my relationship with _______________ transcends the business development opportunity at hand.	_______
Total Your Score	_______

Score	Probable Results
+14 to +20	Congratulations, you have an ALLY.
+4 to +13	He/she is a SUPPORTER.
–10 to +3	He/she is a NONSUPPORTER.
–20 to –11	Be careful, he/she is an OPPONENT.

Figure 2.6 The Contact Evaluator.

reading each question, and based upon the scoring definition, rate the individual in question. Remember to calibrate the Contact Evaluator using known allies, supporters, and non-supporters, adjusting the score ranges appropriately."

"Run the FOX and Contact Evaluators for each individual in your customer contact list, from both your perspective and your competitor's. The quality and extent of your support base will emerge, and be set off in sharp relief against that of your competition. Plotting where customer individuals fall on a Map creates a visual interpretation that can also be quite helpful (Figure 2.7)."

"You should also know, Mary, that there are usually multiple Power Bases in a company. There may be one in each major department and one at the corporate level. Also keep in mind that Power Bases can be situational in nature. A very large purchase, for example, or a specific committee or task force, can create a temporary Power Base. As you move up the value chain, your support base will expand into multiple Power Bases."

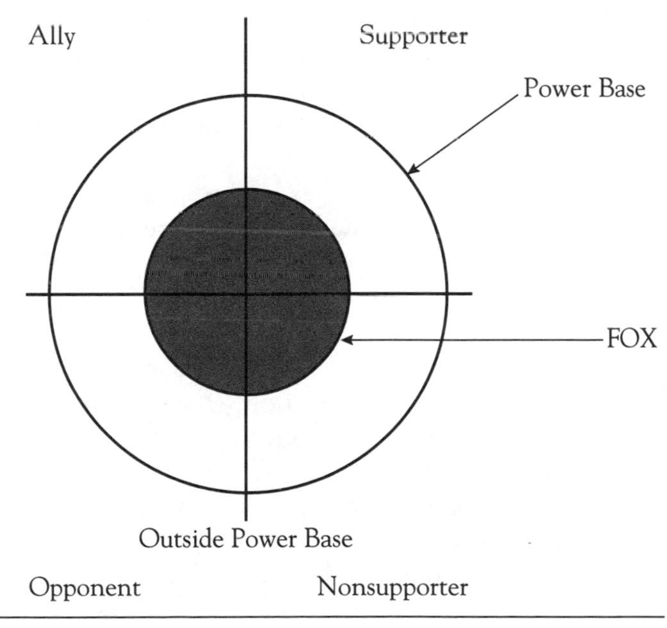

Figure 2.7 Mapping the Support Base.

"That seems like a lot of trouble to go to," complained Mary. "Why is it so important? If I have a FOX in my camp, what is there to worry about?"

Political Competition

"A particular type of dynamic often exists in companies: Political competition. We can characterize this dynamic variously as:

- Power struggles.
- Power plays.

"Power struggles can be healthy in an organization, if properly managed and directed. They are a form of contentious management that brings out the best in people and departments. This assumes, however, that the intentions of the parties are honorable and that the operating philosophy of the people involved is in line with the values and principles of the organization.

"When that is not the case you have a power play, which often operates at the expense of the company and the people involved. An example is where a person initiates a power play, ostensibly for some good business purpose, but in reality to advance a personal goal, one that is out of line with the company's best interest. Perhaps a decision is about to be made to purchase a piece of capital equipment, and the right decision would be supplier A. Yet, the individual opposes A, and strongly supports B, whose equipment is less capable. It may be that he or she perceives a personal advantage in being introduced to, and learning, B's technology. Or it might be that he or she wants to exert influence over the person supporting A, in order to increase his or her own sphere of control within the organization. These motivations are called personal agendas.

"However, not all agendas are bad. The strong motivation to make a project or person succeed, or the desire for advancement, are valid personal agendas. Wanting to build experience with a new technology is not a bad motive, either. It is when the strategy to advance a personal agenda is parasitic or detrimental to the organization that you have a problem. It's also unfair to say that a person initiating a power play is a bad person. A personal agenda is a powerful force in an individual's life because it has been internalized, taken to heart. It then becomes easy for some people to 'drink their own bath water,' where they lose perspective, rationalizing their own behavior and discounting its negative impact on the organization and on other people. It's not that they are bad, it's their thinking that is bad—a malady not uncommon to the egocentric personality."

Sally continued, "Earlier, you asked why you needed to be concerned about Power Bases if you had a FOX in your camp. The answer is that just as there can be multiple Power Bases in an organization, there can be multiple FOXES. Suppose that you do have a FOX as an ally. What if your competitor has a FOX as an ally in her camp as well? Let's further assume that there is a power struggle going on between the FOXES. Who wins?"

"I don't have a clue. They are both very powerful, by definition."

"That's correct, but one will be more influential than the other in a particular circumstance. The question becomes which one is more influential in this particular situation. That FOX will prevail. People possess and wield power for a number of reasons, often because of:

- *Association with authority*, in this case perhaps a corporate FOX, CEO, or Board of Directors.
- *Organizational dependency*, for example, a salesperson who has become a lead performer, causing the company to be very dependent on him or her for a period of time, or an individual who possesses personal expertise in a field that is critical to the company's business.
- *Legal authority*, as in the case of a majority shareholder within a company, or one who has contractual power or owns a patent or copyright granting him or her a special measure of control.

"First, identify the sources of power, then connect them to the two FOXES and you will have your answer. If it turns out that you are aligned with the right individual, life is good. If not, better think about a Containment strategy."

"You know, Sally, I was feeling pretty good about my situation with Alexander Drugs, but now it's clear that I have a lot of work to do, mapping out all the politics of the account. In fact, we will probably include that in our internal planning. One of our internal goals will be to achieve proper political alignment within Alexander. I can also see the focus of several objectives characterizing that goal. For example:

- Identifying all the appropriate Power Bases and finding the FOXES.
- Understanding the personal agendas of those FOXES, and from what source they derive power and influence.
- Determining if any political competition exists within Alexander, and assessing whether power struggles or power plays mark the landscape.

"Now I'm becoming concerned about all this," said Mary. "What if the competition has a better FOX? Maybe you'd better tell me more about Containment."

"Well, when it is clear that you're in trouble from a strategic point of view, and you can't see how to make any class of strategy work, your best option becomes Containment."

CONTAINMENT

"Just as the Divisional strategy is a derivative of the Direct class of strategy, Containment is a variant of the Indirect class. In both cases, you are introducing new issues to the situation, but with entirely different purposes. The purpose of the Indirect strategy is to win an order or achieve some other goal or objective. But the Containment strategy is designed to put everything on hold, to buy time, as long as it does not adversely affect the customer involved. In this way, no one advances, neither you, nor your competition.

"You see, Mary, when we lost the order at Consolidated, it was gone long before we knew it. As soon as the competition indicated that they would consider being acquired, they contained the decision-making process, and by so doing, they contained us. That put them in control of the sales cycle at a value chain level well above us—in fact, out of our sight.

"Well," said Sally, reaching for her notepad, "that's enough on strategies for now. Let's get back to developing the sPlan. Beginning with the most important objective, determine what strategy you think you can count on to be successful. Then identify the necessary tactics to operationalize the strategy. Like objectives, the tactics should be clearly stated, concise, and time-bound, and should indicate who is responsible for their implementation, thereby creating accountability.

"As we build the sPlan, we will undoubtedly reach a point where it will be necessary to differentiate the two, and determine whether something is actually a tactic, or is in fact an objective. I suggest you resolve the question this way: If the task is simple and straightforward, call it a tactic. If it is challenging, complex, and important, label it an objective, which forces you to organize the effort, putting a strategy behind it.

"With the critical Objective-Strategy-Tactic (OST) path completed, you're ready to step back and formulate the overall sPlan strategy."

"Why didn't we do that at the beginning?" asked Mary.

"Until you work through the process of determining what must be accomplished and by when, and on what and whom you're going to count to accomplish it, and then, specifically, what steps you're going to take to do that, you won't have the overall picture. Your sPlan strategy will simply be an expression of the critical path. For example, if the first two most critical objectives center on co-development of a new offering to be brought jointly to the marketplace, then the sPlan strategy will be focused on co-development. When put together, the sPlan at this juncture takes on a form that looks like this:

- sPlan goals and objectives.
- Critical path analysis, prioritizing all objectives.
- Putting a strategy and tactics behind each objective.
- Defining the sPlan strategy.

"Now, that's how you get to the sPlan strategy, but once it has been formulated, you would document and present the sPlan in the following way:

- sPlan goals and objectives.
- sPlan strategy.
- Objectives (by priority), strategies, and tactics.

"There are only two additional steps to completing a world class sPlan:

- Identifying general tactics.
- Testing the sPlan.

"General tactics are tasks like presenting the sPlan to senior management for approval and support. Or setting up logistics, determining when the team will next meet, things like that. Testing, however, is a critically important element of the sPlan, which allows you to move into the future. It begins with looking at whatever could go wrong, for example:

- Management does not approve the effort.
- Critical resources become unavailable.
- The competition launches a counter-attack.
- Funding is removed.
- The customer FOX gets hit by a bus, say, or leaves his company.
- Wall Street experiences a major correction.

"As you can see from those examples, this is the time to consider *all* future possibilities, no matter how far-fetched or potentially damaging to your sales effort. It is not easy. Many people don't like evaluating negatives, or bringing them into the process, even if the ultimate purpose is a constructive one. But considering possible negatives will open the thinking process to include issues that might enable you to identify or be more prepared for what may happen, which is very positive. And Mary, it will do something else for you. We talked earlier about 'drinking your own bath water.' It's easy for a team to get high on their own plan, to become very excited for all the right reasons, but when this causes them not to Test the plan, it becomes potentially dangerous. Looking at the downside will keep you in touch with reality, and keep the team's feet firmly on the ground."

sPlan Goals and Objectives
sPlan Strategy
Objectives (by priority), Strategies, and Tactics
General Tactics
Testing Results

Figure 2.8 The sPlan Schematic.

Sally added those last two pieces, to finalize the sPlan schematic (Figure 2.8).

Mary wondered if Sally would be able to find enough time to continue to help her chart her course with Alexander. She had not yet found the right opening to discuss marketing's future role in the area of value chain management, but she knew that Sally would be very receptive to the idea. But for now, Mary was eager to go off by herself and test some of the theories and tools she had learned from Sally today. It had been time well spent.

"I really don't know how to thank you for all you've taught me today, Sally.

"You don't need to thank me, Mary. I was happy to do it. Our mutual objective is to expand business opportunities for the company. Pooling our effort and knowledge may help St. George keep and further develop the Alexander Drugs account, and that's the way it should be."

Notes

1. sPlan™ is a trademark of Holden Corporation.
2. The Fox Evaluator is available at *www.efox.com/wcs/fox* on the Internet.
3. Power Base® is a registered trademark of Holden Corporation.
4. The Contact Evaluator is available at *www.efox.com/wcs/contact* on the Internet.

CHAPTER

3

The Competitive Salesperson

It had been an intense several weeks for Mary. All the new information she was processing, and the heavy focus on Alexander Drugs, made it difficult for her to cover her other accounts and not let any business slip to the competition. For the first time in her sales career, she found she could not simply shift into overdrive, working harder to push herself through the situation. She was negotiating her way through unfamiliar terrain, and it was requiring a disproportionate amount of her time to assimilate all the new information, distill it, and apply it to her work routine. That created a grueling workload for her, and long hours, but Mary knew that step by step she was making progress, particularly in the areas of:

- How to build Value Statements and Propositions that played to all three organizational levels of a company: Operations, Management, and Executive.
- The principles of Performance Bonding.
- The principles of value chain management.
- Measuring the quality of a relationship between two companies, based upon value.

- How to construct an sPlan, based on value chain management.
- How to measure the strength and size of her support base within accounts.
- How to enhance a support base, using the sPlan process.

Two years ago, Mary not only would have landed the Consolidated deal without difficulty, she'd have secured the business at Alexander Drugs as well. Everything had changed, and it presented a real dilemma. Even with good management support, it was a formidable challenge for Mary to relearn what was necessary in order to sell in today's value-driven marketplace, and still make the sales quota with which she was tasked. Her very livelihood hung on that. *How can I continue to handle all of this?* There was also the unhappy prospect of having to deal with the internal political issues at St. George, which would bring considerable additional stress.

Late at night, unable to sleep, Mary pondered how to handle the new tension in her life, and still manage the rapidly changing direction of her sales career in a capable, positive manner. She decided that in the morning she'd call her friend Josephine Stiller. Jo was the vice president of acquisitions at Newman International Banking in New York, and was a master at overcoming difficult situations through innovative and nontraditional thinking. That's what had brought her to the pinnacle of success at Newman. Jo was Mary's best friend, and they'd known one another for many years—since their college days. She would listen sympathetically to Mary's career concerns, and maybe provide her with just what she needed right now—good, solid advice on how best to proceed.

Newman International Banking was a progressive organization that was currently buying up banks everywhere. Jo was at the helm of that acquisition trend at Newman, spotting new opportunities, negotiating terms, and steering the bank through the legal morass that surrounded most major acquisitions. Before joining Newman, she had been a practicing attorney, working primarily with financial institutions and specializing in bank acquisitions.

Unlike many of her colleagues, Jo was a natural salesperson. Most attorneys disassociated themselves from the sales aspect of building a professional practice, but Jo relished that side of it. If her colleagues talked at all about bringing in new business, they termed it their "business development responsibility." Their euphemistic term for sales reflected the American Bar Association's negative attitude toward attorneys selling their services to the public. But for Jo, sales were sales. "Nothing happens in any business until someone sells something to someone," maintained the practical minded Jo. She also held an MBA from the University of Chicago, which is where she'd met Mary. They'd been roommates there in their undergraduate days. Now Jo was living and working in New York. She was at the top of her game, a place where Mary hoped *she'd* be someday, too. She knew that if anyone could help her work through this problem successfully, it would be Jo Stiller.

Mary called Jo, and they enjoyed one of those long, friend-to-friend conversations where people really connect. Mary was delighted to learn that Jo was scheduled to be in Chicago in a few days on business, and could extend her trip to spend the weekend with Mary. In truth, Jo really couldn't afford to take time away from her pressing concerns in New York at that point, but she'd detected the underlying stress and uncertainty in her friend's voice, and decided to take the time to be with Mary. It would be a great opportunity to renew their friendship, catching up on what was going on in their lives. She'd be happy to see her godchild Arlene, too. But most of all, perhaps she could be of some help to Mary, who sounded like she was at a real crossroads in her life.

A week later, on Saturday, Mary and Jo sat in the Café at the Four Seasons Hotel in Chicago. They had been there since noon, and it was now nearly three o'clock. The time had flown by as Mary unburdened to her friend about the stinging loss of the Consolidated account, and the new dilemma she was facing with how to handle the Alexander Drugs account. Jo listened intently, absorbing not only the details of the two deals, but also her friend's deep concern. After Mary had finished, Jo reflected for a few moments before replying.

"Your focus on value is right on, Mary," Jo began, "I never thought of selling in terms of a value chain, but that is exactly what it is, and it's also what drives business today. I evaluate banks we're thinking of acquiring based upon value, even quantifying qualitative areas like the quality of a bank's customer base, and its employee loyalty, through metrics that I have developed. I believe that there is no other value except that which is measurable, which is what drives my own negotiating approach. I consider it one of the main reasons we have been so successful. On the other hand, I sense here that you are missing something in this approach, and maybe that's what's bothering you so much about your career."

"What am I missing, Jo? I wish I knew myself what's bothering me so much," said Mary.

"Well, let's see if we can figure it out. Everything you've told me today has centered on your concerns about the value that St. George can bring to its customers, present and future. You've talked about the selling implications of value chain management, the company issues of reshaping the business focus at St. George to become more value-centric, and you've also mentioned the internal politics that swirl around that concept. What you have not talked about is YOU—where *you* want to go, what *you* want to achieve, and how *you* feel about your career at St. George."

"That's probably because I really don't know, Jo. I haven't thought much about my own career lately, I've just been immersed in the business I have to land to stay afloat."

"Well, you need to think about it. What about quantifying your own value? I hope you understand that in the world of business, *you* are an asset, one that will either appreciate or depreciate as you navigate your way through every competitive sales cycle, and every internal political encounter or project at St. George.

"No, I guess I hadn't thought of it that way, although I understand what you're saying. I wouldn't know how to quantify my value to St. George."

Sales Currency

"Quantifying your value is not as difficult as you might believe. *Think of it in terms of currency that you can acquire, spend, or borrow.* The more you grow your personal currency at St. George and with St. George's clients, the more you appreciate as an asset to both. During a competitive sales situation, you will either manage your sales value—your personal currency—wisely, causing it to appreciate, thereby increasing your competitive effectiveness, or you will mismanage it, and thereby depreciate as an asset. You can also elect to borrow currency from someone else, invest it wisely, and thereby appreciate your own value."

Mary felt lost. This was totally new to her. "I've never thought of sales, or my value, in terms of banking currency before," she said, "but as I listen to you, it sounds like a plausible analogy. I don't understand about borrowing personal currency from someone else, though. How on earth would you do that?"

"Let's talk about the sources of currency, from a sales point of view," said Jo, "and that will help you understand it. The first is Executive, or chief executive officer, currency. Having met a customer CEO, even briefly, hearing first-hand his or her views on important company topics, gives you currency. In fact, just by that meeting, you may know more about the CEO's views, in certain respects, than do many of the company's own employees. That accords you influence with them as well, and they'll pay close attention as you bring them up to speed on their CEO's thinking. As that happens, you are spending personal currency. If the individual to whom you are speaking is powerful, perceives value in the insight you've just provided, and is of a mind to help you out in return, you have appreciated your currency—your sales effectiveness with that client has increased.

"Or, suppose you are not able to set up a meeting with a customer CEO, on your own, but feel it is important to get the meeting. Working through your own CEO, or maybe your president, you succeed in securing the high-level senior, manager-to-senior manager meeting. When you do that, you're borrowing personal currency from your senior management. If the meeting goes well, giving you the customer's endorsement or support, your currency really appreciates, as that co-relationship is something that you can leverage to produce competitive advantage. To actually capitalize on that advantage to the fullest, however, you need to spend your new currency wisely. For example, overplay your relationship with the CEO, and you can easily damage your credibility and alienate others, which will depreciate your personal value, or your sales effectiveness. Gaining personal currency, lots of it, is key to successful sales—or in my case, negotiating effectiveness with the banks I am acquiring. That's the external perspective.

"Internally, within your company, the same holds true. Your ability to get things done for your customers is directly proportional to the amount of currency you have at St. George. *So currency is a two-way street.*"

Jo outlined for Mary the key sources to building currency, or personal value, within a customer's, or one's own, organization:

1. Relationships—building trust-based relationships with company and customer senior management, particularly those individuals who are in the Power Base, and especially FOXES.
2. Industry Knowledge—developing insight into your own and the customer's industry, identifying:
   - Value chain levels and dynamics.
   - New and emerging trends.
   - Competitors.
   - The emerging role of technology.
3. Political Awareness—recognizing and understanding the political landscape within your company and the customer's organization:
   - Who is in the Power Base.
   - Current political activity, such as power struggles or power plays.
4. Company Effectiveness—the ability to get things done within your company for customers, which in turn creates value for your customers, a function of your:
   - Internal support base.
   - Historical sales performance.
   - Knowledge of your company's business direction.
5. Customer Knowledge—building insight into the customer's business, in terms of their:
   - Financials.
   - Products/services.
   - Business direction, goals, objectives, and strategies.
   - Culture and operating philosophy.
   - History, organizational structure.
   - Resident expertise, as a company.
6. You—developing your personal selling strength, expressed as:
   - Competencies or capabilities, in terms of specific skills and knowledge.
   - Personality-related qualities or attributes that shape your work ethic and impact your performance.

"Earlier, you said I'd be borrowing currency by bringing in my CEO. Why is that?" asked Mary. "How does it get repaid?"

"Good question. As with any loan, you are responsible for repaying the principal, with interest. That is, you have to give increased value back to the lender. In the case of your borrowing currency from your CEO, that means you have to create an incremental increase in business and personal value for St. George *and* your CEO, respectively. Think of it as value in the form of:

- Expected business or sales return, based on securing the order with acceptable terms and conditions, or advancing the development of the account.
- Gratification for your CEO, in that he or she has made a contribution to the business while advancing your professional development, which will improve your effectiveness in the future—creating leverage.

"You may not think it is important, but how the CEO or senior management official feels is as important as the business value created, because those feelings shape relationships, increasing your internal effectiveness within your company," said Jo. "*In selling or negotiating, people tend to focus on the tangible, but it is the intangible that drives the deal, and unfortunately, few people realize that.*

"Take a simple sales call, for example. It's not what you say during the call, or even what you *think* the customer heard that is important. It is how that individual comes away feeling about *you*, in addition to what was said, that will determine the level of support that you and your company or product will receive. The customer may leave the meeting enthusiastic and wanting to sponsor you to his or her upper management. Or, the customer may have been turned off by something and see you as a threat, causing the meeting, and probably its outcome, to go nowhere. *Today we need to open our minds to new thinking and new wisdom, and open our hearts to a new level of caring about people.*

"You know, the most challenging negotiations I encounter, Mary, are those where the people across the table know the power of kindness. Their caring attitude is disarming and, if sincere, very effective in motivating us to reconsider our stance on important issues where we may disagree. Caring is therefore strategic as negotiating currency, even though it resides at the opposite end of the spectrum from those negotiating books that present one hundred and one ways to be a 'killer' negotiator. Blunt and cold 'cleaver' tactics, whether they are negotiation- or sales-focused, won't work in today's marketplace. Use them and you will depreciate yourself in a heartbeat."

Mary had thought a lot about the need to care, and to project a caring attitude, not just as an individual, but as an organization, but she had never thought about managing emotions or customer feelings as a point of focus in negotiating. It made her think about that "meeting from hell" she'd endured with the CEO of St. George and a client a while back. It had never occurred to her, as she sensed the meeting going south with her CEO's curt comments, to step in and try to begin managing the customer's feelings. If only she had tried, maybe saying something like, "We really value your business, but Dr. Tullis is a little concerned about some of these points. Perhaps we can clarify them? We mean no disrespect. . . ."

As she continued to think about it she realized that, even if she had not succeeded, it might have signaled to her CEO that perhaps he should alter his own approach with the customer. This was another lesson learned. Jo's next comment snapped Mary out of her thoughts about that meeting, which still rankled in her subconscious, since they'd lost the order over her CEO's lack of caring about the customer's feelings.

"I sense from what you said earlier that dealing with internal organizational politics also makes you uncomfortable, Mary. Politics can make most people uncomfortable, but they are a fact of life, and you will need to learn how to confront that and work with it. Organizational politics are just one more example of how the intangible drives the tangible. By the time you see it, you can't control it, because it's over and done. The same is true about wisdom. For many it's simply not real, and they miss it completely. So you have to keep this in mind: With organizational politics, it's what you *don't* see that can hurt you most."

Mary knew that Jo was right. Her knowledge of value was now moving into the intangible domain, which, while invisible to most, had effects that were very real, as she had experienced firsthand at Consolidated, and during that infamous meeting between her CEO and a customer. Mary described to Jo what had transpired in that meeting, and then asked, "What happened to me there, in terms of currency?"

"I'm afraid you were reduced to bankruptcy, my friend. Your personal currency, with both your company and your client, was rapidly depreciated. Here's why: Bringing in the top gun is a power move, which should be expected either to excite or to disturb the customer. You never intend for such a meeting to leave the customer in a state of emotional neutrality. But now, having said that—at the meeting you describe, the disturbance was elevated to a personal level by your CEO. That's what blew it up. Just as a CEO or any senior executive can be a significant asset in a meeting, they can also be a heavy liability. When such a person loses or destroys credibility, the entire company loses currency. During that meeting, your CEO gambled and lost all of his currency, depreciating himself, his company, and you. It doesn't happen often, but when it does, it's devastating. So one has to exercise care in bringing such power into play."

"You can bet all your currency that I'll think twice next time," said Mary, and they both laughed. Mary was surprised to find she could finally laugh about it, but in talking about that experience with Jo, she had not only confronted her feelings about it, enabling her finally to put it behind her, but with Jo's help, she had also gained insight and wisdom from it.

Measuring Sales Currency

Jo continued, "Look, Mary, my suggestion now is that you take time to estimate, or quantify, just how much currency you have with certain accounts—like Alexander Drugs, for example. It's not a difficult process, just somewhat nontraditional. I would never go into a negotiation without first going through a similar exercise about myself and my company's relationship with a new bank."

Jo introduced the Personal Currency Tabulator[1] tool and demonstrated how to use it as an account-specific self-assessment of sales effectiveness, expressed in terms of currency. She explained that, as with any non-traditional tool or method, Mary might have to modify it to suit her work, perhaps calibrate it before using it.

"But in general it will enable you to measure your currency level relative to the Operations, Management, and Executive levels of the customer's organization."

Tabulator Questions	Score
1. If you have an ally[1] within the customer's executive management team, enter a score of 10 points; if he or she is a FOX,[2] score 15 points.	______
2. If you have a supporter[3] within the customer's executive management team, enter a score of 5 points, if he or she is a FOX,[4] score 10 points.	______
3. If you can identify the top 3 trends within your customer's industry, enter a score of 10 points.	______
4. If you can identify your customer's top 3 competitors, enter a score of 10 points.	______
5. If you can articulate the customer's corporate goals and objectives, enter a score of 15 points.	______
6. If you can describe your customer's value chain, as they view their marketplace, enter a score of 15 points.	______
7. If you can identify the personal agenda (a political or organizational aspiration) of the corporate FOX within your customer's organization, enter a score of 10 points.	______
8. If you have uncovered a power struggle or power play within your customer's organization, enter a score of 10 points.	______
9. If you have made 100% of your quota for 3 or more consecutive years, within your company, enter a score or 10 points.	______
10. If you have quick access to your executive management, enter a score of 10 points; if to an internal FOX, score 15 points.	______
Total	______

Analysis

If your score fell into the following ranges:	Your currency strength can be considered:
70 and up	Executive level
50 to 69	Middle management level
49 or below	Operations level

[1] Please use the Contact Evaluator (Chapter 2, p. 58) to make this determination.
[2] Please use the FOX Evaluator (Chapter 2, p. 53) to make this determination.
[3] Please use the Contact Evaluator to make this determination.
[4] Please use the FOX Evaluator to make this determination.

Figure 3.1 The Personal Currency Tabulator.

In addition, Mary learned, she would be able to track her improvement within accounts over time—borrowing, building, and spending currency to grow or appreciate in value.

Mary realized that the Personal Currency Tabulator would have applications beyond evaluating her own currency strength. If she applied it to each individual involved with the Alexander sPlan, it would soon become apparent whether or not the St. George team, as a whole, had the necessary currency to create and implement the value that was articulated in her Value Proposition. As she had just learned from her banking friend, *in its most essential form, currency is value*. For her team to be effective in building a stronger account relationship with Alexander Drugs, based upon value and using the Valu-Driver and the sPlan methodology, they would have to possess adequate personal currency. Without it, they could not handle the cost of sales, in terms of value.

Mary couldn't quantify what that cost of sales or required amount of currency would be to create success at Alexander, but now she had the confidence, and the sales tool, to approach it and figure it out—not just for Alexander Drugs, but for any major account in the future. It was a starting point that would help her to understand if, and where, the team was too low on currency. Having identified those areas, she could then detail, or pulse, various St. George executives onto the team on an as-needed basis, forming the company's first virtual account team.

Such teams are dynamic in their structure, allowing the team leader to reconfigure the team on the fly to accommodate changing customer needs, while at the same time maximizing account profitability by avoiding the need for dedicated resources. This becomes particularly important when one is proposing a Value Proposition at the Management or Executive levels. With Performance Bonding, it becomes essential, for risk management purposes.

Later that evening, after ordering in dinner at Mary's townhouse, Jo and Mary resumed their discussion. Jo was curious about where Mary wanted to go with her career, and posed several questions about Mary's role in the company, and where she envisioned herself five years from now.

"At the moment, as an account manager, I am responsible for the penetration and development of specific accounts in the Chicago area," Mary explained. "Up to now my performance has been excellent—I've exceeded my quota every year, received good raises and gained recognition, but now . . . well, it's hard to say what will happen, Jo. I'm concerned about these new trends in our industry, and all that they represent. I'm afraid they might shut me out, or leave me behind."

"Well, you're certainly not alone in your field, Mary, and not alone in your concerns, either. The changes in the competitive landscape are hitting everyone, but therein lies the challenge, and the opportunity."

"I'm afraid what I'm seeing is too much challenge, even though I know that the opportunities are incredible," said Mary.

Jo realized then that her friend was very discouraged, not only about her career as it stood today, but about her future prospects with St. George.

"Well, based on what you have said, Mary, and on my own knowledge of your industry, you're right—the personal and organizational implications of dealing with your changing marketplace will end some sales careers. But don't let that discourage you, because it will also jump-start many others, putting people like you on a fast track. Let me assure you, you're in the right place at the right time to make a difference for yourself, and for St. George, too. So I hope you will capitalize on that. To do that, however, you will need to carefully examine your own capabilities, as they relate to these new sales practices you are working on with your marketing manager and with accounts like Alexander Drugs. You know, in our earlier discussion about currency, and specifically about the Personal Currency Tabulator, we talked about external sources like securing relationships with high-level people, or identifying political activity like power struggles, within an account.

"But you shouldn't forget to look at your own internal sources of currency. By that I mean those that reside within you, such as your:

- Competencies—sales-related qualities, expressed in the form of skills and knowledge.
- Attributes—personality-related qualities.

"*These competencies and attributes enable you to identify, develop, and capitalize on external currency sources to create competitive advantage*. For example, spotting a customer power struggle is very difficult for an outside salesperson, and requires a certain political acumen that enables you to know what to look for, how to interpret and understand what you see, and how to respond. To do that requires that people develop certain competencies."

Political Acumen

"Let's review various sets of competencies, combining them into groups that I'll call Primary Characteristics. Each competency can then be expressed in terms of observable behaviors that enable us to measure the competency, according to four stages of proficiency—the same four stages you described to me earlier that make up the Four-Stage Sales Model. Take Political Acumen, the process of discerning and professionally capitalizing on the political forces within an organization, for example. As a sales- or job-related quality, it has two core competencies, each with four stages of observable behaviors. Characterizing Political Acumen are two core competencies:

1. Develops and utilizes a political map to generate political leverage.
2. Recognizes and capitalizes on political competition within the customer.

"By looking for the observable behaviors, we are able to rate your strength in each competency. That will give you insight into your level of proficiency for the entire Primary Characteristic, like Political Acumen. Because it is Four Stage-based, we are able to understand the relevance of your competency strengths in today's marketplace. Let's revisit the model."

"Reviewing the observable behaviors for each competency, you will see that they are described in terms of four stages that correlate to the Four-Stage Sales Model (Figure 3.2). For example, selling business solutions at Stage III correlates to attaining significant Stage III proficiency in the relevant competencies. Determining whether that level of proficiency exists can be done in two ways:

1. By observing your own, or someone else's, selling behavior.
2. You can participate in a Holden Corporation assessment.

Quality	Stage I	Stage II	Stage III	Stage IV
Salesperson's Intent	To be considered	To make a sale	To create repeat business	To become the dominant supplier
Salesperson's Focus	On the product or service	On the customer	On the competition	On the customer's customers and competition
Relationship with Customers	Casual in nature	Trust-based	Mutual in nature	Symbiotic in nature
Value Chain Level	Low operations focus, providing product or service options	Low middle-management focus, providing applications solutions	High middle-management focus, providing business solutions	High executive focus, providing strategic direction and expertise

Figure 3.2 Four-Stage Sales Model.

"However you score, it's important to note that no stage is better or worse than the others. For example, Stage III is not *better* than Stage II or I, it is simply *different,* just as Stage III selling is different from Stage II or IV selling.

"The first Primary Characteristic, as I have mentioned, is Political Acumen," said Jo. "Like many of these characteristics we'll talk about, you'll see that Political Acumen is as important to what I do, negotiating and acquiring financial institutions, as it is to what you do, selling.

"Earlier, you told me about the new approach to account planning your marketing manager is helping you develop—the sPlan process, I believe she calls it? You described the relationship of goals to objectives. Well, the same is true with Primary Characteristics. They are to competencies as goals are to objectives. Each Primary Characteristic has a specific and measurable set of core competencies. We refer to them as core because they are of central importance in describing the characteristic. For example, you could describe a Primary Characteristic like Political Acumen as an array of competencies; however, there are only a couple that are highly dispositive, or essential. That keeps things manageable. Lets look at one of them (see Figure 3.3)."

Qualities	Stage I	Stage II	Stage III	Stage IV
Salesperson's Intent	To be considered	To make a sale	To create repeat business	To become the dominant supplier
Salesperson's Focus	On the product or service	On the customer	On the competition	On the customer's customers and competition
Relationship with Customers	Casual in nature	Trust-based	Mutual in nature	Symbiotic in nature
Value Chain Level	Low operations focus, providing product or service options	Low middle-management focus, providing applications solutions	High middle-management focus, providing business solutions	High executive focus, providing strategic direction and expertise
Core Competency	**Stage I**	**Stage II**	**Stage III**	**Stage IV**
Develops and utilizes a political map to generate political leverage	Does not routinely distinguish influence from authority; little ability to generate political leverage	Identifies who is in the Power Base structure	Aligns with the centers of influence (FOXES) and "hooks" their personal agendas	Working closely with FOXES, acts as a catalyst to successfully complete their agenda

Figure 3.3 Four-Stage Model with Political Acumen Core Competency.

"You can see, Mary, that all this is based upon the distribution of *influence* within the customer's organization, as opposed to authority. You can find individuals at senior levels who don't have influence commensurate with their titles and, conversely, people at operating levels who are very powerful, with the ability to exert significant influence. If we put it into a matrix, it would look like Figure 3.4."

"Focus, in terms of the three core competencies, is on the Power Base, where influence is the common denominator. It sounds simple, but influence, unlike authority, is not visible. Only the *exertion* of influence can be observed. So one needs to develop the acuity to recognize when influence, particularly in the absence of authority,

POWER BASE	
Influential Authoritarian	Noninfluential Authoritarian
Influential Nonauthoritarian	Noninfluential Nonauthoritarian

Figure 3.4 Influence-Authority Matrix.

exists. As you already know, the person wielding the influence will be a FOX (Figure 3.5)."

Mary said, "I believe that FOXES are among the most powerful individuals within an organization. They also are the most difficult to identify, because their influence exceeds their authority to such a great degree. They nearly always maintain a low profile."

"You're right. The Influence–Authority Matrix we discussed helps us find them, but there are other ways, too, and I'm sure you know that it's important that you do find them wherever possible. FOXES are smart enough not to exert their influence openly in

Influential Authoritarian	Noninfluential Authoritarian
FOX	
Influential Nonauthoritarian	Noninfluential Nonauthoritarian

Figure 3.5 FOX Influence-Authority Matrix.

another's territory. For that reason, the best way to find and identify them is through two FOX Hunting practices:

1. Power Base tracking.
2. Spotting a FOX-like profile.

"And you know that people who are part of the Power Base are there because of their association with a FOX, who is at the center of influence. Usually they are networked very closely, which is what makes tracking possible. Find a person in the Power Base and if you're skillful, that individual will lead you to a FOX. Also, it is useful to know what FOX-like characteristics you're trying to spot. Here is a chart that formalizes what I look for when I go into a new bank and want to understand its political infrastructure (Figure 3.6)."

"These characteristics also help to identify people who have the power of a FOX, but who live on the dark side and are to be avoided at all costs," warned Jo. "Whenever I don't see Number 8, high integrity, Number 11, people-oriented, Number 12, good listener, and Number 15, not egocentric, yet the individual is clearly very powerful, I do not proceed with a bank acquisition without a plan to replace that person. That's how strongly I feel about avoiding the political dark side of a FOX. Having said that, remember that FOXES drive organizations, and understanding how to deal with them and with internal politics in general is key to successful negotiation and selling.

1. Results-Oriented	2. Rarely Surprised by Events
3. Can Work in Exception to Policy	4. Calculated Risk Taker
5. Delegates Well	6. Strategic Thinker
7. Well Respected	8. High Integrity
9. Very Well Connected	10. Well Organized
11. People-Oriented	12. Excellent Listener
13. Communicates Well	14. Diplomatic
15. Not Egocentric	16. Personifies the Organization's Operating Philosophy

Figure 3.6 FOX-like Characteristics.

"In fact, if you connect the core competencies for Political Acumen and the Four-Stage Sales Model, you can see that people at Stage I are focused on selling products or services, as opposed to building competitive advantage based on proper management of a sales cycle. That is, formulating competitive strategy, achieving the correct political alignment, or engaging in competitive sales tactics to outrun a competitor—the type of activities that describe a Stage III approach to selling. But don't think of Stage I selling as the exclusive domain of a new salesperson. There are many instances where Stage I selling is very appropriate. For example, your marketing department might decide to run certain products through a Stage I channel of distribution, which is particularly appropriate for commodity-type products. Remember that Stage I is not measured against the other stages, it is just *different*.

"Between Stages I and III, we have the more solutions-focused sale, which brings you higher up on the value chain, but as in Stage I, your success still depends on the quality of what you're offering. That's why you don't see any ability to produce political leverage at Stages I and II. Competitive advantage is based upon the offering, its price, and the salesperson's interpersonal skills, not on how the salesperson and his or her company is managing the sales cycle or account development effort.

"Each of the stages in these Models is cumulative, so at a Stage III, for example, we are suggesting that a person has Stage III, II, and I ability in a particular core competency. In addition, we can group Stage I, II, and III core competencies under the umbrella of *servicing demand*, taking on a strong competitive orientation as you reach Stage III. At Stage IV, however, life changes. Now, you've stepped into the domain of *creating demand*, the ability to identify and develop opportunities of which the customer may not even be aware. Often, it means creating the budget to support an acquisition. It is a prime example of where a Value Proposition is critical to success, particularly as it relates to justifying the new allocation of budget or funds. This is where it might be critical to operate as a political catalyst, as identified in the Stage IV observable behavior for the core competency, *develops and utilizes a political map to generate political leverage*."

"You already know that a catalyst is something that causes a reaction to happen that would not otherwise occur by itself. Salespeople, at Stages I, II, and III, are by definition sales catalysts in bringing together the customer and their products, services, or solutions. At Stage IV, salespeople, sales teams, and the companies they represent take on a different kind of catalytic role. In the creating demand role, they become a catalyst for change within the customer's organization, operating in a consultative capacity. But that means more than uncovering new opportunities to create value for customers, developing them, and tracking results.

"For example, in your case, Mary, within St. George, if you want to get something done, it may be necessary to 'light a fire' under people, gaining their attention and securing their support. Everyone is extremely busy today and just getting on the right person's radar screen can be a challenge. That's where becoming an organizational catalyst comes into the picture.

"Or, take a company where you understand the political structure and have identified the basis for a power struggle. Perhaps two departments have a history of competing with each other in a healthy way, possibly for resources, or in terms of control in launching new initiatives. Instead of following the traditional methods of organizational consulting, you determine how to spark interest on the part of both groups, interfacing with their respective FOXES while maintaining a politically neutral position. If you are able to capture interest from both FOXES, where they see how taking ownership of the project will advance their individual agendas, you have become a catalyst. But remember two things:

1. You are not *creating* the competition, or the power struggle, you are the spark that *ignites* what is already there.
2. It's important that you remain *neutral* in the process. If you get too involved or take sides, you will soon find yourself in an unmanageable situation."

Mary began to think about what would be required for her to be a catalyst at St. George. *Is the environment there right for change? Who could act as the spark to ignite change? Could it, or should it, be me? And if it turns out to be me, could I remain neutral, as Jo says a catalyst must?*

Realizing that she had prodded Mary into some serious introspection, Jo excused herself to step outside for some fresh air and a cigarette. Mary poured herself a glass of wine, and wandered out to the deck off her bedroom. She knew she was in an ideal position to drive change within St. George, yet in her heart she was still committed to avoiding focusing on internal concerns. Her goal was not to reshape the company, but rather to influence it and its operations to the extent necessary to support her sales requirements in this new market atmosphere. She had no desire to go near the political dark side of St. George Pharmaceuticals. And even if she flirted with the idea, Mary knew there was no way she could remain neutral—she had enough difficulty as it was maintaining neutrality in an account, and the accounts weren't the ones who wrote her reviews and approved her raises and promotions. As an employee of St. George, she knew that neutrality simply wouldn't be possible. *No indeed. And anyway, it's not my mission. Let someone else drive the change that's needed at St. George. Who needs that headache?*

Her decision made, Mary felt herself relax. She went outside to join Jo. "It's a beautiful evening, and Arlene is spending the night with a girlfriend tonight, to give us time to talk. Why don't we go for a walk?" she suggested.

"Fine," said Jo. "You can bring me up to date on how Harry is doing at school."

"Well, I haven't heard much from him lately. You know how it is with boys Harry's age—they only call home if they need money, or are really homesick, but if Harry's learning half as much as I've had to learn these past few weeks, he's doing very well."

Note

1. The Currency Tabulator is available at *www.efox.com/wcs/currency* on the Internet.

CHAPTER

4

Competency Profiling

The next morning, Mary and Jo decided to drive over to Mary's office, where they could find better facilities for illustrating what they had been discussing the previous evening. Jo went immediately to the white board and began sketching on it.

Building a Competency Map

"Let's take a look at several Primary Characteristics, including Political Acumen, and an example of their respective observable behaviors, to create a partial Competency Map. This Competency Map reflects what is required to be successful, as determined by the marketplace, for your position as account manager. You'll see that many of the Stage IV observable behaviors are shaded, and there's a reason for that. Not too long ago, Stage III competencies would have been sufficient to support that position. However, today value chain management has changed all that. Taking point on a major account now requires competency levels that eclipse those required in the past.

"The good thing about this Map is that it's flexible. As new market trends emerge, the Competency Map can be changed to reflect the new sales capabilities required to meet the sales challenges created by those trends. That keeps the Map current, in a 'self-correcting' way, which becomes the basis for determining how strong you are competitively, given today's marketplace. Let's take a look at a partial Map, based on four Primary Characteristics. We could easily include six more, that I will mention briefly, and construct a complete Map for your position, but for an example today, let's select only four. The entire list of basic Primary Characteristics looks like this:

- Political Acumen—discerning and professionally capitalizing on the political forces within an organization.
- Business Savvy—insight relative to business issues and trends along with their corresponding industry and customer implications.
- Executive Bondability—establishing a relationship and sustaining credibility with senior executives.
- Change Agency—being a change agent by influencing and shaping an organization's strategic plans and direction.
- Competitive Adeptness—maximizing competitive advantage while professionally putting competitors at a disadvantage.
- Resource Optimization—maximizing the return on the investment of company resources.
- Leadership Effectiveness—mobilizing others to advance a common vision.
- Management Effectiveness—the ability to get things done through others.
- Product/Service Proficiency—understanding the function, features, and benefits of your products/services.
- Communication Effectiveness—the ability to express ideas and information clearly to create action.

"Our partial Competency Map for your position will incorporate only the first four Primary Characteristics, the lightly shaded boxes indicating what is required to be successful. This is of course based upon the present marketplace. Let's take a look at them, starting with Political Acumen (see Figure 4.1).

"In its totality, Political Acumen covers the political spectrum, from being able to see the political dimension within an organization, like who has power and is competing for more of it, to knowing

Core Competency	Stage I	Stage II	Stage III	Stage IV
Develops and utilizes a political map to generate political leverage	Does not routinely distinguish influence from authority; little ability to generate political leverage	Identifies who is in the Power Base structure	Aligns with the centers of influence (FOXES) and "hooks" their personal agendas	Working closely with FOXES, acts as a catalyst to successfully complete their agenda

Figure 4.1 Partial Account Manager Map—Political Acumen.

how to generate competitive advantage from that knowledge and insight. Moving across that spectrum, we begin with Stage I.

"A Stage I level of proficiency reflects a nonpolitical view of the world, where more authority appears to equal more power. It is a level shaped by what is tangible, not by what is real.

"A Stage II proficiency includes an awareness that authority does not always rule begins to emerge at this level, along with a desire, but not the ability, to capitalize on that awareness.

"At Stage III political awareness and ability converge. The individual is able to align with FOXES, quickly building insider status in accounts.

"At Stage IV the individual, for all intents and purposes, becomes part of the Power Base.

"Now, I started with Political Acumen as the first Primary Characteristic, but I did not actually intend to present them in order of priority. I am not even sure that priority is relevant, because it is the stages of proficiency that are most important. For me personally, in my situation, politics is at the center of what goes on in life. For example, in your case, Mary, you may not have the ability to develop an effective sales strategy, but if you are aligned with a FOX, he or she will probably guide you in the right direction, creating a virtual strategic ability, as it relates to that specific sales situation. Have you ever seen that demonstrated in your sales work?"

"Yes, definitely," said Mary. "In one account, a senior manager provided me with guidance throughout the sales cycle. At the time, I didn't understand it, but later I recognized that I had lucked out and found my way into the Power Base."

"That's exactly what I mean," said Jo, nodding. "Okay, now let's look at Business Savvy. Figure 4.2 is a Map that lays out one of the core competencies you should know about."

"Like the Political Acumen spectrum, Business Savvy proficiency ranges from building business knowledge and insight, to competitively capitalizing on that which has been built so as to provide enhanced value to a specific customer. Again, that range is characterized by four stages of ability.

"The Stage I level reflects a general understanding of the customer's business.

"Stage II reflects an advance in capability: This is the first level where a salesperson is able to link a specific sales situation to the customer's business situation.

"At Stage III the salesperson becomes a business resource for the customer. Interacting with customer senior management, he or she is able to contribute to, or map value into, the customer's business plan.

"At Stage IV the focus shifts beyond the customer's business plan to the thinking behind it, actually helping to shape the plan as it relates to the supplier's business and the customer's strategic direction.

"You can begin to see the relationship between operating at different levels of the value chain and having the right stage of Business Savvy to support those operations. In addition, you will find a relationship to Executive Bondability: Without a minimum Stage III level of proficiency in Business Savvy, a salesperson generally

Core Competency	Stage I	Stage II	Stage III	Stage IV
Understands and analyzes the cusstomer's business plan and financial position	Has a general understanding of customer's financial position, but no access to their business plan	Builds a business case for a specific product/service using cost-benefit analysis, linked to a customer's current need	Contributes value to the customer's business plan or its implementation	Utilizes business knowledge to create a mutually beneficial partnership

Figure 4.2 Partial Account Manager Map—Business Savvy.

will not have the business credibility necessary to build sustainable relationships with senior customer management. Now, having said that, let's talk about Executive Bondability, and Figure 4.3 shows you a Map that can help you assess it."

"The continuum of Executive Bondability proficiency begins with the ability to see the world as executives see it, then moves to the point of being able to generate strategic value for customers and competitive advantage for yourself, as a salesperson. Take a closer look at the four stages.

"At Stage I, while the executive role is understood to some extent, it is not one to which the salesperson relates, or could in any way leverage.

"Stage II is the first one where the salesperson begins to connect the management of sales situations, by building customer middle management relationships.

"At Stage III that connection becomes stronger and elevates to customer-executive management.

"At Stage IV a longer-term perspective, and a focus on providing significant and nontraditional value to customer organizations, set the stage for demand creation. That is, identifying new opportunities for customers to advance their businesses, which also produces new sales opportunities and long-lasting executive relationships.

"We talked about how Business Savvy is linked to Executive Bondability. Now, can you see how Executive Bondability is also linked to Political Acumen?"

"I think so," Mary responded. "I know that if we can't reach high levels in an account, we can't get the organizational exposure that's often necessary to map out the Power Base."

Core Competency	Stage I	Stage II	Stage III	Stage IV
Assumes an executive perspective	Understands the executive role	Understands the executive role and its impact on a sales opportunity	Understands executive issues as they relate to the customer's business plan	Capitalizes on his/her understanding of executive issues to build long term relationships

Figure 4.3 Partial Account Manager Map—Executive Bondability.

"That's exactly right. FOX hunting is almost impossible without the ability to establish and maintain credibility at executive levels. All three Primary Characteristics then interrelate, which is why you see mostly Stage III and IV levels of proficiency required for success as an account manager in today's marketplace. Now, I'd like to go into all ten Primary Characteristics that I believe should make up the Competency Map for your position, but in the interest of time, I'll address just one more that I think is especially relevant to you, Mary. That characteristic is Change Agency (Figure 4.4)."

"Like the others, Change Agency ranges across a spectrum from driving minimal change within the customer's organization and your own company, to generating momentum within both organizations to produce value and competitive advantage. At one side of the spectrum, then, is Stage I."

"In looking at Stage I, recall from the Four-Stage Sales Model that the focus at Stage I is on a product or service, which does not leave much room for change management.

"Stage II is characterized by a focus on networking and on informally driving operational changes within your company, and a customer's organization, with the intent of advancing a specific sales situation.

"At Stage III the salesperson is focusing on building sales momentum, often by influencing groups of people, and business practices and procedures, that will translate into increased value for customers, and add momentum to a sales effort.

"Stage IV is the partnership level of Change Agency. It is designed to create momentum within and between companies.

Core Competency	Stage I	Stage II	Stage III	Stage IV
Ability to influence change in his/her own organization	Reacts to change in his/her own organization	Understands the change process; influences change as it relates to a specific customer	Drives change as it relates to a specific business initiative	Drives change as it relates to the organization's strategic plans

Figure 4.4 Partial Account Manager Map—Change Agency.

"I hesitate to use the word partnership, as it has developed a negative connotation of late. All too often, businesses and salespeople view its meaning as, 'we'll give you lip service, designate your account with a fancy name, like Signature or Platinum or Partner (or some other important sounding label) and in return, you give us all your business.' However, if you look past that to the essence of partnership, along the lines of what you mentioned earlier with the sPlan, then you'll understand what I mean here by the word partnership.

"Connecting Change Agency to the other Primary Characteristics enables you to see how they interrelate. There is no way salespeople could even begin to drive strategic change in customer organizations, or within their own companies, without the necessary Political Acumen, Business Savvy, or Executive Bondability to accomplish the job. In order for you to be successful in driving change within St. George, Mary, you would need to be at the proficiency levels indicated on the Competency Map for your account manager position in all four of these Primary Characteristics."

Mary remarked, "I know that there is a Holden Corporation Architectural Assessment that enables salespeople to measure their ability in terms of Primary Characteristics, including those we've mapped here, but I have not participated in it."[1]

"I have," said Jo. "It produces a confidential Competency Profile, based on a series of questions that are linked to the core competencies. You not only find out where you are in terms of selling effectiveness in today's marketplace, relative to your position, but also receive insight into your standing in the selling community. That's of particular interest to you, because we often wonder if we stand alone in trying to deal with these new industry trends and challenges."

Mary was concerned about how she might rank in such an assessment. "Can you lead me through a number of questions, so we can estimate where I am on the four stage continuum?"

Competency Profiling

"Sure. Be happy to," Jo replied. "I'll ask you a series of questions to augment what I believe I already know about you, and we'll create an estimated Competency Profile on you, okay?"

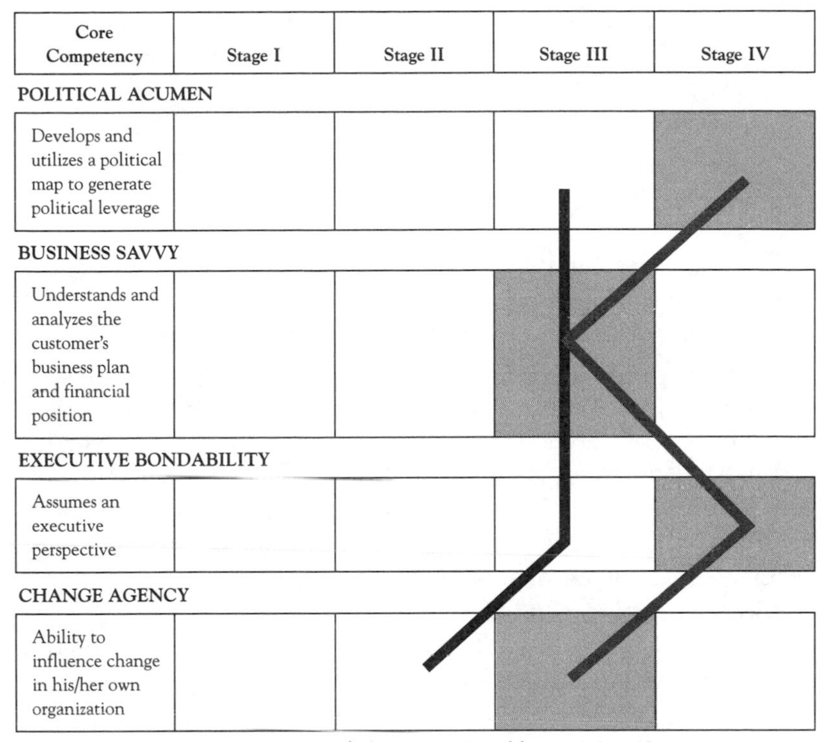

Figure 4.5 Mary's Partial Account Profile-to-Map Comparison.

The process took about forty-five minutes, and covered only a part of the four Primary Characteristics they had discussed. When they had finished, and they reviewed the results, Mary saw that her perception of herself and her competencies before the assessment was very different from what she was now seeing carefully mapped out.

Jo had drawn Mary's Stages of Competency results in black, and the Map Requirements in grey, then superimposed them to create a graphical comparison (see Figure 4.5).

Mary had believed she would score much higher than she actually did when Jo interpreted the results for her.

"In the area of Political Acumen, your ability is actually below what is required to be successful. It is not that you are not skilled, it's that your skills are at this moment behind the market, which means two things:

1. You will need to compensate for the difference between your Profile and the Map. Therefore, you will need to *borrow currency* in those areas, so that current sales efforts are not compromised.
2. You will need to work to develop competency in those areas, through training and practice.

"The key is to lean on the right people at St. George—those who can assist you in accounts so that your success is not paced to your new learning curve in closing the gaps between your Profile and Map. When that happens, your increased currency, albeit borrowed, can make you look like a Stage IV salesperson. You know, most people don't develop from one stage directly to another, they first move through a *virtual* stage. Let me give you an example. Suppose I am basically a Stage II salesperson, let's assume a high Stage II. One day, I bring my manager into an account to meet with upper-level customer management. What am I doing?"

"Borrowing currency," Mary replied.

"Right, and when I do that, my manager develops insight into certain political and business issues that I was not aware of within the account, but which I fully understand when debriefed by him later. I would not have been able to do what he did, but when he explains it to me I not only get it, but can alter my future selling efforts appropriately. Okay then, suppose a few days later, I run into another of my company's managers, and she asks me how we are doing in the account. In my response, I casually share what is happening on the customer's political and business fronts, and how we are adjusting our efforts accordingly. To that manager, I will *look like* a Stage III salesperson, even though I'm not yet there. As long as I am tethered to my manager, and gaining wisdom from him or her, I will be able to operate at a virtual Stage III. Remove him or her from the equation, and I'm back down to Stage II."

"Hmmm. I'm not sure I like that virtual stage at all," said Mary.

"Well, don't despair. I believe that people experience the steepest learning curves, accelerating their development, when they experiment their way through virtual stages of growth under the wing of an effective coach."

Jo again examined Mary's Profile-to-Map comparison. She turned to her friend with a smile, "Mary, in reality you're mostly Stage III, with some Stage II and if we included additional core competencies, I'm sure some Stage IV. The challenge will be to catch up to the market, developing the necessary skills and knowledge to deal with and capitalize on today's industry trends—to become a virtual Stage IV in the short term, and a real Stage IV in the longer term. This is where your natural attributes kick in."

Sales Attributes

"I recall your mentioning sales attributes as a source of internal currency," said Mary, "and I understand the importance of having strong interpersonal skills in selling, but what is their relationship to the core competencies?"

"Personality-related characteristics, while difficult to measure, can have the same effect on a salesperson as does a good manager/coach. Just as the manager can help create virtual performance, the presence (or absence) of certain attributes can move a person's virtual performance up or down. Suppose your Political Acumen averages to a Stage II, but you are driven to succeed, and you're not shy about bringing in your manager and other resources to assist you. While your actual level is Stage II, your performance, although virtual, increases to a Stage III or IV. On the other hand, a salesperson may possess a Stage IV average capability in, say, Business Savvy, but because of an inherent lack of drive, his or her virtual performance is Stage II. Drive, as an attribute, is critical to performance. In negotiating, as well as in sales, we could both list a number of such natural attributes that affect performance level, from drive and energy, to integrity, to the ability to empathize with other people."

Integrity and Performance

"I agree with what you're saying, Jo, but how can you link integrity to performance?"

"In our work, integrity is critical. If there is one good reason, there are a hundred, but here are just a few:

- When your sales efforts require that you operate at a virtual Stage of performance, you're going to make mistakes. When those mistakes occur, your intent will be visible. High-integrity people have high-integrity intent. As a result, their mistakes become more recoverable, as customers respond to the spirit of their intent, creating a strong learning environment and accelerating their sales development.

- FOXES normally seek out and align with people of high integrity. *A salesperson with low integrity will always have a difficult time "hooking" the agenda of a* FOX. Hooking takes place when a salesperson provides value that advances an agenda, and is recognized by the customer individual as such. When a FOX recognizes and acknowledges that value, you have "hooked" his or her agenda. FOXES will rarely depend on people they cannot trust.
- To get things done within an organization requires building a support base. Absent personal integrity, that base rests on sand. A powerful person with low integrity will not survive in an organization over the long haul. Ultimately, lack of integrity will erode his or her support base, causing the individual's performance, credibility, and reputation to degrade.

"In the position of CEO, personal integrity will not only influence the individual's performance, it also will impact the company. Authority, influence, organizational dependency, contractual protection, knowledge of accounts, strong core competencies, any form of currency you can name, Mary, will ultimately depend upon, and grow, only through personal integrity. Your personal integrity, and your education, or what you've learned in life, are among the few things you truly own, that no one can take away from you. You know Mary, the best thing you have going for you is *you*. Your attributes, and especially your integrity, are at the core of your sales success. They are what will get you through this difficult time."

"Thanks for those kind words, but at the heart of it, *I think my real strength is that I care*. That's an attribute that no one seems to discuss these days, yet when I look back to the big push for quality in corporate America a few years back, it all came down to one thing. Companies, including St. George, trained everyone in the area of quality processes and philosophy. Now, it's ISO 9000, but in my opinion, the real benefit to all that training and work was that it got a lot of people to *care* about quality.

"You just talked about FOXES and their emphasis on integrity, Jo. I believe that behind or within every really successful FOX you will find a caring person, one who cares about the business, cares about people, and cares about doing what is right. For me, caring is a prerequisite to integrity. Nevertheless, everyone will tell you that they care—and for the most part they do. The problem lies with what people care about. For most, its themselves, then others and their company. *It may be too much a sweeping generalization, but I believe that people are either givers or takers. Giving people care, without thought for themselves. Takers give, in order to eventually take.*

"You know, Jo, I'm no FOX, but I really care about this business and St. George, and you've certainly opened my eyes to the areas where I need to put some major effort into self-development. I can also see where the concept of building these Competency Profiles and Maps can be central to success in any company function. They actually explain to people, in an understandable way, what is required to be successful in a position. A person can find exactly where there are gaps in competency, and learn where they need to focus more effort on self-development. Every person is different. This highlights individuality, and spotlights the areas where more training and coaching is needed. And after all, how can anyone take ownership for their own development if they don't know what development is required?"

"You're absolutely right. Speaking of development and training, until recently at Newman Banking, we didn't train people, we 'sheep-dipped' them. Everyone received the same training, whether they needed it or not. It didn't matter if one employee's individual needs were different from another's. In defense of the company, however, no one knew what development gaps existed at the individual level. As a firm, we were ignorant of such precision training and development concepts. But that's not the case today. When it comes to training, we now have three rules:

1. Train people only in their gap areas, to create congruence between their Profile and Map.
2. Never train people beyond their manager's ability to coach, because that limits virtual performance potential.
3. Always take a closed-loop approach, employing metrics to measure how much and how well people implement what was

taught. If there's no accountability, no real *training* will have been accomplished.

"I can tell you, as a result of that approach, our revenue per employee and margin per employee has gone up, and is now the highest in our industry. That's not because we have fewer people. It is primarily due to our ability to do a better job than anyone else, and in less time. That means more work output, and ultimately more fun. For years, we talked about empowerment. Now we have operationalized it, with Competency Profiling and Mapping at the heart of the process."

Mary stood up and stretched. "Speaking of fun and empowerment, I'm ready for some of both right now. We have only half a day left of this weekend. Let's call it a day and go enjoy ourselves. Knowing when to kick back and relax is definitely a Stage IV competency—and if it isn't, it should be."

"I'll see that it's added to the Map when I get back," laughed Jo, as they locked Mary's office, and left.

Note

1. The Architectural Assessment is a Holden Corporation sales diagnostic service with a database of over sixty-thousand salespeople, managers, and support people.

CHAPTER

5

Creating Value through Technology

The time Mary and her friend Jo had spent together had been extremely productive. Mary now understood that changes in the marketplace had outstripped her abilities as an account manager. It had been painfully evident in the gaps between her Competency Profile and Map. The good news, though, was that she now knew what she hadn't known before—and knowledge is the first step to wisdom. Yet she still didn't know how she would begin to close those gaps. Mary took stock of her situation.

She had good sales management support from Mark Avery and Jim Watkins, she knew, but what about her personal currency with St. George, as a company? The loss at Consolidated could be distilled down to a two-fold gap problem—hers and St. George's. If the market had outrun her own sales capabilities, it had certainly outrun the company's. Did executive management understand that a large organizational gap existed, evident in the value chain misalignment with Alexander Drugs, potentially one of the company's most important customers? Mary knew that with hard work and some training, she could close her personal development gap, creating Profile-to-Map congruence, but if St. George was not moving in the same direction, at the same speed, the results would be like rolling a big rock uphill. The weight of trying to push the company along, to motivate it, and lead it into new territory, would become an unbearable task.

In the week or so following Jo's return to New York, Mary had completed the first draft of the sPlan process. They had spent nearly two days in the sPlan session with the representatives of Alexander Drugs, and everyone was optimistic about its successful implementation. The next step, on Mary's side, would be to review the draft with St. George's senior management and hopefully get them to ratify it. But after several attempts to schedule a meeting, she began to feel that the top management at St. George was not really aware of the importance of this account, and therefore not supportive of what was taking place. Already, she was feeling reluctant even to take the Alexander planning process to the next phase. She had learned a long time ago that when something doesn't go right after several attempts, the people involved were either *unwilling* or *unable* to perform. In street language, "unwilling" translated to *conspiracy*, a desire to cause or allow something to fail. "Unable" translated to *incompetent*, a lack of ability to perform the needed task.

Of course, the problem in setting up a meeting could be one of logistics, the difficulty of scheduling a meeting among such a busy group of people, but Mary didn't think so. And if the real issue was one of unwillingness or inability, that was very disheartening to her, in light of her ultimate goal with Alexander Drugs.

Mary discussed the situation with Sally Loxner, and they decided to bring Jim into the loop. This meant Mary had to move into the dark pit of corporate politics. It also meant she and Sally would be going around her boss, Mark. Mary was determined to speak to him about it first, but even so, it was an uncomfortable situation for her. She knew that with Sally in agreement, Mark would have little choice but to support their wish to bring Jim into it, but how would he feel about it? After all, Jim was Mark's immediate boss.

How would I feel if I were in his shoes, wondered Mary? She recognized the need to consider Mark's feelings, and decided to set up a face-to-face lunch meeting with him. Ordinarily, they corresponded by voice mail—or recently, by company e-mail. This led her to another thought: a few months ago, St. George had hired a new chief information officer (CIO), Danilo Salenger, who had installed the new e-mail system.

Shortly after he had come on board at St. George, Danilo had asked Mary why a salesforce automation initiative, begun several years prior to his joining the company, had not succeeded. Mary had avoided going into any detail at the time. *Danilo just might be the right person to contact now,* she thought. If she could not get to senior management personally, with a face-to-face meeting, she might be able to accomplish what she needed by using technology, namely, their new e-mail system.

With Danilo's help, Mary created a report that included a draft copy of the sPlan, and attached it to an e-mail in which she outlined the project. *Okay,* she thought, *it won't manage individual feelings, or give me personal visibility in the eyes of top management, but at least it will get the request for action onto the table.* Dick Chainy would receive a copy, along with an invitation to comment and approve the draft, as would the rest of the sPlan team. Mary felt that if this worked, the new e-mail system also would be very helpful to her later, in managing the implementation of the Alexander sPlan, especially the coordination of activities and tracking results.

Mary was very pushed for time, but she felt she needed to meet again with Danilo. She wanted to feel him out about his long-range vision of technology at St. George and the role he envisioned it playing, particularly in the areas of sales and marketing. Sally was interested too, and so they arranged to meet a few days later at the St. George Technology Center, located at their corporate headquarters offices.

The first hour of the meeting was spent briefing Danilo on the concept of value chain management and other industry trends that were forcing the company to operate and sell differently. They explained how St. George needed to reshape itself to become more value-centric in the marketplace, underscoring the urgency that it be done now, not "sometime in the future," if St. George wanted to maintain its competitive position in the rapidly changing pharmaceutical industry.

"Danilo, can you help us with this?" Sally's face reflected her concern. "You know we're excited to finally have e-mail in-house, and that's a big step for St. George, I know, but it's only one step up the technology mountain. We need technology to give us competitive advantage, and we need it now. We need to automate everything we have told you about, including sales tools like:

- Contact Evaluator.
- FOX Evaluator.
- Value Potential Evaluator.
- Value Statement and Proposition Templates.
- Performance Bonding Models.
- Currency Tabulator.
- Valu-Driver.
- sPlan process, including a means to collaborate on sPlan implementation."

Danilo was accustomed to servicing strong demand for applications by users, but he had never seen such eagerness to merge the latest business practices—in this case, sales and marketing practices—with the latest in technology. He was intrigued. It was an ideal opportunity for him to create new Intranet (a company or private form of the Internet) Web-based solutions, which was his real focus at St. George. This meeting with Mary and Sally was an affirmation to Danilo that he had joined the right company after all, something he had been questioning lately. He was pleased to find at least a few forward-looking managers at St. George.

Initially, after his discussions with St. George's top managers and executives, particularly the chief operating officer, Dick Chainy, Danilo had resigned himself to taking a more traditional approach to salesforce automation. He planned to incorporate features like contact management and a marketing encyclopedia, which would keep the sales organization apprised of product and service updates, along with competitive product announcements and customer industry information. He had intended also to tie the system into the company's back-end or data warehouse, enabling the field salesforce to retrieve information on order processing, shipping status, and even commissions earned whenever they wanted to access that data. Installing just those two systems would be a giant step forward for St. George Pharmaceuticals. Danilo hadn't really given any thought to new processes like team selling, or integrating sales or marketing methodology, let alone these new concepts and tools that Mary and Sally had brought to the table today.

Basically, Danilo had been focusing on sales operating efficiency, not sales effectiveness. He was trying to reduce the amount of paperwork for salespeople and to get information out to them faster so they could better manage their time. Those things were certainly very helpful, but now he realized they were not nearly enough.

The Technology Gap

The same kind of gap that Mary had mentioned in her own personal development, and the organizational or company gap that separated St. George from the marketplace, could be seen affecting Danilo, his workgroup, and their technology. *The Technology Center itself was positioned too low on the value chain for St. George's growing needs in the marketplace.*

Danilo stood, went to his board, and began to outline technology values for them. "I realize that just as you two talk about the value chain for customers, there is also a value chain for technology. It reflects different levels of value to you, as users, and to our company as a supplier in the marketplace.

"At the first level, we have *data.* Data is a set of points in a domain," he explained, sketching a diagram on his board. "You're probably familiar with the concept of data mining, which centers on getting the right data at the right time."

Sally looked over at Mary and shrugged. Mary smiled, feeling reassured. Sally didn't know what Danilo was talking about, either. They both had something to learn here.

"At a higher level, you have *information,* which is data with some purpose attached to it, like an accounts receivable (A/R) report, intended to help people manage aging of accounts. But at a higher and infinitely more interesting level, we enter the world of *insight.* Insight is a human capability, whereby information is processed to produce timely and relevant value.

"Suppose you're studying those accounts receivable reports, and you begin to see a trend that suggests that a certain type of customer is always late in making payment to us. Upon further investigation, you discover that the cause of the delay does not lie with the customers in this group, but rather is due to one of our own company policies, a policy that is inherently incompatible with how companies in that industry do business. This root cause analysis requires human insight, an ability that every technology expert would like to emulate using Artificial Intelligence (AI). But for now, it still requires expert knowledge in whatever subject matter or field you're analyzing. So, I guess your challenge to me today is to move as quickly as possible to the *insight* level of the value chain for every internal strategic project at St. George. I'm afraid I have neither the budget nor the required personnel to accomplish that. My answer to you is that I hear you, and I agree with you. However, we will have to be very selective in our applications focus, and you will have to help me get the executive support I need to increase my budget to accommodate your needs. You'll also have to be my experts in the areas of sales and marketing. Fair enough?"

Both women nodded. Danilo looked squarely at Mary. "There's something I want to know. I asked you about it once, but I didn't get much information."

A Failed Attempt

"I'm still curious about what happened with the salesforce automation initiative several years ago. I've been told by others that it failed, but I haven't been given any concrete reasons. Most of what I have heard has been anecdotal in nature, and not specific. I sensed that you were reluctant to discuss it with me earlier, but I'd really appreciate some insight on it now."

"I think maybe I can answer that for you, Danilo," interjected Sally. "It began just before I moved into marketing as director. I must say it had strong upper management support. Dick Chainy was the principal sponsor of the project." Sally turned to Mary. "You might remember the Global Med Care account. That was covered by a salesperson who left St. George and took the account with him. The salesperson didn't do anything wrong, he waited out his non-compete period and then went into Global, selling competitive products." Sally returned her attention to Danilo.

"The problem was that we, as a company, did not know very much about Global. When the salesperson left, he took away with him the knowledge of the account, which resided in his head and not in our system. Dick decided after that incident that account information would be viewed as a company asset and not remain the personal property of the salesperson handling an account. He suggested that account information be recorded, updated, and shared with the right people so that, ostensibly, we could be more responsive to customers. Who could argue with that? However, in my opinion there was something else behind that, which I will share with you, with the understanding that this is strictly in confidence.

"Dick has never viewed the salespeople at St. George in a positive light, even before that account manager left and took the account with him. It is somehow fixed in Dick's head that salespeople work short hours, buy too many lunches, and are substantially overpaid. He recognizes that we need them, but only because someone has to be out there interfacing with customers. He has no idea of the groundwork it takes to develop an account, or the persistence, depth of knowledge, and sheer drive required to land a large, highly competitive deal. Moreover, he isn't interested in learning.

"If given his choice of expanding the R&D budget or committing resources to revamp sales approaches—and believe me, the idea of marketing runs a close second behind sales in Dick's mind—it would take him about one epsilon of time to sign off on the R&D proposal."

"Do you think that might be why I have not heard anything on the Alexander sPlan draft being approved?" asked Mary.

"Possibly," replied Sally. "Look, even if he does give you the green light, I'm not sure Dick will really understand or appreciate what you're trying to do with the Alexander account. I'm glad you are planning to meet with Jim about it. Here's why.

"When the Global account problem surfaced, Dick was furious. He could foresee the salesforce holding the company hostage, with its captive account information and key customer relationships. Not everyone agreed with him, but in any event, a committee was formed to evaluate needs, and it also was tasked to design the new system. The committee was comprised of several people from the Technology Group: Jim Watkins as VP of sales, a finance person, and one representative from the field sales ranks, a person who was somewhat technically oriented. Jim was designated chairman of the committee, with Dick having executive oversight responsibility for the project.

"After months of discussion, a preliminary design began to emerge that, not surprisingly, reflected Dick's negative attitude toward salespeople. It was a design based on several priorities and areas of focus:

- *Roll-up reporting* of sales field activities to management, which included who was calling on what customers, account information, sales forecasting, win/loss reporting, competitive information, and more; and
- *Time management* tools for the field, enabling them to file peoples' names, telephone numbers, addresses, and the like, while also keeping track of scheduling, meeting notes, and follow-up, when required.

"It all seemed reasonable on its face, but behind the design there appeared to be one objective—to reduce St. George's dependency on its salesforce. At a time when we needed to be moving closer to our customers and our marketplace, increasing what we expected from the field organization in terms of converging the interests of our customers and ourselves, we were essentially planning to over-regulate, and ultimately distance, the sales organization. A better converging-interest focus might have led us to the value-oriented thinking we're now talking about. Instead, emphasis was placed on compliance with new sales operating procedures that essentially put salespeople on a tight leash. Even the time management capability that was provided had strings attached: Daily reports had to be generated for management, identifying who was doing what. *Worse, nothing in the design translated into value for customers.* The technology design became one gigantic electronic surveillance paper mill, so that management could see everything the salesforce was doing, every minute."

"Sounds like a lot of Big Brother activity to me," remarked Danilo.

"Exactly," Mary was glad that Sally had taken on the task of enlightening Danilo about the failed project.

"So, how did the field respond?" Danilo wanted to know.

"Well of course they saw too little value, as far as helping them be more successful, coupled with too much corporate exposure for them. In addition, the daily, weekly, and monthly reports they were required to complete and file came at the direct expense of face-to-face selling time, which they believed would decrease their ability to perform.

"Publicly, no one could argue with the stated intent of the project, and no one really wanted to take on senior management, politically. So the field began to look at the situation from a business point of view, and they approached sales management with a common voice, saying that they would do everything possible to make the project a success, but would need quota relief to compensate for the lost selling time.

"Management came back with the argument that the new software, particularly the time-management capability, would increase sales efficiency, extending the capacity of the salespeople. The theory was that the increased sales overhead, in filling out the necessary forms, would be offset by increased operating efficiency. Of course nobody in sales bought that."

"So what happened?" asked Danilo.

"Wisely, Jim decided to reconfigure the committee," said Sally, "by adding two more salespeople to it. I understand that you were invited, Mary, but you elected not to become a formal member of that committee."

"That's right, I said I was willing to help in any way possible, but did not want to serve as a committee member. It had become a political hotbed, and I had no desire to climb into it," said Mary.

"I don't blame you." Sally was sympathetic. She said to Danilo, "The design was then revised to add more value for the salespeople, giving them the ability to track orders, along with providing other information that introduced a customer service component into the design. That enabled the field sales group to see some direct customer value to the system. In addition, the daily reporting requirement was dropped."

"So then, why did the system fail?" asked Danilo. "You should know, Mary. You worked with it."

Mary knew Danilo deliberately had put her on the spot. He was letting her know she shouldn't expect help from him on her project, if she refused to offer any help to him from her end. Fair enough. She drew a deep breath. "It failed for a number of reasons, Danilo," she said. "First of all, we never were sure what management really wanted from us. For example, it was not practical to fill out the account profile form for all accounts or all sales situations, yet we had no guidance or protocol suggesting when we should or should not use the form. There were no stated criteria. That left it to individual discretion. We in the field were not properly trained or informed on the new system.

"I know that technology alone cannot succeed. If you don't communicate and establish the proper behaviors to support the technology and make it work, there will be no positive results. Human insight is still needed. Recently, my neighbors bought a new alarm system for their house. Three weeks ago they were robbed during the night, while they were asleep. Guess why? They didn't arm the security system on the nights they were at home! So they had the right system, good technology, but poor training about using it. And the result? Disastrous.

"So that's what happened at St. George. The field sales people ended up filling out the forms when management was involved in an account, or just before our forecasting sessions, but even then only on the high probability sales opportunities. Basically, if management was looking, we filled them out. If not, we didn't.

"Secondly, it was not clear *how* management was going to use the system or *if* they were going to use it at all. For example, if we knew that management was going to review certain reports and then use the information to develop insight, in order to help us to be more effective, the field would have developed the necessary behaviors or practices to support them. It could have molded how we operated. Instead, we heard and saw nothing. That generated mistrust. It did not take long for rumors to spread that people and their performance would be evaluated using the new system. The *visibility* that management wanted into sales turned into *exposure* from the salespeople's point of view, creating accountability that we'd never had before. And that brought resistance, even dishonesty in some instances, which was the beginning of the end.

"For example, on the win/loss form we had to complete, if a salesperson didn't win, he or she would either not fill it out, or else would check 'Dropped Out,' suggesting a "no decision" by the customer. *Eventually, the system was perceived as one that rewarded dishonesty and mistrust.*"

"And management allowed that?" Danilo asked, surprised.

"Well, if anyone was challenged for not cooperating, and not using the system, they would just blame the system itself, which in truth never performed a hundred percent. I'm not saying that was right, Danilo, but in truth, there were always software bugs that created a frustrating waste of time, and our hardware wasn't all that reliable either. So the field sales reps always had a somewhat legitimate out, or a channel of complaint, which threw the management pressure and focus off them and right back onto the Technology Group. It evolved into almost a tactical interdepartmental war at St. George. I surmise that's why you're here and your predecessor is not."

Mary's frankness took Danilo aback. He looked a bit shaken. *Why did I say all that?* Mary chided herself. Obviously, Danilo now had visions of being assassinated professionally by a group of scheming salespeople! It caused the cold wind of political reality to blow through the room, and on Danilo in particular.

Danilo was intelligent and confident, and he understood what Mary was saying. He didn't take offense at her openness. He was grateful to both of them for enlightening him about the pitfalls that had entrapped his predecessor. He would not allow himself to suffer the same fate.

On every project Danilo organized, he always took great care to align new practices with new technology. He formulated those practices through focus groups and individual interviews, in conjunction with senior management's involvement and, above all, a strong communications plan. That tended to silence the grapevine, while enabling everyone to understand and appreciate what was going to happen, why, and what was expected of them as individuals. The approach was not foolproof, but it had worked in the past and he believed it would work at St. George.

It was time for a break, but Danilo needed to know more. These two women were more apprised of what was happening in the marketplace today than anyone with whom he had spoken so far, but the picture was not yet complete.

"If you will bear with me a little longer, I would like to get a better grip on salesforce automation priorities, as you see them." Danilo smiled at both women, pen poised over his notebook. "You first, Mary."

Formulating Value-Centric Technology Strategy

"All right, Danilo." Mary couldn't help smiling back. She liked his spirit. "Let's see. . . . We'd like *insight-level value technology* on projects that impact the generation of value for our customers or competitive advantage for ourselves. All the sales tools we mentioned earlier fall into that category. We'd also like to automate the various sales methodologies that we will be employing in the future."

"What do you mean by 'various' sales methodologies, Mary? I thought we used only one, the Power Base approach," said Danilo.

"That's right, at least for the moment," said Sally, "but in the future, if all goes well, St. George will be implementing several sales methodologies, as we achieve better alignment between our company and the marketplace in a value-centric manner. In addition to looking at our customers from a traditional point of view—how much do they buy from us, where are they located, and what industry are they in—the marketing department plans to propose that we characterize them in terms of the value chain.

"Each level on that chain will constitute a market segment, so that we can effectively organize our sales and marketing efforts to align St. George with those segments—probably three or four in number. That will enable us to maximize the right type of value for the right customers, while creating maximum competitive differentiation. As you probably know, that impacts elasticity of demand, allowing us to max-out our margins, especially since we will be able to identify which customers we should invest in for the future.

"I suspect that currently we are under-invested in accounts that have tremendous potential, and in some cases we have probably over-invested in accounts that are never going to move up the value chain. Getting our market alignment right may even drop our cost of sales. I'll talk more with both of you about this later, but it will certainly mean restructuring the sales organization, if Jim agrees. That way, each market segment will be known for its own set of sales requirements within our organization, influencing not only sales methodology but other sales and service practices, and each segment will create the need for specific Competency Maps to define what is required to be successful in the various sales positions. Those Maps will tell us what core competencies will be required to support the implementation of the various sales methodologies."

Danilo took notes as they spoke. "Okay, I think I've got the gist of that. Anything else?" He looked expectantly at Mary, but Mary was thinking about one of Sally's comments on the sales organization and restructuring it. She seemed so confident, so authoritative.

Could Sally be a FOX at St. George? With a jolt, Mary re-engaged with Danilo.

"Sorry, Danilo, I got distracted for a second. Let's see." Mary rechecked her notes. "We'd also like to have *information-level value technology* on projects that impact the customer service function, like billing, order processing, and so forth, as well as for any applications that impact sales efficiency, like contact management or tracking leads. In that way, the *insight-level value technology* will drive sales hit rate and margin, while the *information-level value technology* will drive up customer responsiveness at their operations level, while helping us to be more efficient, thus increasing our capacity to sell more. Together, these levels address both effectiveness and efficiency, giving us a clear, value-centric technology strategy. Sally and I believe it's a strategy that will create alignment among:

- Our technology value chain;
- How we need to sell to each market sector, in terms of sales practices, including sales methodology; and
- Customer buying patterns that reflect where they are on the value chain.

"In short, this will put technology, selling, and customer buying into the right value-centric relationship to one another."

"I see what you mean." Danilo was excited about the technology vision they were presenting to him, but he wanted a concrete example of an *insight-level* application, as Mary and Sally envisioned it, in order to feel really comfortable with the idea.

"Take one of the sales tools, for example," he began. "How do you see the insight piece of the application operating with it?"

"Well, from my point of view," said Sally, "you can take the Contact and FOX Evaluators. Each requires that the salesperson enter a point evaluation from +2 to –2 for each of the ten questions. When you automate those tools, if you could make provision for the salesperson to comment as to why each answer was rated as it was, it would provide insight into their thinking. If the sales manager is clear as to the behaviors, that is, he or she explains to the salespeople when it is appropriate to comment on the scoring, it could be used to perfect the salesperson's judgment in making those scoring decisions. After all, a tool is only as good as its input.

"Here's an illustration. Let's say that the sales manager asks that new salespeople, or individuals working on highly competitive deals above a certain dollar amount, fill in the comments field for each question of the Evaluators. Since the Evaluators are updated throughout the sales cycle, that means that at the end, as part of a win/loss discussion, the sales manager already will be able to see where the salesperson's assessment of his or her support base was accurate, or inaccurate. It could provide us with two key indicators:

1. Identification of a training need; and
2. Identification of a coaching need.

"In both cases, the longer term results that will follow the needed training or coaching will be an increase in sales. If the competitive perspective is brought into play, the results could be even more impressive. By that I mean running the Evaluators on the competition's contacts, to determine the extent and quality of their support base and how it is changing throughout a sales cycle.

"Now we could go a step further, albeit a big step. If we were able to index the two Evaluators, thereby creating artificial intelligence-type insight during the sales cycle as to what will most likely happen next, we will reach the top of the technology value chain. It might be a prediction that a competitor, implementing a Direct strategy, will switch to a Divisional strategy, as the system recognizes the competition's shrinking support base in relation to ours. That would provide new insight for the salesperson, which is very exciting."

Automating Value-Centric Sales Methodology

"It *is* exciting," agreed Danilo, obviously caught up in the idea. "Now tell me, how would you envision automating sales methodology, using *insight-level value technology*? I'd like us to take your ideas and build a *technology blueprint*. First we'll need to define the purpose of the application, then break it down into modules, or components."

"Okay. There are two sales methodologies in which I am most interested," said Mary. "The first, which you won't find surprising, Danilo, centers on how to engage and defeat competition in a highly competitive sales situation. Think of it as being *deal-focused*. The second is a bit fuzzier. It centers on the penetration and development of major accounts, which you could think of as *relationship-focused*. In the first case, the purpose of the competitive selling methodology is to:

- Increase hit rate,
- Reduce sales cycle times,
- Reduce the need for discounting, and
- Reduce cost of sales."

There ensued a discussion wherein all three of them contributed to building a component blueprint to be automated. When the list of components was completed, it consisted of the following:

- Value Selling-Tool Set—incorporating value-oriented sales tools, along with the building of specific data bases for the trending and reporting of information and insight.
- Opportunity Profile—providing the necessary account information to support sales campaigns.
- Qualification—utilizing specific criteria to determine quantitatively whether a sales situation should be pursued, based upon the quality of the business and whether or not it can be won within a reasonable time frame and under acceptable terms. This process of qualifying the opportunity would take place several times throughout the sales cycle and again at the win/loss review. Again, trending and reporting were intrinsic to the module.
- Strategy Analyzer[1]—providing guidance and direction in the area of strategic formulation, testing the salesperson's strategy using AI. In general, they agreed this was still a very challenging area for sales professionals.
- Confidential Win/Loss Review—a private assessment of what took place, with the intent of creating a closed-loop system, linked to other system components in order to provide significant insight or introspection into self-performance and developmental needs.
- Contact Management—incorporating available features, with the addition of support base management, where the quality and

extent of the sales professional's support base, and that of the competition, is tracked over time.

- Marketing Encyclopedia—accessing the Internet and other sources to provide the field staff with real time updates on accounts, competitors, internal St. George product information, and company news.
- Sales Forum—enabling sales professionals to communicate and exchange ideas on various topics, as a threaded discussion.
- Confidential Individual Sales Performance Reporting—providing sales professionals with confidential information and trending of their personal performance.
- Pipeline Management—graphically displaying the salesperson's position in a sales cycle, according to specific phases, which are then aggregated and fed into a funnel report, identifying all sales activity, by phase.
- Management and Executive Reporting—enabling senior personnel to receive summary reports particular to their areas of interest, such as marketing, manufacturing, finance, corporate business, and sales management, along with customer service.

The configuration they had developed was leading-edge. However, with the possible exception of the Artificial Intelligence functions, Danilo knew he could build it. His thinking was to create a series of Web-based applications, consisting of the individual components. In that way, salespeople would simply go to the St. George Web site, enter their security password, and gain access to the set of sales tools and competitive sales methodology components, along with their own personal databases on accounts. To ensure a high level of system security, this would all take place behind the company's firewall.

"I think we can do this for you, or at least something pretty close to what you've outlined to me today," said Danilo.

"Well, in that case, I'd like a couple more bells and whistles, if you don't mind," said Mary.

At that, Danilo couldn't help laughing. "Don't they always? Well, it never hurts to ask. What else do you need?"

"In addition to these components, I would like to see four other capabilities incorporated into the system:

- Extensive System Help—By this, I mean a user could click on "help" messaging that would go beyond explaining what something is, perhaps providing actual questions to ask in order to get the information necessary, or an in-depth tutorial on a particular sales or marketing subject.
- Sales Management Help—Similar to what you mentioned when you talked about having a comments field for each question of the FOX and Contact Evaluators, I would like to see the ability to comment provided throughout the critical system components, with flags that I can set, so that comments are automatically brought to my sales managers' attention. In that way they can review my judgment in certain areas and proactively assist me.
- Fast Track—This would be an abridged version of the system, for use with repeat-order sales situations, or noncompetitive opportunities that don't require the more comprehensive strategic analysis components.
- Security—A strict security protocol, providing need-to-know access as necessary along with confidentiality provisions to ensure privacy at the salesperson's level regarding certain components of the system.

"That means detailed win/loss information should be available only to the salesperson, with only roll-up reporting of win/loss information available to the salesperson's immediate manager. I know that's counter to what St. George has instituted, but my belief is that salespeople will embrace the system only if it has a setup for proprietary input of information reserved to them and them alone, information they believe helps them develop personal strategies for winning accounts."

"In the case of the second sales methodology, which focuses on major account management," Mary continued, "I would explain its purpose as:

- Enabling the sales team to operate in a Demand Creation mode, as opposed to Servicing Demand on an individual opportunity or deal basis;
- Enabling the team to go very high on the customer's value chain and implement Performance Bonding, where appropriate; and

- Creating competitive immunity within an account, minimizing the risk of competitive displacement."

They began to build a component blueprint to support automating the major account management process. An especially attractive aspect of the Web-based approach was that it consisted of a cluster of applications or components resident at the Web site, which could be used to support set processes, which could be mixed and matched as appropriate. For example, the major account management process would have to include the ability to access certain components they had identified to automate the competitive selling methodology. That meant maximum flexibility, a far cry from the traditional salesforce automation systems of the past, where the field staff had been forced to change sales methods to suit the technology, instead of the other way around.

"In today's marketplace," said Mary, "the fast-changing market rules everything, and companies must have the flexibility to change along with it. Competency Maps change, sales positions change, and with them, sales methodologies must also change. Therefore, technology has to be flexible, too. It has to be quickly and smoothly adaptable to changing methodology. The market does not allow time to wait weeks, months, sometimes even years, for reprogramming applications. Technology, through its ability to adapt easily, can produce strong competitive advantage for a company—quickly moving up and down the technology value chain to formulate highly flexible technology strategies to meet the sales and marketing needs of today's marketplace. That will take a lot of strategic planning by your techno-wizards, Danilo. But it's the way of the future."

"I know. But this is a tall order you're pulling out of the wish book, Mary. Especially here at St. George. Just so you understand that. Other than that, the sky's the limit." Danilo knew he was faced with a challenge he could really get his teeth into.

"We do understand, Danilo, and we know there will be limitations, but we might as well go for broke while we're at it," Sally said, jumping back in to lead the discussion. They began configuring the major account methodology. It did not take long for them to come up with the two necessary components:

1. Valu-Driver—enabling a company to assess the quality of its relationship with a major account, based on the customer's

perception and that of St. George. It would become the basis for joint account planning, particularly in building an sPlan, and would be extremely effective in expanding and strengthening a salesperson's support base within an account.

2. sPlan—allowing the creation of joint St. George-customer multiyear value-centric account plans, with tools to support the generation and implementation of the sPlan, such as a process guide and various templates and tools to assist in the coordination of tactics and the allocation of resources.

Sally and Danilo were deep into examining the feasibility of a tangent component. Mary sat back for a moment, and began to revisit her earlier thoughts about Sally Loxner. *Is Sally a FOX?* If so, she was connected in some way to a high-level of authority at St. George. *Who?* Mary wondered. She began to think, viewing St. George as she would an account. It was a first for Mary, as she mulled over everyone at the top, and finally concluded that, if Sally was truly a FOX, it could mean only one person—Dr. Tullis, the CEO. If that were true, it would put Sally on a par with Dick Chainy, or maybe even slightly higher, in her influence.

Mary's highest-level corporate relationship was at the level of vice president, with Jim Watkins. Mary decided to run the FOX Evaluator on Sally. That would tell the story, and reveal whether or not she had a connection to the CEO. Since they had just been discussing the FOX Evaluator, Mary couldn't resist the temptation to open her notebook, and do a quick run-through on Sally (see Figure 5.1).

Bingo! I knew it! Mary was elated to find that Sally had scored in the FOX range, but decided to make one final test.

"Sally, we've not discussed how senior management might feel about this approach of Web-based sales applications. What about Dr. Tullis? Do you think he will be supportive? How about Dick Chainy?"

"Well, Mary—I don't want to speak for Dr. Tullis, but I know he'll give this design we've developed today a fair examination, especially if Jim Watkins is on board with us. You may not be aware of it, but I was the one who recommended Danilo to Dr. Tullis, based upon my knowledge of his work with a former employer. Dr. Tullis knows that Danilo's expertise lies in building Intranet applications, so he is clearly predisposed to our approach, as far as the technology

Score	Definition
+2	I am confident that this is true.
+1	This is most likely true.
0	I don't know.
–1	I doubt that this is true.
–2	I am confident that this is not true.

Fox Evaluator Questions	Score –2 to +2
1. *Sally* has exerted influence outside of his/her organizational authority.	*+2*
2. *Sally* has knowledge of his/her company's mission and business goals, as evidenced in his/her working—directly or indirectly—to advance them.	*+2*
3. *Sally* is an effective risk taker, showing an ability to access and manage risk.	*+1*
4. *Sally* demonstrates integrity, in being unwilling to compromise his/her company or individuals within the Power Base to advance his/her own aspirations.	*+2*
5. *Sally* is a good listener.	*+1*
6. *Sally* can appropriately and successfully work in exception to company policy.	*+1*
7. *Sally* influences important decisions before they are made formal.	*+2*
8. *Sally* has a close relationship with others who posses expertise that he/she personally does not have, but that can be important.	*+1*
9. *Sally* is not arrogant about his/her knowledge or accomplishments, as evidenced by his/her willingness to have others receive the credit for accomplishments.	*+2*
10. *Sally* is diplomatic in how he/she operates, as evidenced by rarely taking people on in a confrontational manner.	*+1*
Total Your Score	**15**

Score	Probable Results
+14 to +20	*Congratulations, you have found a FOX.*
+7 to +13	He/she is not a FOX, but is in the Power Base.
–20 to +6	He/she is outside the Power Base.

Figure 5.1 Sample Completed FOX Evaluator.

part of it. Dick might be another story. He hired our last CIO, who did not work out, as you know. However, Dick most certainly will have a voice in what we do, so we'll need to lobby for his support. I believe Jim Watkins will be very supportive, and might help us win Dick over if he shows signs of balking."

"Well, then, how do you suggest we proceed on this?" Danilo was addressing Sally. "This package you've proposed is not only extensive, it's very expensive, so getting approval on it won't be easy."

Danilo knows she has influence, too, thought Mary.

"I would recommend that we approach Jim Watkins as soon as possible with this blueprint, and the idea of creating a task force. A committee that can take what we have developed here today, our blueprint, and shape it into a workable project plan. One other thing I would suggest, with Jim's approval, is that you be the person to head up that committee, Mary."

Mary was stunned. "Why me? Wouldn't Danilo, or you, be a better choice?"

"I don't think so. You and Jim have a good relationship, and you have your finger on the pulse of the new and emerging trends within our industry, more than anyone. You're becoming proactive in the area of value chain management and have done more with customers, in that regard, than anyone else at St. George. In addition, you are developing an excellent working knowledge of the sales tools we want to automate."

Mary sat back. Her first impulse was to refuse, flat out. But now she hesitated. *How can I say no to a FOX as connected as Sally, one who has enthusiastically supported me and my needs?* If she agreed to Sally's request to head up the task force and it went well, their relationship could evolve to one where Sally might become a strong ally and mentor. Mary detested corporate politics, but she knew the power of having a FOX as an ally.

She was about to thank Sally and accept, albeit with reluctance, when thoughts of her father came storming into her dissonant brain. George Gagan was retired from business, but in his earlier years he had been a pilot for a major airline. After twenty-five years of service he had been promoted to Captain of a 747, flying the Chicago-to-London route. He was good at what he did, and loved his work, but when the industry went into a slump in the late 1980s, life had changed for Mary's dad.

It was during that time that every airline was cutting costs wherever possible, including doing everything legal to reduce maintenance costs. Over the years, George had become good friends with people on the ground at Heathrow and O'Hare airports. He knew what major cutbacks in personnel had done to alter maintenance procedures, and he also knew the risks inherent in putting cost above safety. Other pilots ignored it, but George had grown up with the fundamental belief that *money follows.* It follows hard work, integrity, and innovative endeavors. He could never put money ahead of safety.

At a company meeting, George had voiced his concern. It had a rallying effect with some of the other more senior pilots. Then, exactly six weeks later, George's airline had cut back its Chicago-to-London route and moved him to a feeder airline subsidiary, flying a prop plane to some backwoods destination. He was devastated, having suffered the biggest setback of his career. What had happened to him, Mary knew, was more than just political in nature—it was political censorship, conducted with surgical precision.

An ancient philosopher once observed that in order to establish and maintain control of a province, a ruler had to create and maintain fear among the powerful, and do so quickly and decisively. He suggested that to do that, the ruler would single out a specific person, kill him, and destroy his property. If more than one powerful person was attacked, or any kind of significant burden was placed upon the rest, it would create a "common grievance," which was to be avoided at all costs, since that usually led to resistance, or even revolt.

The medieval statesman and philosopher Niccolo Machiavelli remarked in his treatise *The Prince,* "men are less concerned about offending someone they have cause to love than someone they have cause to fear. . . . If a ruler has reason to take a life he should do so, . . . but refrain from the property of others, for men are quicker to forget the loss of a father than the loss of a patrimony. . . . "[2]

It was with Machiavellian precision that the airline had cut George Gagan down, all but destroying him, and striking fear into the hearts of the other pilots—fear that the same fate might await them if they voiced their concerns. As Machiavelli and other strategists have long observed, fear makes the vulnerable knuckle under, and when they saw what happened to George Gagan, there was no further discussion of maintenance procedures by the pilots.

What remained in the wake of his demotion was the hardening of her father's heart, and a broken spirit. George Gagan was a sad political victim, forced to ride out his time to retirement while banished to a distant corner of the company. It had affected Mary deeply to see her father's anguish.

Now, she wanted very much to say an enthusiastic "yes" to Sally, and accept the challenge. She knew it was the right thing to do. It also was the logical and street-smart thing to do, but when she tried, the only words that came out were, "I can't, Sally. Sorry, but I just can't." With that, Mary excused herself and left the meeting, obviously emotionally distressed.

Like Danilo, Sally was momentarily stunned by Mary's unexpected negative reaction. However, she was smart enough to know that there had to be something else behind Mary's refusal, something she didn't know about.

In true FOX-like style, Sally would not take Mary's refusal and emotional departure personally, nor would she hold it against her. Instead, Sally decided to put the committee idea on hold for a few days. First she'd talk to Jim, and maybe revisit it with Mary later. She'd also try to find out what distressed Mary so much that she'd flatly turn down what Sally thought was a wonderful career opportunity for her. Sally finally broke the silence that had prevailed since Mary's departure.

"I don't know what it was that upset Mary so much about heading up the committee, Danilo, but rest assured, she'll be a part of this project, and a definite asset to it, too. I think we both want that."

"You're right. For some reason she's resisting leaving the field, but like you, I feel that having Mary on the development team, even if she doesn't head it up, is critical to getting this project effectively developed and implemented. So I hope you'll be successful in bringing her around on this. Keep me posted, will you? Meanwhile, I suggest we move forward with this draft blueprint. I'll get it ready for review."

"Good. I agree. And thanks, Danilo. I knew we were doing the right thing to bring you on board."

Notes

1. A form of Strategy Analyzer is available at *www.efox.com/wcs/strategy* on the Internet.
2. Machiavelli, *The Prince* (First published 1531), trans. Daniel Donno (New York: Bantam Books), Chapter XVII, p. 60.

CHAPTER

6

Segmenting the Market

Mary had received e-mail acknowledgments from everyone on her team, indicating that the Alexander Drugs sPlan was under review. To her pleasant surprise, Dick Chainy asked his executive assistant to call Mary personally, advising her that the COO had received the Alexander sPlan and was looking forward to discussing it further with her.

Well, maybe the problem in scheduling a meeting to review and ratify the sPlan before really was just one of logistics, she thought. It felt good to know that it was finally in place and under review, particularly as she was keen to get back to Alexander Drugs. At the same time, the e-mail attachment of the sPlan proposal was probably one of the longest electronic transmissions any of the managers had received since the system was installed. It consisted of a brief history of the account, followed by an Executive Summary, that covered:

- *The Valu-Driver:* What it is, why it was employed for Alexander, and what the results were, particularly the divergent perceptions of St. George's view of the value they were providing and Alexander's view of what they were receiving from St. George.
- *Company-to-Company Alignment*, identifying the four key areas of:

    Reward,

    Risk,

Accountability, and
Philosophy.

- *The sPlan structure,* consisting of:
  sPlan goals and objectives,
  sPlan strategy,
  Objectives (by priority), strategies, and tactics,
  General tactics, and
  Testing results.
- *Mary's Currency Tabulator Rating,* that placed her squarely at a "middle management level" of compatibility, in terms of the personal value she could bring to the account. She noted that as a result of this assessment, one of the St. George sPlan Objectives focused on bringing her to an "executive level" of currency. Otherwise she, as the Alexander Drugs account manager, would be too low on the Alexander value chain to operate effectively.
- *The Executive-Level Value Proposition,* that articulated quantitatively a first-pass expression of the value that St. George could potentially provide to Alexander Drugs.
- *The Value Potential Evaluator,* which showed, on a scoring range of High, Reasonable, Emerging, and Weak, a very "Reasonable" potential to successfully build and implement an effective Value Proposition with Alexander. Again, Mary had noted that as a result, one of the St. George sPlan Objectives was centered on moving that score upward, to the "High" category.

In developing the Executive Summary, Mary had provided a brief abstract, to signal to the recipients that value chain management was a great deal more than simply talking to customers about value. She underscored for them that it was a systems-oriented approach to creating, defining, and realizing value, one that would involve not only Mary Gagan as the account manager, but St. George Pharmaceuticals as a company.

She hoped that in reading the Summary top management would see the multifaceted nature of the proposal, and understand that if any one segment of the system or plan was off kilter, the result would be a fast trip down the customer's value chain for St. George, like a child jumping onto a wet pool slide. In her cover note, she had indicated they should read the Executive Summary before delving into the longer document attached, the full-blown sPlan jointly developed by Alexander Drugs and St. George.

Choosing the Approach

Back in her office in the marketing department, Sally Loxner ruminated about her meeting with Danilo and Mary. *Why had Mary been so emphatically negative?* Perhaps the concept of setting up a task force to support the automation of the field sales organization, even assuming that Jim would be supportive, was the wrong approach. The discussion had centered around how to marry new sales practices with new technology. Sally knew that their thinking was very progressive, yet when it came to implementation, they had reverted to traditional thinking that focused on salesforce automation. *It was not the salesforce that needed to be automated,* she realized now, *it was value chain management that needed to be brought to life, using leading-edge, worldwide Web-based applications. Was that what had upset Mary?*

The ideas put forth in their meeting still applied, but would now be just one segment of an overall effort. Sally thought about it for a while, then began making some notes. As she did, the idea became clearer. After an hour of thinking, writing, and re-writing, she had the basis for a plan. Value chain management at St. George would consist of nine clearly defined and phased activities that could be loosely grouped into three categories:

Category One: Approach to Market

- Phase One—Carefully segmenting their marketplace, according to value chain level;
- Phase Two—Characterizing the buying patterns for each segment; and
- Phase Three—Translating buying patterns into sales processes or methodologies.

Category Two: Front-End Structure

- Phase Four—Determining the optimum approach to each market segment, in terms of organizational structure, based upon the sales methodology most appropriate to a given segment;

- Phase Five—Defining sales roles and positions on a per market segment basis;
- Phase Six—Identifying the necessary levels of currency, by sales position, to ensure alignment between an individual's personal level of value and the customer's value chain level; and
- Phase Seven—Establishing the marketing role, in terms of specific practices on a per segment basis.

Category Three: Front-End Infrastructure

- Phase Eight—Synchronizing recruiting and selection, performance management, and compensation practices with sales positions, aligning the human resource function with sales; and
- Phase Nine—Aligning the technology value chain with the sales, marketing, and human resource practices on a per market segment basis.

Seeing clearly now the opportunity to automate and operationalize the concept of value chain management, Sally contacted Jim to discuss the idea of the three categories and nine phases. She had a second agenda for their meeting, though she didn't mention it when she called him. She wanted Jim's input on what might be bothering Mary, as well as his view on what it would take to entice Mary to head up the project, if he gave it a green light.

They met the following afternoon in Jim's office. He was intrigued and enthusiastic when Sally briefed him on their meeting with Danilo, and her new concept of categorizing the phases of value chain management.

"It still needs work, Jim. How do you feel we should characterize the various value chain levels?" Sally asked.

Defining Value Chain Levels

"Well, why don't we look again at that Four-Stage Customer Model, and use it as the basis for describing what level of the value chain a customer is currently on with its suppliers? We have to keep in mind, however, that we are dealing with a dynamic situation for most companies, so they could be at one level of the chain today, and another tomorrow. We need to take that into consideration and evaluate customers on the basis of where they are currently, then try to gauge reasonably the level to which they could evolve, with our assistance. In many cases, that might afford us the opportunity to shape new buying patterns within accounts, if early on we can position ourselves at one value-chain level above them."

Jim got out a notepad, pulled the Four-Stage Customer Model from a file, and began to build around it, scratching out his thoughts (see Figure 6.1).

"At Stage I, the customer is clearly focused on the product, or in some cases on service value that is prepackaged. The emphasis here is on product features, where the primary value lies in the presence or existence of features. These offerings may also include product training and a few months of warranty value, all for a defined price. In our new world of value-centric thinking, I view this type of customer as a Commodity Value Level account. That is not intended to be a negative connotation. We have quite a few very large Commodity Value Level customers, some of whom may have the potential to move to Stage II. That potential would be reflected in their individual Value Potential Evaluator scores. Applied to their Operations and Management levels, the VP Evaluator would give us a reading pretty quickly. If there is potential, we will most likely see an Emerging score on the range of High, Reasonable, Emerging, or Weak. We'd then designate that account a Commodity Value Level

Quality	Stage I	Stage II	Stage III	Stage IV
Customer's Intent	Solve a problem	Acquire a solution	Capitalize on a business opportunity	Create a new business opportunity
Buying Focus	Product or service features	Product or service benefits	Supplier expertise and resources	Supplier strategic ability and commitment
Relationship	Vendor on demand	Characterized by trust and commitment	Strong mutual dependency	Business partners and advisors to each other
Customer Value	Low cost, quick fix	Able to purchase reliable solutions	Able to co-develop and create custom offerings to solve complex problems	Receives insight into business issues and creativity in addressing them

Figure 6.1 Four-Stage Customer Model.

(CVL) Plus, or CVL+. If the score range is Reasonable or High, it becomes a CVL++ or CVL+++, respectively. The more plus signs, the more potential to move up the value chain, and the more we should be considering investing resources to move up the value chain ahead of them.

"Stage II is a bit different. It identifies customers at the Solutions Value Level, where value is directly derived from a product, as in product benefits, and in support services that, when combined with the product, create a solution. Now we have moved up one notch on the value chain, to where the customer is usually trying to solve yesterday's problems today. Nevertheless, they are dependent on us to provide good service and support, which brings trust into the equation. That's why, even at Stage II, we try to 'sell the company,' promoting the fact that St. George cares about our customers and their business, and that we have the resident expertise to provide the quality and responsiveness they require. It's at this Stage that Value Statements begin to play a role, as they speak to the quality or effectiveness of our solutions. Again, if an account has potential, using the VP Evaluator at the Management level of the customer's organization, I consider them a Solutions Value Level (SVL) Plus Plus, or SVL++ account for a Reasonable score, and SVL+++ for High. You will note that a double plus sign, and not a single, is required to indicate potential. The reason for that is, at a Stage II, Solutions Value Level, you would expect a minimum Emerging rating at the customer's Middle-Management level, otherwise they have not reached the Stage II, Solutions Value Level yet."

Sally had been taking careful notes as Jim talked. "You know, I think this might work, Jim."

"Well, I'm just thinking out loud, really, but I believe it can work, as I posit these theories against the Model. Anyway, to recap, we've visited two levels of the value chain, each with a designation reflecting the customer's potential to move to a higher level, which gives us an indicator that we might want to be adding to our investment in them, and leading the effort wherever possible. The two value levels we've discussed today are:

1. Stage I, Commodity Value Level, with the potential to move up indicated by a +, ++ , or +++, and
2. Stage II, Solutions Value Level, with the potential to move up indicated by a ++ or +++.

"Now, why don't we take a break for a quick lunch, Sally? I'm starved," said Jim. "We can talk some more about this as we eat."

Sally was impressed with Jim's idea of using the Four-Stage Customer Model and the Value Potential Evaluator together, as a basis for pinpointing accounts that were ready to be considered for the concept of value chain management. She was already mentally into the next step.

"In my view, Jim, the third level—Stage III—should be the Business Value Level (BVL), where the focus is on business solutions that address today's problems. As opposed to the Stage II SVL that you described, which is more centered on solutions that solve operational problems at the lowest possible price, a BVL solution carries the purpose of enhancing or strengthening the customer's business itself, by solving a specific problem, or various problems. At this level, as you know, customers are very concerned about the cost of ownership in relation to return, or yield improvement. So it's easy to see how Value Propositions can come into play here. As a quantified expression of value, Value Propositions focus on achieving measurable results and would therefore be extremely appealing to the BVL customer. Building and introducing a Value Proposition also sets the stage to begin the process of drawing a line from the value chain level at which we are currently working with them, and the level at which they reside with their customers."

"You think we can do that, using this approach?"

"I'm pretty sure we can," said Sally, "but I'll come back to that thought in a little bit. If we run the Value Potential Evaluator on the Management and Executive levels of the customer's organization, it will, as you indicated earlier, give us insight into their potential to move up the value chain, and will provide us with an indication of whether or not Performance Bonding might be a viable option with them. Using your system of plus signs, Jim, I'd look for a Reasonable score to verify that the customer really is at a Stage III BVL, which would be BVL++, and a High score to indicate the potential to move up the value chain, which would be BVL+++. So if we added that to your list, we'd have three stages of value chain levels:

1. Stage I, Commodity Value Level (CVL), with the potential to move up indicated by a +, ++ , or +++;

2. Stage II, Solutions Value Level (SVL), with the potential to move up indicated by a ++ , or +++; and
3. Stage III, Business Value Level (BVL++), with potential to move up and possibly introduce Performance Bonding indicated by a +++."

Jim was nodding and taking notes as he finished his sandwich. Sally pushed her salad aside and plunged on, her excitement over the idea evidenced by the enthusiasm in her voice. She was so caught up in thought, she didn't want to be distracted by lunch.

"The highest level on the value chain, then, would be Stage IV," she continued, "and that could be expressed as . . . let's call it a Strategic Value Level (STVL), where the focus is on strategically advancing the customer's business, and our own, by addressing tomorrow's challenges, opportunities, and problems. As an example, take the sPlan process I told you about earlier. When we conduct an sPlan session with a customer, we would open with a discussion of our two businesses and our industry in general. In talking about existing and emerging trends, and how they could impact the customer's business practices in the future, we are of course operating at a strategic level.

"Taking it further, when we provide specific guidance and direction about how the customer can modify existing practices and introduce new ones in order to advance their business, stating them as sPlan goals or objectives, we are attaching direct value to the strategic guidance that we're providing to them."

"I can see that, and agree with your choice of Strategic Value as a header for the fourth stage, given that example. Any other ideas?"

Sally thought for a minute. "Well, another STVL example might be outsourcing. At the low end of the value chain, our company is simply moving product. As we move up, we can begin to provide value that results from the customer's *use* of that product. Go up another value chain level, and the value we provide must not only increase, but become wider in scope. In some cases a supplier like St. George, focusing on yield improvement, will incorporate another company's products—even a competitor's—with its own, integrating them to produce a better quality solution—perhaps a more effective one—for the customer. Outsourcing gets us to the very top of the value chain, in that we are not providing the customer with the means to produce value, we are providing the value directly."

"In other words," said Jim, "We take over a complete function for a customer, freeing the customer to focus on core business, allowing them in turn to move up the value chain with *their* customers."

"Exactly," said Sally. "Look at St. George. We might hire a large computer services company to take over and run our Technology Center, or bring a company in to run our telemarketing function for us. That frees us up to concentrate more on new product development, or acquisitions, or to expand into new markets. More and more companies are moving up the value chain, making acquisitions of other companies to give them the "bandwidth," or scope of offerings, that will enable them to move into outsourcing and reach the STVL.

"As you know, Jim, the higher you go on the chain, the more value you provide, while enjoying increased competitive differentiation. Enhanced value and differentiation mean better elasticity of demand, which means more margin, and increased protection from the threat of competitive displacement. At the Stage IV STVL, anything we do will lead to a symbiotic relationship, a stage where disengagement would be painful for both supplier and customer."

"So," said Jim, who had been writing and diagramming as Sally spoke, "pulling it all together gives us four major value chain level designations, based on the Four-Stage Customer Model. (See Figure 6.2.)

Stage I, Commodity Value Level or CVL, with the potential to move up indicated by a +, ++, or +++

Stage II, Solutions Value Level or SVL, with the potential to move up indicated by a ++ or +++

Stage III, Business Value Level or BVL, with he potential to move up, and possibly introduce Performance Bonding, indicated by a +++

Stage IV, Strategic Value Level or STVL, the top of the chain

Figure 6.2 Four Stages of Value Chain Levels.

They left the cafeteria and went back to Jim's office, to develop a more formal design of their new concept.

"This value structure would give us the ability to look at accounts and vertical markets on a continuum basis," said Jim. "It also should allow us to draw a value chain line from ourselves, as a supplier, to our customer, and from our customer to our customer's customers, something like this." Jim sketched out an example for Sally (see Figure 6.3).

"You can see in this example that we are positioned to provide value at the Commodity, Solutions, and Business levels. Alexander, however, is positioned to provide value at two levels, suggesting that their market could be segmented into two groups:

1. Transaction-driven, price-sensitive retail product purchasers, and
2. Relationship-driven, value-oriented solutions customers, like insurance companies.

"You will also note that we are currently one notch above Alexander on the value chain—that is, we are able to provide more value

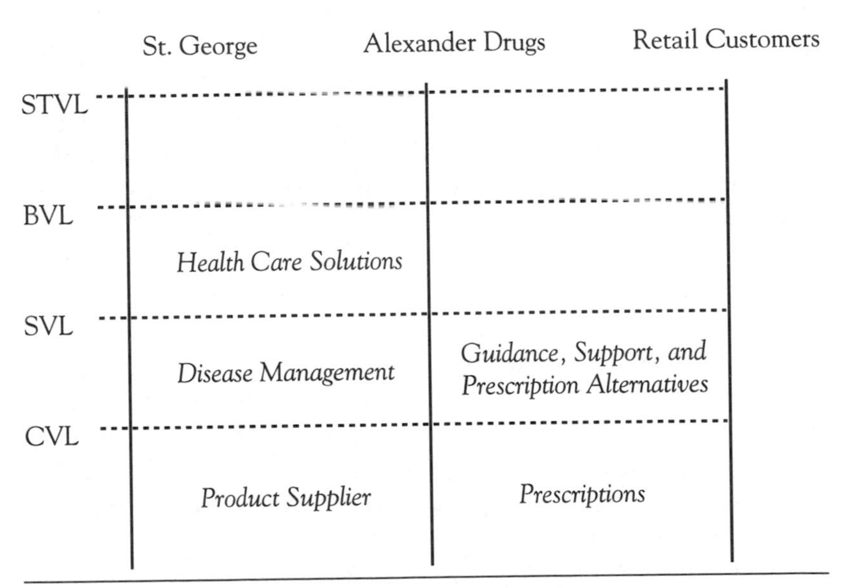

Figure 6.3 Sample Value Chain Continuum.

than they currently need—which is important in establishing ourselves in a leadership role."

"Mary will be pleased to hear it, since that's where she had intuitively figured we were, and that's what brought her to the idea of the sPlan proposal for Alexander Drugs," remarked Sally.

"Well, she certainly got us off the dime and moving again with that idea," said Jim. "It's been a long time since I've felt this fired up about a project."

"I feel the same way. You know, I mentioned vertical markets earlier," said Sally. She looked again at Jim's sketch of the Value Chain Continuum. "I think that just as you drew the Value Chain Continuum for Alexander here, we might also draw it for a drug store chain vertical market, within a particular geographical area. That gives us the ability, in marketing, to align all the appropriate departments of St. George with specific market segments, from sales, to manufacturing, to R&D, to finance. In that way, we are essentially treating a vertical market like an account."

"I see what you mean," agreed Jim. "We could use this base model for a lot of other things. Another thought: It might also be useful to mention in our initial model that the value chain continuum could also consist of a number of value lines from a supplier into different divisions or groups of a company. In today's marketplace, a customer might participate in multiple market segments, and therefore need to be treated as multiple accounts by a supplier in keeping with a value-centric point of view.

"For instance, we could be at a Stage I CVL with one division of an organization and at a Stage III BVL with another division or group of that same company. When that happens, our recommendation should always be that we build an account sPlan, to ensure proper value segmentation and focus."

"What about our existing market descriptions," asked Sally, "the ones that define accounts in terms of customer industry, sales volume, and St. George product mix? Would we have to change those?"

"No, I don't think so. Value chain market segmentation is an overlay to what we have been doing," Jim explained. "I'd just recommend that we add the appropriate value chain level designation to certain accounts or groups of accounts, where these groups are defined by their industry."

"That would work," agreed Sally. "We could segment our markets very effectively on the basis of value, but it will require a team effort. One person I think we'd need to have on that team is Mary Gagan. I wanted to talk to you about that, too, Jim.

"In our meeting with Danilo, I brought up the idea of a task force to investigate and handle this whole project. Mary surprised us by saying that she couldn't participate, much less head it up. She seemed hesitant to shift her focus away from the field. At the same time I sensed, as did Danilo, that she has a deep interest in, even a passion for, what we are trying to do here. Actually, she's the one who raised this whole issue with me. If anyone in the field understands the importance of value chain management, it's Mary. Maybe she is still hurting too much from the Consolidated loss, I don't know. But something is bothering her very much, Jim. Do you or Mark have any idea what it is? Is there some reason she can't leave field sales right now to do this?"

"Not really. I kind of agree with you that it's more than the loss of the Consolidated sale, Sally. Mary just has not been herself lately, and Mark and I have both noticed that. We think she may have decided it's time for her to leave St. George, or perhaps she feels that the company will not become value-centric in its thinking and operations quickly enough to keep pace with the market, and has become discouraged about trying anything new.

"My guess is that she sees this Alexander Drugs sPlan project as necessary for her success with that account, but also feels it's a long shot at St. George, and fraught with internal politics. So she is weighing her options. I hate to say it, but bottom line, she's correct in her evaluation of the situation, and you and I both know that."

Sally and Jim both sat there a moment, reluctant to say anything more, but each understanding the other's thoughts. Then Jim said, "Tell you what. I'll talk to Mary tomorrow, see if I can get to the bottom of what is really bothering her, or at least find out where she stands with St. George. Then we can determine how best to proceed on all this."

"That sounds good, Jim. And we need to bring Danilo in on what we've developed here today, too. Above all, and I know you'll agree with me on this, I don't want St. George to lose talent like Mary's. She has a good educational background, a fine performance record, and shows excellent intuitive abilities and a knack for strategic planning. Those characteristics should not be lost, nor underutilized. And I think that's what we'd be doing if we left her in field sales and didn't try to move her along.

"You know her a lot better than I do, Jim. Please talk to her, and find out whatever you can. Meanwhile, I'm going test the wind at corporate headquarters, and see what needs to be done to move St. George off the dime, too, and into a spirit of change. Let's touch base again next week."

CHAPTER

7

The Value-Centric Transformation

Jim had been doing a lot of thinking about his discussion with Sally, and their characterization of value chain levels to create specific designations. The ability to communicate with the field sales organization regarding which accounts to invest in, and to what extent, would prove invaluable. It meant they would be able to match their selling efforts and resources to each account, or in some cases to groups of accounts that resided on the same value chain level, particularly if they were part of the same vertical market.

More important was something that Jim didn't realize until after his meeting with Sally. Every year, Jim and all the senior managers went through a planning and budgeting process, which for him consisted mainly of forecasting and costing.

Dr. Tullis, their CEO, would develop a corporate statement of direction or strategy that would be presented to the senior team during an off-site corporate planning meeting. That direction would then be discussed and modified, and by the end of the second day, everyone would agree on what St. George was counting on to be successful during the following year. It was a good process, led by an independent facilitator, that enabled the department managers, directors, and VPs, like Jim and Sally, to enhance their business plans during the two days that followed. It was also during that time that the managers normally broke away to meet with their key people and determine what changes were necessary to better advance St. George's business strategy. On the fifth day, everyone reconvened and presented their plans for approval by Dr. Tullis and Dick Chainy.

Putting Strategy Back into Strategic Planning

It was Saturday, and Jim was sitting out in his back yard, listening to the birds chirping and the wind rustling through the leaves on a beautiful July day. With the kids at soccer practice and his wife Miriam away doing errands, he had time to sit and think without interruption. Today, his mind was on that annual meeting.

The yearly planning process was important, certainly, and very helpful in managing St. George's business, but it had become a routine, almost boring, process. Jim would take last year's numbers and bump them up to reach what Dr. Tullis needed, while other managers would set a budget, go into the "strategic planning session," and then squeeze out costs to align with the next fiscal year's "corporate direction." This was a euphemism for how much margin they would be required to generate during the following fiscal year. It was all tactics, and darned little strategy.

There would be some discussion of what initiatives to pursue, and that was helpful, but the process was definitely not strategic in the true sense of the word. To be fair, in the past it had never needed to be strategic. If a company performed well, it would get its share of business, and sometimes more. Today, as they had seen with Consolidated Hospitals, a supplier could do everything right and end up with nothing.

Mary's instinctive reluctance to head up the value chain development task force is understandable, thought Jim. *This is more than a task force. If we are to become strategic as a company, recognizing the power and necessity of becoming value-centric, it will require a top-down commitment to change, and that will not be easy at St. George. Management is pretty entrenched in the old ways, the old methods.*

With the radiant sun warming him, and the symphony of birds in the background, Jim was happy to be out of his work environment and in an atmosphere that was conducive to introspection and intellectual honesty about the situation. Lip service support from Dr. Tullis would not be enough. The CEO would have to experience the power of value chain management, internalize it, believe in it. Dick, on the other hand, was almost certain to be opposed to it. He would never support an initiative that would transfer more control of the business into sales and marketing.

A Missed Opportunity

There was a time when Jim could have challenged Dick, and perhaps prevailed, but that time was long gone. His chance to establish himself as part of the Power Base had passed. He had allowed himself to be intimidated by the COO, who was the kind of man who enjoyed inspiring fear in his subordinates and who believed that the world orbited around him, as evidenced by Chainy's two favorite subjects—himself and what he did.

Jim knew that Mark had always wondered why he didn't go to bat for him, back when Dick had quashed Mark's enthusiasm and plans for his sales region, shortly after he first joined the company. There were times when Jim could see it in Mark's eyes, and it almost made him sick. *My own political naïveté, seen in the clarity of a bright summer day,* he thought. *But maybe it's not too late to move into the Power Base, right the wrong, and spearhead an effort to put St. George Pharmaceuticals on a path to reshaping itself.*

"OK, so I blew it," Jim spoke aloud, and forcefully, startling the gray squirrel foraging under a nearby tree. "But Sally has the ear of Dr. Tullis. She's the only person I know right now who could take Dick on, and win. The power struggle alone would focus Dr. Tullis on value chain management, enough that it would be certain to get a good hearing from him. That means Sally Loxner, not Mary Gagan, should probably be the one to head up this task force."

Jim began to see a glimmer of hope in that idea. *With the full weight of the sales organization behind her, and the help of Mary, in particular, Sally just might be able to pull it off. I know Dr. Tullis respects her, she's the only person in the company who can just show up at his office and visit for a while. She's the one he values as an internal sounding board. We'd certainly need Danilo's backing, but Sally and Mary seem to have that locked.*

Jim paced the back of the yard. The gray squirrel scurried around, occasionally looking at him, but for the most part it ignored him and went about hunting for seeds. Jim didn't realize he was still talking out loud.

"It's not going to work. What am I thinking? A Direct strategy will require heavy superiority, and even with Sally, Mary, and Danilo, it's not enough to ensure victory for our side. No, we'd have to go with an Indirect strategy, one that doesn't telegraph our intentions. Sally is right, the challenge ahead of us is not one of automating the sales organization, but rather automating value chain management. But to do that, we'll need a strategy that focuses on sales.

"If we can launch a project around salesforce automation, then later, as we get into it, redefine selling, or maybe just drop the term 'selling' altogether and concentrate on value management, we could make this work. It might even help with Dick if we distance the project from a focus on sales, per se. Alexander Drugs, and maybe one other account, could participate in the task force, enabling us to bring the voices of our customers into the process. Who could argue with that, given the acknowledged need within St. George to become more customer oriented? Especially if Mary is as successful as she already seems to be, in working with Alexander to produce the account sPlan."

Suddenly aware that he was giving a speech in his own back yard, Jim looked around guiltily. No one had seen or heard him, except the squirrel and maybe a couple of birds. He sat back down, his thought process at full steam, and tossed a pretzel toward where the squirrel had been working.

On second thought, Sally is right. Mary should head up the task force. Without Mary taking the lead, capitalizing on her firsthand knowledge of value chain management, Sally will not take on Dick Chainy over it, of that I'm sure. Mary's role in this is of pivotal importance. I'll call her first thing Monday morning, and see if I can change her mind.

Jim felt good. He believed that he could really make a difference for St. George, and he was ready to put his job on the line, if necessary, to do what was right. Also, he intended to share his thinking on this with Mark, and apologize for not backing him that other time. He heard a sound behind him, and turned to see what it was. Miriam was coming out the back door into the yard.

"What are you doing?" she asked.

"Nothing much. Listening to the birds, talking to a squirrel, and trying to figure out how to make St. George Pharmaceuticals change course and become the best company in this business," he replied.

"Well that's nice. Do you think maybe your little friend the squirrel will help you wash the car, while you're at it? I mean, if you ask him nicely?"

Jim laughed. "Nah, I doubt it. He listens well, and works hard, but I think car washing is out of his field of expertise. I better just do it myself."

Managing Value

Jim was still on an optimistic high when Mary came to his office on Monday afternoon. He felt as though he'd had a vision, and he wanted to communicate that vision to Mary and secure her support. But first, he needed to update her on his meeting with Sally, and get her thoughts on the value chain categories that they had designed.

He took his time explaining them, soliciting her input at each step. Mary was quick to grasp the new designations, and able to cite account examples for each category. She became more enthusiastic as the design unfolded, and Jim realized that gradually she was joining them in taking ownership of the value chain concept for St. George. He was elated. This would bring her aboard, he was sure of it.

"Now," he continued, "I need your help in defining the buying patterns for each value designation so we can determine the optimum approach for mapping into those patterns. You'll note that I am not saying how to 'sell' into them. I believe that in today's marketplace, life has changed so much that the word selling is something of a misnomer. We are now in the value business, as it relates to pharmaceuticals, disease management, and health care. *We don't*

Stage	Designation	Low Potential	Medium Potential	High Potential
IV	STVL	NA	NA	NA
III	BVL	NA	NA	+++
II	SVL	NA	++	+++
I	CVL	+	++	+++

Figure 7.1 Value Chain Levels with Potentials.

sell any more, we create and competitively manage value. You're not an account manager so much as you are a value manager for your customers. So, let's look at how we can do that at each level of the value chain."

"Fine. Say, who put all the sugar into your cereal this morning, Jim? You're positively hyped. But don't get me wrong, I agree with you on this, 100 percent. The question is, will the top management at St. George agree with us?"

"We'll get to that."

Jim went over to the white board and sketched out the four value chain designations in ascending order, along with an explanation of how to rate an account's potential to move up the value chain (see Figure 7.1).

The Entire Buying Process

"Now, let's take the *entire* customer process of making major acquisitions and map it into the value chain to identify various buying patterns. The way I see it, there are ten phases to this 'inside-out' process, starting with the customer's senior management."

CORPORATE PLANNING

"This is where the company is formulating its future direction and expected growth, both organically and inorganically—deciding what businesses to be in and what businesses to divest, and assessing their financial and market position relative to competition, industry trends, emerging opportunities, and threats. Also, with what we now understand, that planning should include how well the company is aligned with its markets on the value chain."

FORMING CORPORATE INITIATIVES

"Operationalizing corporate direction is accomplished through the formation of corporate initiatives—often, many more initiatives than any company could implement in any year or, perhaps, several years. But that's not a problem. The purpose, at this point, is to identify all possibilities. Each initiative can be expressed as an Objective-Strategy-Tactics blueprint, or snapshot, that clearly articulates the initiative's aspirations or objectives—what the company is counting on to be successful, in terms of strategy, and what major tactics or actions are required to ensure that success. It's not a detailed piece of work. At this point, the blueprint is not intended to be a plan graven in stone."

SELECTING CORPORATE INITIATIVES

"The initiative blueprints present management with enough information to determine which ones are critical to the successful implementation of the corporate strategy. It is a process of qualifying initiatives and looking at alternatives. A company may evaluate the possibility of developing a new technology internally, or may instead decide to acquire a company that already possesses that technology, in order to move into it more quickly. Other initiatives may focus on a redeployment of company resources, a launch into a new marketplace, or a restructuring of the sales and marketing organizations to create better alignment with the marketplace.

"While this approach to determining which initiatives stay and which go sounds very straightforward and logical, it is nonetheless one of the most difficult processes to implement well," said Jim. "Not because of the process itself, but because of what is behind it. As you know, Mary, there is no true language of company politics, apart from what Holden developed back in 1979. Many of those terms have become part of the general business lexicon now. But even if our management knows and understands those terms, they would never use them openly."

"Well, I did learn about them at the Holden Power Base Selling seminar, but I've never used them that much, myself. They were in the Participant Guide, I believe."

"Yes, well I'd revisit that, if you still have it. It's important. Political expression exists in business, in terms of what initiatives people support and those that people oppose. As a result, nowhere are corporate politics so intense as in the high-level competition of corporate initiatives. It is in this phase that the initiative blueprints are built into *plans,* with people's careers made or broken in the battle to establish relevant value, cost effectiveness, and manageability of the competing initiatives.

"These are factors based upon assumptions, which are in turn based upon an individual's judgment, which is a function of a person's wisdom and insight, hopefully evidenced by their track record in a particular area. Basically, then, selecting initiatives becomes a turf war. Do you follow me?"

"I think so," Mary replied. "I can see that the process is very subjective, like a customer's buying criteria, even though it looks objective, as they identify a number of specific factors using a decision-making matrix." Mary sketched out her idea for Jim. "For example, suppose you have three competing companies and three decision-making criteria, like the one shown in Figure 7.2.

"Which do you want to win? Assume X is reliability, Y is price and Z is performance ability. If you want company A to win, you make X and Y more important than Z. If, instead, you like company B, you make X and Z most important. On the other hand, company C will prevail if Y and Z are judged most significant. The point is that the weighting is subjective, so the supposedly 'objective' process will say whatever you want it to say."

	Company A	Company B	Company C
X Capability (Reliability)	Strong	Strong	Weak
Y Capability (Price)	Strong	Weak	Strong
Z Capability (Performance)	Weak	Strong	Strong

Figure 7.2 Decision-Making Criteria Matrix.

"Good," said Jim. "You've got it. Okay, now, let's go to the next phase."

IDENTIFYING SUPPLIERS

"Once corporate strategy is in place, key initiatives have been identified, and plans developed behind each selected initiative, the company is ready to identify and evaluate outside resources in order to produce a list of qualified suppliers. This is the first external manifestation of what is otherwise a very guarded internal process.

"Various Requests For Proposal (RFP) will be generated and distributed to suppliers," said Jim. "The intent is to characterize fully what is required to ensure the success of each project assigned to a supplier. However, as you have already noticed, while the process appears to be organized and objective, it is actually subjective. This creates a wealth of internal political opportunity, giving birth to power struggles and creating new political alignment opportunities for people, particularly around very important initiatives that will be outside-supplier dependent."

"I cringe whenever an RFP for a significant deal hits my desk," said Mary, "especially when I didn't know it was coming. Nine times out of ten, it is written around a competitor."

"Very true, yet some buying patterns, as you will see, don't require that you pre-wire the RFP. Now, let's go to the short-list phase."

SHORT-LISTING SUPPLIERS

"Getting to the right short list is a priority, as it is too difficult and time-consuming to evaluate thoroughly every qualified supplier. Internal politics intensify here, with power struggles surfacing and personal agendas strongly linked to the success of particular suppliers. This creates a challenge for senior management, as many of these evaluations are run by middle management, where the risk of a power struggle degrading into a power play is very real.

"While the criteria for determining whether a supplier will make it to the short list may vary by initiative, the process will always distill down to three critical factors:

Short List Critical Factors

- Understanding.
- Commitment.
- Ability.

"Any two of these factors, without the third, will still allow a supplier to fail," said Jim. "Let's say that the supplier fully *understands* what is required to ensure the success of a particular project and is *committed* to that success, but does not have the necessary resources or *ability* to carry out the necessary responsibilities. What happens? Or, suppose that they do have the resources or *ability,* and they *understand* what is required to create success, but are not able to give a *commitment* to assigning those resources. Perhaps they are *committed* to other customers. What then? And lastly, take the situation where the supplier is *committed* and has the *ability* to make good on that commitment, yet lacks true *understanding* of what the company wants and needs to accomplish with the project. Success will be difficult.

"They may have the best intentions, but maybe they're new to the business. On the other hand, being new to the business may be an advantage for the company, as the supplier must realize a 'home run' with the project, needing a strong success to accelerate their business, specifically market penetration, by using the company as a reference. *The danger is that a supplier will have enough ability or experience to give the appearance of understanding, getting through the short-list filter, but not enough ability to do the job."*

"What you have just talked about reflects what I strive for with my proposals when engaging strong competition," said Mary. "I have not used your three operative words of *understanding, commitment,* and *ability,* but I recognize their value."

"I suspect that what we have been talking about formalizes what you have been doing informally, Mary. That explains why your proposals have been so effective. These three critical factors all need to be present to ensure success.

"Separating fact from fiction, and especially from opinion, becomes critical at this juncture, requiring that the short-list filtering process have some built-in discerning ability. This means two things for those who are tasked with doing the evaluating. They must:

- Ask the right questions, and
- Require proof statements for every supplier response."

"But what if the company representatives don't ask the right questions? Or don't have the *ability* to ask the right questions?" asked Mary.

"Aha. The same three critical factors that govern who makes it through the short-list filter apply to the individuals doing the evaluating. This is probably the main reason major corporate initiatives fail—company representatives tasked with evaluating the means of achieving those objectives are missing one or more of the three critical factors, *understanding, commitment,* or *ability.*

"Now, *understanding* and *ability* can be assessed, based upon past performance, but assessing *commitment* is another story. How do you determine effectively the nature and extent of a person's *commitment?* Certainly, motivation is a factor, with recognition and reward quickly coming to mind, but more telling than that is the perceived professional mission of the individual, and the extent to which it overlaps that of the company and the project at hand.

"Second to the mission-driven nature of the individual is his or her personal agenda, and whether or not the project advances that agenda. Last, in my opinion, are reward and recognition. They are very important, to be sure, but they come third on this list."

"With what I know about Performance Bonds, if and when I have an opportunity to build and implement one," said Mary, "the first thing I will look for is customer *commitment,* followed by *understanding* and *ability.*"

"That's wise. Now, let's move to the next phase."

SELECTING SUPPLIERS

"The process intensifies as the company gets to the point of making a final decision. On a major initiative, this phase of the process may informally involve individuals throughout the company at various levels, many of whom are not formally a part of the supplier evaluation process. At the end, the decision is usually based on which supplier best demonstrates and proves their *understanding, commitment,* and *ability.* But behind all that, within the procuring company is an array of internal issues that influence and characterize what the company requires in *understanding, commitment* and *ability.* I like to think of these as a food chain of issues, that resides first within the company department conducting the supplier evaluation, and extends up into corporate headquarters."

The Customer Food Chain

"The customer food chain is a hierarchy of formal and informal issues that move up and down the Operations, Management, and Executive levels of a company. Look at it this way. The RFP reflected a set of project requirements, some of which are HOT. Graphically, it can be viewed like Figure 7.3.

"In this model, each black dash is an operational issue or requirement that qualified suppliers must address. The issues identified as black boxes are HOT, in that they are:

1. Critical to the success of the project, reflecting 'must have' capabilities or qualities, or
2. Reflective of company evaluator biases, perhaps stemming from past experiences, strong philosophical viewpoints or personal preferences.

"The second level of the departmental food chain consists of business issues and like the operational issues, some of the business issues are HOT (see Figure 7.4)."

"Some of these 'HOT' business issues or considerations will drive some of the operational issues or requirements. For example, manufacturing capacity requirements might drive system speed, or through-put requirements for a piece of capital equipment being purchased. As such, we can link the two types of requirements together with solid vertical lines, forming the first level of the 'food chain.'

"Above the business issues in our hierarchy will be a number of political issues or factors, and some of those also will be 'HOT,' in

Figure 7.3 Level One of the Departmental Food Chain.

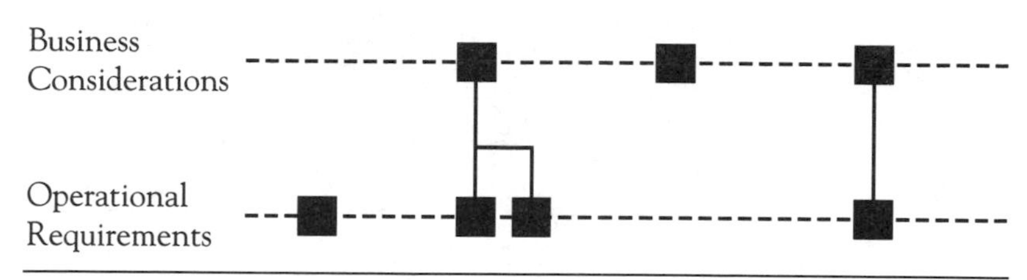

Figure 7.4 Levels One and Two of the Departmental Food Chain.

turn driving various business considerations, and forming the next food chain level.

"Thus, political issues connected to an individual's personal agenda, or power struggles, or power plays, will filter down through the world of business issues, where politics finds its legitimacy, and emerge as an epicenter of operational issues. It looks something like Figure 7.5."

"At the corporate level, another food chain exists. Different from that of the departmental level, it begins not with operational issues, but with higher level business issues, the type that go into formulating the company's corporate strategy. *These business considerations are tied to those of the departmental food chain and, not surprisingly, some are HOT.* Behind them reside various political factors, a subset of which link to and drive the HOT business considerations (see Figure 7.6)."

"Tying those departmental business issues to corporate level business issues is generally my goal when I bring in senior

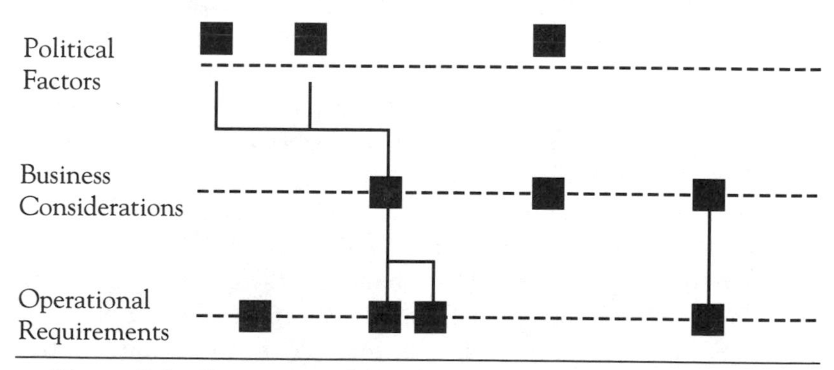

Figure 7.5 Departmental-Level Supplier-Selection Food Chain.

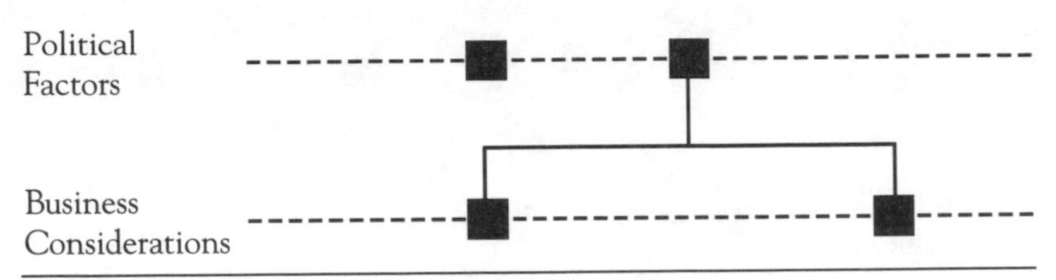

Figure 7.6 Levels One and Two of the Corporate Food Chain.

St. George management," Mary said, nodding. "*It is a way of tapping the power of corporate and bringing it down to the point of sale.*"

"Exactly, but I'm not so sure Dr. Tullis and Dick Chainy see it that way. In any event, the corporate and departmental levels become connected to create one long food chain, as we will see in Figure 7.7."

"At the very top of the corporate food chain are cultural issues that reflect the values and operating principles of the company. Those govern how things get done. A talented new manager may be the architect of an excellent initiative, only to find its merits significantly discounted due to lack of alignment with the company's operating philosophy.

"At the same time, in today's marketplace, it's not uncommon for senior management, specifically FOXES, to be working to change company culture, perhaps becoming more customer or value-centric, for example. The point is that major initiatives often carry with them a desire and need to shift the thinking of the organization in some meaningful way, which makes certain values or principles HOT, strongly influencing the corporate political and business issues that, in turn, filter down to the departmental levels of the food chain."

"Each of these issues throughout the departmental and corporate 'food chains' are tied to people, many of whom are not part of the formal evaluating and decision-making process as it relates to selecting a supplier. Yet, their views will directly or indirectly influence the selection process, and the final decision.

"Keep in mind that it's not unusual that a 'decision maker' at the departmental level who is outside of the Power Base, might not have a clue about what is really going on in a major acquisition, relative to the food chain. But those of us in sales must not only understand

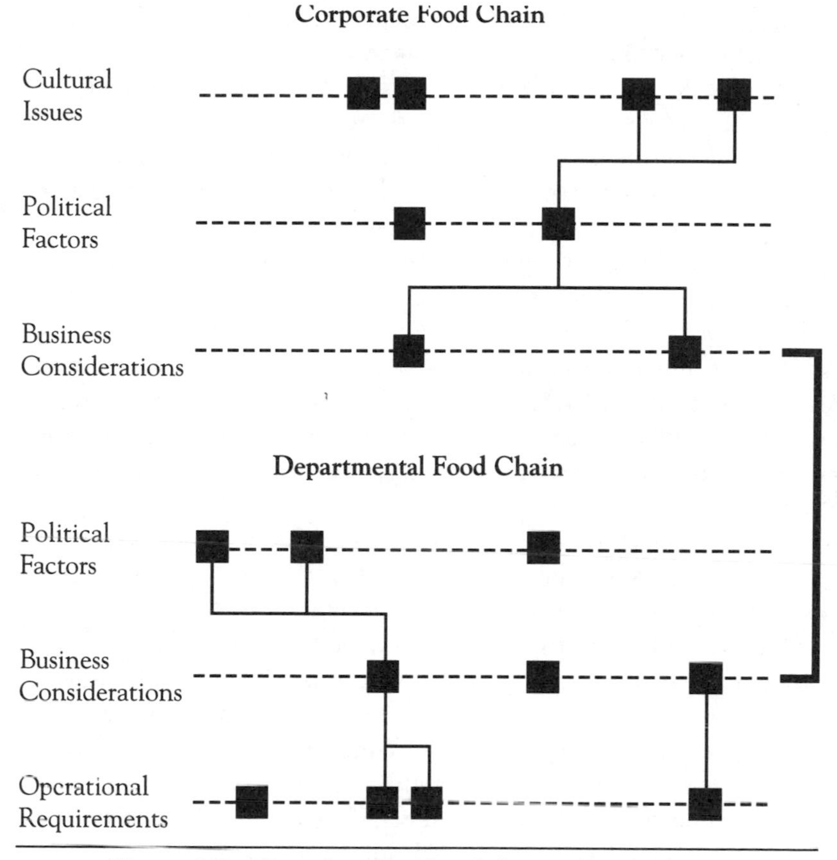

Figure 7.7 Complete Supplier Selection Food Chain.

that phenomenon, we must have some command over what happens."

"If we're not in the Power Base," said Mary, "how can we possibly influence the outcome?"

"We'll talk about that later," said Jim. "Right now, I'd like to elaborate on the next step in the process, which is negotiating contracts."

NEGOTIATING CONTRACTS

"At this phase, we look for a give-and-take process leading to a legal expression of the company-supplier relationship. Based upon shared and balanced reward, risk, accountability, and philosophy, a legal agreement, or contract, should emerge.

"As you know, Mary, this very tricky part in the selling process looks and sounds a whole lot easier than it is. Just when the supplier thinks all has been said and done and the business is won, the company's internal counsel may well be brought in to negotiate terms and conditions. Making matters worse, many salespeople tend to avoid bringing legal counsel in earlier, viewing contract negotiations as an administrative exercise, rather than a sales or account responsibility.

"When customer counsel is brought in and important corporate initiatives are involved, some legal considerations or terms will be considered extremely important, or HOT." *At that very moment, another level of the food chain springs to life at the departmental levels."*

"I have never seen the legal people brought in early in the negotiation phase," said Mary, "even though it makes sense to do so, to avoid problems and misunderstandings later."

"You're absolutely right. Somehow, we must find a way to convince our executive management that our legal people, who tend to focus only on legal issues and to be company-oriented, need to create a better balance between what is almost by definition an adversarial stance on everything. I'd like to see them become more value-centric and customer-oriented. They could become a nontraditional source of competitive advantage for us, by becoming involved in the *entire* buying process with our salespeople.

"I believe that every manager at St. George, and every person that plays a role in our internal buying process, including legal people, should in some way be connected to the marketplace, so that they understand the market dynamics that impinge upon our company's ability to sell, operate and survive," said Jim.

"We may be right, but somehow I don't see that happening at St. George in the near future," said Mary. "Do you?"

"All we can do is put it forth as part of our overall proposal for change, and try to make it happen," said Jim. "Whether or not the initiative succeeds will depend on the corporate food chain. But to continue with our present project, the next phase in the process concerns the implementation of the project that has been negotiated and contracted."

PROJECT IMPLEMENTATION

"Once an agreement is reviewed by legal and signed, the project plan is put in place and the implementation team formed. Then the company is ready to launch the project. Supplier *understanding, commitment,* and *ability* now become evident in their actions as the effort moves through a series of benchmarks on its way to project completion."

TRACKING RESULTS

"In this phase results are tracked. The company accumulates data and looks for trends that give valuable insights into how successful the project is, and how successful it might continue to be in the future. A major project, one engendered by an important corporate initiative, will always demand a Value Proposition. It may be constructed by the supplier of choice or developed internally, but in any event, a Value Proposition should always be part of the process, in order to justify the effort. That means measurable results are identified early in the process, along with the metrics necessary to actually measure those results. Metrics, in this situation, are the predetermined tools and the processes that employ them, in order to gather relevant data.

"In addition, I think we should be producing internal project Performance Bonds to our executive management wherever possible, tying them to our compensation in terms of bonus, where the amount is proportional to the business value a successfully managed major project produces. I know that sounds a bit radical, but creating clear accountability, linked to reward and recognition at all levels, could move some of the food chain out of the shadows, thereby increasing overall manageability to further enhance the project's success. You know, Mary, I believe that what we are being asked to do by the marketplace, in terms of value chain management with our customers, has equal applicability internally."

"That's a real departure from our present operating norms," said Mary, "but it is worth considering."

She knew that the level of accountability Jim was outlining would be a bitter pill for most of the St. George organization—in truth, it would be a political nightmare. She wondered if Jim realized how much of one. But she just nodded, not wanting to get him off track and into a discussion of company politics.

Jim continued, "The last phase of the process is probably one of the most important for us, the sales professionals. It has to do with learning from experience. All too often, the end of a project is the end of the project. But when that happens, we don't learn all that is possible from the experience. We do not build wisdom derived from the nuances, which become clearly defined and audible only through post-project analysis."

ANALYZING RESULTS

"This phase ties back to the corporate plan and initiatives, creating a closed-loop perspective on what has occurred during the entire internal buying process. Time pressure, and the need to move forward with new initiatives and projects, are key factors that often delay a post-purchase analysis, but this is an area where an excellent supplier can play a helping role."

Defining Customer Buying Patterns

By studying the process Jim had outlined, and by basing their analysis upon phases of the entire company buying process at the three general levels of organizational structure within a company—Operations, Management, and Executive value chain levels—Jim and Mary were able to identify some specific company buying patterns. Together, they designed a worksheet that would help define those buying patterns.

"This worksheet (see Figure 7.8) will of course vary from company to company," said Jim, "but here at St. George, the Executive team drives the early part of the buying process by setting company strategy and identifying major initiatives to implement that strategy. Management overlaps the Executive team somewhat, and is mostly focused on lining up the right resources and expertise to support the selected initiatives. Operations, on the other hand, is involved from the time suppliers are identified, all the way to analyzing results."

"This chart will help us recognize who is involved in what phases of the process, along with the type and extent of supplier

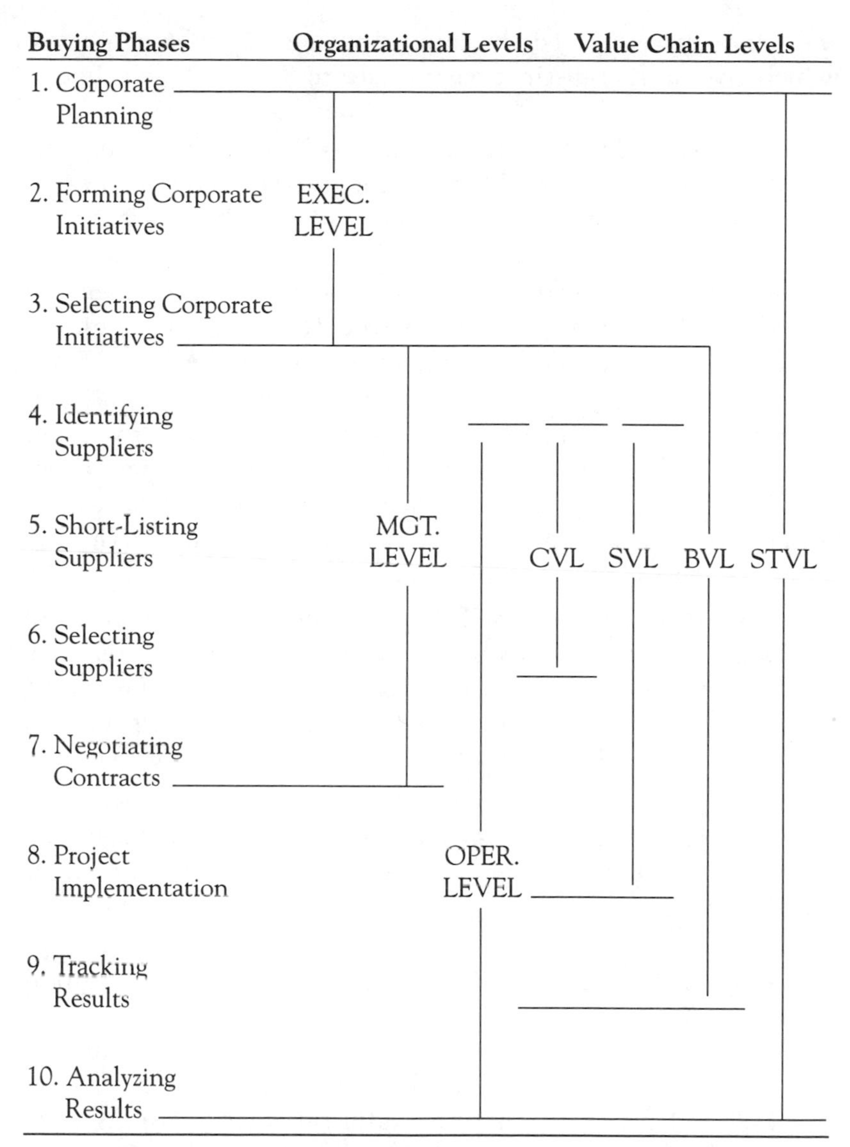

Figure 7.8 Company Buying Process/Patterns Chart.

value necessary to feed the buying process at different phases, which gives us four distinct buying patterns:

1. Commodity Buying Pattern (CBP)—Operations driven, with Management support. Management involvement is limited to the identification and selection of suppliers by the company.

"For simplicity's sake, let's refer to it as the *blue pattern*. It sounds simple, I know, but that one word, *blue*, then communicates the entire concept," said Jim. "The other patterns are:

2. Solutions Buying Pattern (SBP)—Still Operations driven, but with a wider scope of Management involvement, from supplier identification to project implementation. As such, there's more middle management input into the selection and activities of the supplier. This is the *green pattern*.
3. Business Buying Pattern (BBP)—Reaches up into the ranks of Executive, in terms of which corporate initiatives are selected, and funnels down through all aspects of supplier interaction with Management, to tracking project results with Operations. We'll call this the *red pattern*.
4. Strategic Buying Pattern (STBP)—Covers all phases of the company buying process, and involves all three: Executive, Management, and Operations levels. This will be the *yellow pattern*."

Using a marker, Jim underlined each pattern title with its appropriate color.

"Does this mean that we could actually classify our accounts in terms of *blue*, *green*, *red*, or *yellow* buying patterns?" asked Mary.

"We can, but keep in mind that different buying patterns could exist at different times for different departments within a customer's organization, so it could be unfair to characterize a company in terms of one buying pattern, even though a supplier may be selling into only one pattern at a given point in time. That's why it is critical for us to understand these patterns, participating in the ones that make sense and helping customers to shape new ones that bring us higher on their value chain, ahead of our competition, with the ultimate goal of helping those customers move up *their* customers' value chain, ahead of *their* competition.

"But let's put off getting into how best to sell into different buying patterns until another time. I think we've covered enough technical points for one day. I know we've replowed some familiar ground in this process, but I wanted to share some of these ideas with you, Mary, because I believe that our future as a company lies with value chain management.

"At the same time, like you, I recognize that getting the right kind of support from our executives, and driving the internal change necessary to be world class in this area, will not be easy. But I believe that ultimately it is doable. That is, if Sally and I can have your help, Mark's, and hopefully the backing of the entire sales and marketing organization."

Mary tensed. She knew what was coming next—the dark side of company politics.

Confronting Internal Politics

"I know that Sally has mentioned this to you before, Mary. She told me that you refused her initial suggestion. But I hope you will keep an open mind about this, and reconsider your refusal. Like the rest of us, you are vitally interested in your own future. I also believe that you are concerned about the well-being and the future of St. George, as a company, in the world marketplace. Sally and I both know that you care about what is happening, and what will happen.

"If you would be willing to play a significant role on a new task force that Sally, Danilo and I will recommend to Dr. Tullis, we could put St. George on a trajectory that will make it one of the most exciting and forward looking companies in this business."

Jim noticed that Mary had leaned forward to prop her chin on her hand, and was looking at him, waiting. The body language signaled that she was still open to persuasion. Her expression was unreadable, and she wasn't smiling and nodding in agreement, that was for sure. However, she hadn't said "No" and slammed the door like she did with Sally, either.

"Let me elaborate a bit on our thinking, Mary, before you make a decision one way or another. This effort would exist initially as a straightforward salesforce automation project, based upon value chain management. That shouldn't cause much political heartburn at the outset. It's our belief that as the effort really gets rolling, there will be an opportunity to shift the project emphasis away from selling per se and onto value chain management. That would be operationalized through new technology, following the lines you, Sally and Danilo discussed, factoring in some additional directions Sally, and I refined the other day, and those you and I have developed today.

"In fact, it is at that point that I'd like us to look at redefining sales roles to be more value management-oriented roles. Today, selling is all about value: Identifying customers and market sectors by value chain level, looking at the buying patterns those levels create, the sales methodologies that map into those buying patterns, and the competencies necessary to successfully implement the methodologies. Selling to value is so different from traditional selling that the very word "selling" will become a misnomer. Instead, we are in the business of creating and competitively managing value.

"Mary, what I'm saying is that we have the opportunity to do something very significant, and like Sally, I would like to see you heading up the task force that will drive that change at St. George. I think it's a wonderful opportunity for you, personally."

Mary drew a deep breath. She had never seen Jim so intensely committed to an idea as he was to this one. She thought back to what they discussed earlier. It was evident that both Jim and Sally had the three necessary components to get this project off the ground—namely *understanding, ability, and commitment.* Mary felt she had only one component—*understanding. Were commitment and ability her missing links?* Jim and Sally both believed in her *ability* to do it. So that left only one—*commitment.* What Jim had said earlier about that echoed in her brain: "*Certainly, motivation is a factor, with recognition and reward quickly coming to mind, but more telling than that is the perceived professional mission of the individual, and the extent to which it overlaps that of the company and the project at hand.*

"*Second to the mission-driven nature of the individual is his or her personal agenda, and whether or not the project advances that agenda. Last, in my opinion, are reward and recognition. They are important, to be sure, but they come third on this list.*"

Mary felt she needed a lot more time to think about that and to evaluate her own professional mission and her personal agenda before she would consider leaving what was familiar to her, what she knew she could do well, and embarking upon a whole new road full of political potholes. She tried to keep her tone neutral, noncommittal in fact, as she responded to Jim.

"I understand, Jim, and I want you and Sally both to know how much I appreciate your vote of confidence, but I am first and foremost a salesperson for St. George. Accepting this position to lead the task force would mean leaving the field, right?"

"Yes it would," Jim responded, "but only for a year. And your compensation would remain the same, including what you would have made in commissions for that year."

"To whom would I be reporting?"

"Sally Loxner. We both agree that she should steer this project at the corporate level, so I feel it would be best for you to report directly to her."

"Hmmm. That would make it a staff position. Jim, I appreciate all you're trying to do for me, and for St. George, and I think the project should proceed. But I'm not cut out for this kind of staff job. I like the field, and my freedom to operate there as I think best. Besides, you know how I feel about getting internally focused. I absolutely hate the idea."

"You mean you hate getting involved in anything that smacks of internal politics, don't you?"

"Yes, that's exactly what I mean. I'll do it only to the extent necessary to support my accounts. I'm not good at it, and 'hate' may be a strong word, but I definitely don't like it."

"You're wrong when you say you're not good at it, Mary. Actually, you're very good at it. Just look at what you have been able to accomplish with your customers, and how much good you've been able to do here at St. George when you put your mind to it."

"I know, but it's not the same. I'm just beginning to learn how to become an effective catalyst for change *within accounts,* but those are situations where I am able to maintain neutrality, not getting too involved in their internal politics. At the end of an account visit, I return to St. George, with my neutrality intact. How could I possibly remain neutral driving change here, when St. George writes my paycheck? Neutrality is not possible.

"In an account, if I blow it, it may mean losing an order, at worst a whole account, like Consolidated. And yes, I recognize that I could be reprimanded, or take a pay cut, or be fired for that. It's still a lot different from getting fired, or wishing you were fired, because some manager decides to make your life miserable day in and day out, reducing you to flying some feeder route out in West Podunk."

"What? What feeder route? Forgive me, Mary, but I don't know what you're talking about."

"Sorry. I know you don't. It's, well . . . nothing, never mind. It's personal. Ignore it."

"Mary, what is your real concern here?" Jim knew that there was something else, an underlying concern that was forcing her away from the project. "What is your specific objection to the project? 'I don't like politics' is too vague for me to accept. What is this about feeder routes and West Podunk?"

In trying to uncover specificity in Mary's concern, Jim did just what Mary would do in a sales situation when a customer voiced an objection about price or some other aspect of the deal, but they knew it wasn't the real reason. New salespeople might react only to the objection, never knowing what was behind it, but not Mary or Jim. They knew enough to dig for the real cause.

"Jim, you know that I'm reasonably good at what I do because I understand and believe in what I'm doing and I'm confident in my ability to perform, or to learn what is necessary to perform. I'm also committed to winning, and helping St. George and the customer win, too. Now, if fear enters that equation, it's over for me. I cannot do my best work in that environment. Dealing with tough issues or fierce competitors doesn't frighten me, but the dark side of corporate politics on my own turf is a specter that I simply don't want to see raised in my personal life, let alone be forced to deal with on a day-to-day basis."

"I see. Well, I can understand that, Mary, and certainly I can relate to it. It was not so long ago that I ran into that specter of political fear myself, and like you, I backed away. It was not the right decision, and I regret it now. But my situation was different from yours. I was not working for a FOX, and quite frankly, I did not have your innate wisdom."

"Thank you, but I wouldn't credit my wisdom all that much, Jim. You're a lot wiser than I am. But I have good friends who have counseled me well on this subject, and a lot of personal exposure. Look, I know Sally is a FOX—I ran the FOX Evaluator on her. And please don't get me wrong—I also appreciate the fact that under her wing, and yours, it could all work out for me, and for all of us, but that's a logical response to the offer.

"Unfortunately, my problem is more an emotional one, a personal one even, and I recognize that. It's a commitment issue. I'd like us just to leave it at that for now. I promise I'll think more about it, but at this point, I honestly don't believe I can leave the field and become a staff person, even though I respect what you're doing. I like Sally a lot, admire her agenda, and could work well with and for her—I just don't feel I should."

Jim knew that it was time to draw back and not press the issue further at this point. He understood where Mary was coming from, just as he knew the sting of politics she had so vividly described. However, she hadn't given a definite "no," and she'd asked for more time to think it over. He remembered his own words to her earlier: "Now, *understanding* and *ability* can be assessed, based upon past performance, but *commitment* is another story. How do you effectively determine the nature and extent of a person's *commitment*?"

He knew that Mary was as committed to the idea of transforming St. George into a value-centric organization as were he and Sally Loxner. But for some personal reason he hadn't yet discerned, she was inordinately fearful of committing herself to the political maneuvering that change would entail. He'd have to leave it at that for now.

CHAPTER

8

Selling to Value

That night was another sleepless one for Mary, after her meeting with Jim. She was concerned that her reluctance to head up the task force might alienate key supporters like Jim and Sally, perhaps increasing the chances of a negative encounter with the political specter she was trying to avoid. Finally, her emotional consciousness gave way to fatigue and she drifted off, but restful sleep was lost that night in a sea of turbulent dreams. One particularly vivid one involved her friend Jo. It was a dream about an accident so tragic and frightening that it woke Mary at 4 A.M. Peering at the clock, she decided she might as well get up, begin the day, and end one of the worst nights she had ever spent. When everything was right with her family and work, Mary felt on top of her game, but when trouble struck in either, her life went into a tailspin. That was always the downside to having a caring personality.

At work during the next few days, Jim and Sally remained patient. Neither pressed the issue with her, which helped Mary. It appeared that her relationship with them was secure. Perhaps her reluctance to head up the task force might not be made into a big deal at St. George after all. In any event, she began to feel better about the situation. Mary was a very genuine person, and at times she wore her emotions on her sleeve. To sell effectively, she needed a positive outlook. Reinforcement came when she learned that Dick Chainy had approved the Alexander sPlan. Also, some of the others who had reviewed it submitted praise, along with excellent suggestions and comments. Mary incorporated many of those suggestions into the final draft. Now the time had come to take the ratified sPlan to Alexander Drugs for their final approval. Mary was feeling more confident as each day passed, but she couldn't shake a sense of foreboding about Jo. As soon as she got home tonight, she would give Jo a call.

The presentation to Alexander senior executives went very well, even better than Mary could have hoped. For the first time at St. George, a jointly developed, value-centric account plan had been built with an important customer. It was a significant accomplishment for St. George, for Mary, and for Alexander Drugs, because it put St. George ahead of their competition in the understanding and implementation of value chain management.

Arriving home that evening feeling exhilarated about her success with Alexander Drugs, Mary was smiling as she picked up the phone and checked her voice mail. The first message was from Jo, and from the tone of her voice, Mary could tell her friend was down about something. Reminded of her dream a few nights before, Mary immediately returned the call, but it was almost an hour before she could reach Jo.

Accepting the Call to Action

"Mary," said Jo, "I'm so glad you called. It's been a horrible day for me. I've been demoted at Newman."

"What? Oh, Jo, I can't believe it. Not you! How did that happen?"

Jo tried to laugh, but her laugh ended on a catch that sounded suspiciously like a sob. "I could say 'I wish I knew', but actually, I've figured it out. After all the discussions we had that weekend about politics, and all the counseling I gave you about finding and aligning with FOXES, building political acumen and personal currency, I goofed on those very issues myself. I left myself open and vulnerable. Remember when I said it's what you don't see that hurts you most?"

"Yes, I remember that."

"Well, that's what got me all right. Oh, they told me it's just part of a restructuring, but I've reexamined everything, and now I'm certain that it happened because a certain executive saw me as a threat to his career, or maybe his ego. As you know, Mary, I came up through the ranks at Newman International pretty fast. And I had a solid track record in the acquisitions field. That success, coupled with strong recognition from our CEO, is what fueled my career growth at Newman. A few months ago our CEO announced that he would retire at the end of this year, and at the time I wasn't too concerned. But what I did not think about was the impact on my job of losing such an important supporter in the Power Base of the organization. I suppose I figured that, since I knew that I had a good support base, with a number of people behind me within the bank, I'd be okay."

"I would have bet on that too, Jo. Surely the CEO retiring couldn't have caused this to happen?"

"It certainly could, and for the most obvious reason. Secure in the support of the CEO at Newman, I ignored the principle, 'be close to your friends, but be closer to your enemies.'"

"Well, I know you need to be careful of your enemies," said Mary. "In a sales situation, they can feed information to your competition, but even so, I find it better to try to win my enemies over whenever possible."

"Well, maybe you should have been counseling me, instead of the other way around, when I was there."

"I can't imagine that, Jo, but tell me exactly what happened," said Mary. "I still can't believe this."

"Believe it, my friend, because it's true. I haven't decided yet what I'm going to do about it, but for the moment, I just need to absorb the shock. Here's what I figure happened. There is one senior executive at Newman that I never really got to know very well. As it turns out, he's been tapped as the new CEO, which is fine by me. But what I did not anticipate, Mary, was that he would immediately begin setting up his new organization, and that I would not be included as part of it, due to another executive, Allan Crenshaw, who is probably one of my worst enemies at Newman. Crenshaw is in the inner circle of the new CEO. He's also an egotist, and has shown open jealousy of my success and annoyance at my positive relationship with the outgoing CEO. Ergo, he's now in, and I've been dumped out in the cold, demoted to a peripheral position at Newman International. Crenshaw finally got his revenge."

Mary was deeply saddened about her friend's situation. Worse, the political specter that for Mary personified everything evil about corporate politics, the antipode of a FOX, had struck again. First her father, and now her best friend. Mary internalized things like that. She was the type of person who genuinely celebrated another person's success when things went right for them, and conversely, she deeply felt their loss when something went wrong. Other people in her office would actually feel better about themselves when a friend or colleague got into trouble. And when something went right, they would say the correct words, like "congratulations," or "well done," but deep down they didn't mean it. They were primarily shallow, ego-driven people whose image of themselves often went up when others in their work environment fell down—the kind of people who celebrated the failures, rather than the successes, of their co-workers and friends.

For Mary, those types epitomized the dangers of corporate politics. She'd worked with many of them, but had remained aloof from them personally. Jo, like Mary, was a sincere and caring person, who did her job well. She had brought value to Newman, and did not deserve to be cut down by petty political considerations. The two friends talked for a long time that evening. Mary tried her best to wrap a protective blanket of caring and understanding around Jo.

Later that night, she remembered what Jo had said: "Be close to your friends, but even closer to your enemies." Mary knew that Jo was right. Never allowing yourself to get close to people you don't like is the wrong approach. The challenge is to care about people who don't deserve it. Mary realized that Jo was telling her that the only way to beat the specter of politics was not to run from it, but to embrace it, and by doing that, defeat it. Jo Stiller was one of the most politically astute people Mary knew, and if Jo attributed her own setback to not taking the time to get close enough to key people, like them or not, Mary knew that there was a lesson to be learned from that experience.

That night, Mary reviewed her own situation. Finally, she decided that she was ready to tackle her fears. Now, with God's help, the hunted would become the hunter. Mary had been strengthened in her new determination partly because of the lesson of Jo's unhappy situation, but mostly because of the need to restore her own sense of self-esteem. She realized that the specter's principle weapon was fear, and fear had to be conquered to defeat it. To her own amazement, Mary slept soundly that night. The next day, she accepted the offer to head up the task force.

Jim was delighted, and although neither he nor Sally really understood what had happened to make Mary change her mind, he was glad she had. The three of them met to discuss the project, and Mary's strong commitment was evident.

"Before we get into details about the task force and my role in it, Jim, I'd like us to go back and review the buying patterns we discussed at our last meeting," said Mary. "As I recall, we characterized those patterns according to:

- The 10-Phase Buying Process, or buying life cycle of a company, beginning with the Corporate Planning Phase and ending with the Analyzing Results Phase;
- The three organizational levels, Executive, Management, and Operations, that identify who participates in the various Phases of the buying life cycle; and
- The four value chain levels, CVL, SVL, BVL, and STVL, which overlap the Buying Phases and company organizational levels."

Creating Value Chain Language

"Defining those gives us the ability to define customer expectations and the opportunity to shape those expectations, in terms of how we at St. George should interface with customers at different value chain levels," said Mary. "You simplified all that with your color code, which would facilitate our internal communications. Can we look at those again?"

"Sure," Jim responded. "Basically, the four color codes look like the sketch in Figure in 8.1."

"In essence, these codes tell us what customer activities we should be involved in, and what type of value we need to be providing, in order to be aligned with the customer on a particular value chain level. It also makes very clear what we have to do to 'notch up' to the next highest level, in order to build a true company-to-company relationship, to change the ground rules on a competitor, or to move into a leadership position, focusing

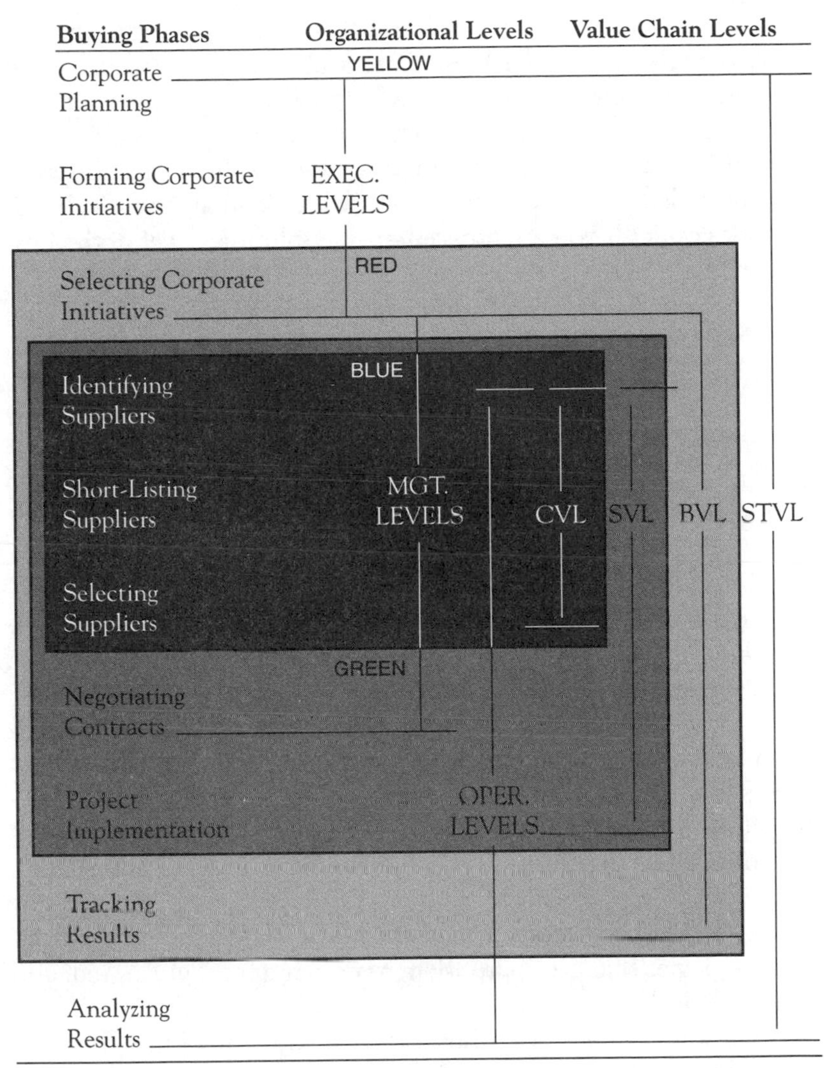

Figure 8.1 Color-Coded Company Buying Patterns. (Yellow has no screen, red is the lightest screen, then green, and blue is the darkest tone.)

on demand creation with an account in which we want to invest for future returns."

"So to be at the highest level of the value chain with an account," said Sally, "we need to map into a yellow buying pattern, that involves St. George in the customer's Corporate Planning, Forming of Corporate Initiatives, and so on, right through to Analyzing Results."

"Exactly," said Jim, "but suppose that a yellow pattern doesn't make sense? You run the Value Potential Evaluator and decide to go with a red pattern. At that point, you want to be involved with the customer during the phase when they are Selecting Corporate Initiatives and carry on through Tracking Results. It is a different buying cycle from yellow and, as we will talk about later, a different sales cycle. If you are focused on the solutions level of the customer's value chain, reflecting a green sales initiative, the cycle will be even shorter, beginning when the customer is Identifying Suppliers and ending when they move into Project Implementation. You can see how the amount of sales involvement or investment in an account changes, depending upon where you are on the value chain.

"The smallest amount of sales work, and the shortest sales cycle, is required for a blue buying pattern, or value chain level. In fact, I believe that commodity type products or services are really more marketing driven than sales driven."

"That's true," Sally agreed. "At the blue level, we depend more on marketing to create 'pull' in the marketplace, then service the demand created with techniques like telemarketing, indirect channels like third-party distributors, and e-commerce, where we will use a future St. George Web site to advertise products and accept orders electronically. In some cases, salespeople might be involved in selling certain products or services into a territory, but the margin to provide blue value, as you know, will not support very much in the way of cost of sales."

"Let's build on that point," said Mary, "and look at the sales methodologies that are appropriate to creating blue, green, red, and yellow value."

Mary was clearly very enthusiastic. Jim and Sally knew they had made the right decision in nudging Mary along to accept the task force position.

Selling to Blue Value

Jim went to the chart up on the board. "Let's take selling to blue value first, and look at it from several points of view, building on the blue customer buying pattern that we have identified:

- First, compare the Four-Stage Customer Model to the Four-Stage Sales Model for the Stage I level (see Figure 8.2).
- Then go to the sales methodology that most effectively maps into a blue buying pattern.
- Next, examine how much sales currency is necessary to implement a blue sales methodology.
- Finally, look at the competencies required to implement a blue sales methodology.

"If we like that approach, we can apply that format to all the value chain levels." Mary and Sally nodded their approval.

Jim continued, "Remember, all this stems from the buying patterns that characterize our marketplace. These patterns are fostered by the new and emerging value chain levels that are producing new opportunities for us and our customers. As those trends change, buying patterns may also change, influencing everything that we are about to discuss. Now, let's examine the Models."

"*Selling directly into these accounts is primarily an exercise in numbers.* Most of these sales situations are short cycle, probably three to four sales calls each, where you're dealing with a fairly large number of accounts. You pulse in, quickly move to the short list, and either get the business as the selected supplier, or move on. *As a result, sales efforts in this commodity market space are principally managed through a pipeline.*

	Stage I	
Quality	**Sales**	**Customer**
Salesperson's Intent	To be considered	Solve a problem
Salesperson's Focus	On the product or service	Product or service features
Relationship with Customers	Casual in nature	Vendor on demand
Value Chain Level	Low operations focus, providing product or service options	Low cost, quick fix

Figure 8.2 Stage I Sales-to-Customer Comparison.

"Because of the number of accounts, it becomes very important to determine three things:

1. Whether or not there is a product or service fit between what you are selling and what the customer needs.
2. Whether or not the funding is present to support the purchase.
3. Whether the timing of the buy will be short-term, or long-term. Those answers will give you a quick reading as to whether or not you should pursue the sales opportunity, again based on:
   - Product or service fit,
   - Funding availability, and
   - Decision timing.

"Most often, this assessment is done over the telephone. In some organizations, it is accomplished through a telemarketing operation, using a structured approach. Specific questions are asked and the responses rated, usually on a scale of + 4 to –4, or something similar, creating a range and a point score for each question. The points are then added up to indicate if the opportunity is a qualified one to pursue. If it is, the opportunity enters the pipe, which consists of a number of phases. Typically, you see something like Figure 8.3.

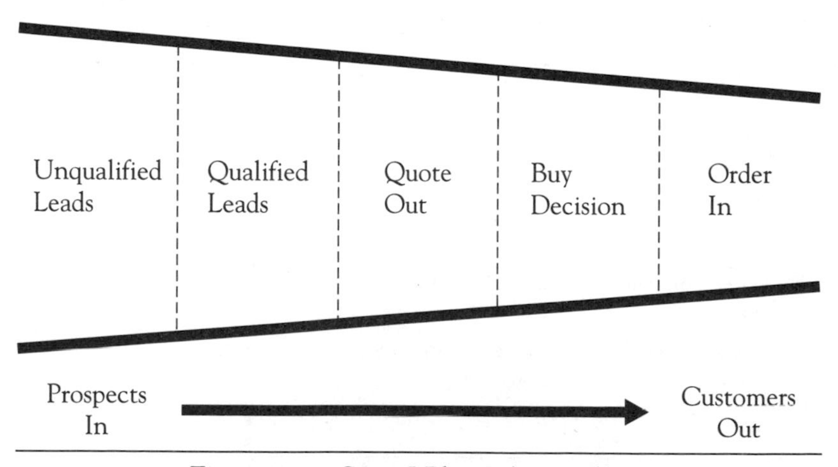

Figure 8.3 Stage I Blue Sales Pipeline.

"Once qualified, the lead is followed up by a salesperson, or maybe a channel partner, such as a third-party distributor. During that first call, the qualification assessment is verified, the customer's needs are discussed, the product or service is presented, and a link is set to the next step in the sales cycle. It may be a product demonstration or a presentation where a quote is provided to the customer.

"You'll note I did not say proposal here. In the world of blue value, it is generally not necessary to formally convey understanding, commitment, and ability, as you and I discussed a couple of weeks ago, Mary. The customer wants a low cost, quick fix, as expressed in the Stage I Sales Model. Price, features, and availability often rule the day here. If possible, the next phase will be collapsed right into this call, where the salesperson asks for the order. If not, a link will be set to the next call. That is, the next meeting is set up, making sure the right customer individuals are involved, before leaving the current meeting. In that way continuity is established, keeping the sales cycle as short as possible. Linking is also important at this point in the sales cycle to ensure that a 'close condition' will exist when you return.

"Remember: To make a buy commitment, the customer must be ready, willing, and able to make that commitment.

"*Ready,* in that they have reviewed their options, in terms of possible suppliers, *willing,* in that they are prepared to make a decision with the full support of management, and *able,* in that the funding is present to support a commitment to purchase, and they are authorized to make that commitment."

Establishing the GLOS Ratio

"When we purchased our copier for the sales office, for example, I spoke to the salesperson from the copier company. In my view, they sell mostly to blue, dealing with issues like price, print quality, reliability, and size. I may be understating their business with that view, but the salesperson explained to me that he received about one hundred and twenty-five leads per week. Those unqualified leads distilled down to approximately twenty-five qualified leads, which in turn produced the opportunity for five presentations or product demonstrations per week. Out of those five, he would generally close one deal, on average.

"Let's use those numbers to create a GLOS ratio: G, or gross leads in the pipeline out of which come L, qualified leads, and from them we get O, opportunities resulting from those leads, and finally S, actual sales. The GLOS ratio for his product at the blue level is then 125:25:5:1 or, in short, 25 to 1 for qualified leads to close, giving us an indication of sales effectiveness.

"From a currency point of view, not much is required. It's always nice to have, but even with it, selling into blue doesn't provide very much time or opportunity to spend it. Selling ability, however, is a different matter. Here, success is a function of demonstrating proficiency at two levels:

1. Managing the pipeline, which is key in managing a sales territory, and
2. Selling tactics, which can serve to improve the GLOS ratio.

"What causes most pipelines to fail is a lack of willingness or ability to purge sales opportunities that are not advancing in the pipeline, or that have become unqualified. When that happens, the pipe begins to bulge and sales are lost due to lack of attention. Purging the pipeline regularly will ensure that the right opportunities get the right attention.

"At the selling tactics level, a different set of skills and knowledge is called for to ensure success:

- Qualifying sales opportunities, using specific criteria, as we have discussed;
- Preparation and execution of structured sales calls, involving probing techniques, objection handling, asking open and closed questions, and linking;
- Presentation skills;
- Product and/or service knowledge; and
- Closing and blocking skills. Blocking is where you eliminate one of the three closing states I mentioned earlier—that the customer must be ready, willing, and able to make a commitment. Eliminate any one and you will contain the sales situation,

inhibiting the competition from closing the business if they are 'last in.'

"Each of these areas of tactical selling proficiency can be viewed as Primary Characteristics, or job-related selling qualities, made up of core competencies that, in turn, express themselves in the form of four stages of observable behaviors. I know that you are already familiar with that concept, so I won't go into more detail on it now.

"Attributes like the ability to deal with rejection, personal drive, and others also become important, with integrity again at the top of the list, particularly impacting a salesperson's ability to handle objections and close business.

"Integrity is a salesperson's most significant asset when it comes to engendering customer confidence."

Selling to Green Value

"Okay, let's look at the green pattern. Selling to green gets a bit more involved, because here we move into the sale of solutions that are more operationally specific in meeting customer needs. That is, customized solutions. *At green, mass customization ability is a supplier requirement.* It enables companies to produce customized offerings for relatively large numbers of accounts, creating a stronger operational fit with their needs. This is achieved through a customizing process that is very well structured, or codified, to support replication of the process. Software called configurators automate that process, moving you up on the value chain, as can be seen with the Stage II Sales to Customer Comparison Models (see Figure 8.4). It also moves you down, from the standpoint of the number of sales opportunities or accounts that a salesperson can effectively cover.

"This will be true all the way up the value chain, as value level is inversely proportional to the number of accounts that can be effectively covered by a sales professional."

"In the green pattern, the sales cycle often begins at the same point as a blue pattern commodity value sale, with receipt of an RFP or sales lead. It then continues through the sales cycle and into the Negotiating Contracts Phase, where issues relating to service, support, customization, pricing, and other business terms

	Stage II	
Quality	**Sales**	**Customer**
Salesperson's Intent	To make a sale	Acquire a solution
Salesperson's Focus	On the customer	Product or service benefits
Relationship with Customers	Trust-based	Characterized by trust and commitment
Value Chain Level	Low-middle management focus, providing applications solutions	Able to purchase reliable solutions

Figure 8.4 Stage II Sales-to-Customer Comparison.

and conditions may be addressed. That's where the negotiating process becomes an overlay to the sales process. Then, it's on to Project Implementation, where supplier support can play a key role in implementing the solution.

"*All too often, this is the Phase that gets the least supplier attention, yet what happens here is the first step in the next sales situation.*

"The green sales methodology kicks in upon receipt of an RFP, or a lead with a more extensive qualification of the opportunity. Still concerned about fit, funding, and timing of the purchase decision, we now focus in on the customer's understanding, commitment, and ability to make the solution successful, from the point of view of their role in implementation. This adds *customer competency* to the list of qualification criteria, along with *customer resource availability*. Thus, the qualification criteria might be expanded to look like this:

- Product or service fit.
- Funding availability.
- Decision timing.
- Customer competency.
- Customer resource availability.

"Again, a point scale can be used very effectively to determine if implementation of the solution is likely to be successful. While this qualification is taking place, a series of in-depth discussions, focusing on the customer's needs, will also occur. This enables the salesperson to configure a solution and build a Value Statement, which becomes part of the proposal. Unlike the blue pattern, where a quote would typically be generated, we have stepped up to a proposal which is based upon supplier understanding, commitment, and ability, and which will hopefully match the needs and desires of the customer, as determined during the green qualification process. The proposal, along with customer references, will lend credibility to the Value Statement, on which the salesperson is often counting to win the business. However, like blue, green generally does not depend on sales strategy to produce competitive advantage, as the sales focus is on the customer and the product or service offering, as we saw in the Four-Stage Sales Model.

"The sales cycle advances with presentations, customized demonstrations, and other sales activities that create alignment between what the supplier can provide and what the customer needs, consistent with the customer's decision-making criteria.

"Advancing to the close, blue sales cycles tend to peak very dramatically, with a customer decision made fairly quickly, once the ready, willing, and able status is present. Again, that's why blocking, as a sales technique, is so important in that environment.

"In green, sales cycles are characterized most of the time by a softer peak. Sales professionals here tend not to close the business in an explicit fashion, which, while common, is not necessarily prudent.

"*Massaging a sales situation down to a soft close may be less stressful for some sales professionals, but it is also less effective, more risky, and generally an indication that the negotiating process phase will be viewed by the salesperson as an administrative task, often leading to late-cycle discounting and problematic contract terms and conditions.*

"As you can see, the sales cycle is longer and a bit more involved in a green than in a blue sale, but it can still make sense to set up a pipeline to manage the advancement of opportunities. Its structure, and its GLOS ratio, are similar to what we discussed earlier, with the addition of more phases to support the longer sales cycle."

"That's pretty much how I manage my sales opportunities now," commented Mary, "but I have a question. I can understand why you use the color designations to facilitate communication, but I'm not sure I am comfortable with them, though I'm not certain why."

"Perhaps because it sounds to you like an oversimplification, Mary," replied Jim. "Let me ask you this: How would you like to see these value chain levels, buying patterns, and sales methodologies labeled?"

"I'm not sure. I agree it needs to be succinct, but a little more explanatory. What do you think, Sally?"

"Well, let's see. I guess my vote would be to use descriptive designations for each pattern, like Commodity, Solutions, Business Solutions, and Strategic, where Blue would be Commodity, Green indicates Solutions, Red is for Business Solutions, and Yellow denotes Strategic. We use those terms anyway, and it would be more descriptive of what we mean than simply giving it a color designation."

"I like that idea," Mary agreed, and Jim nodded his approval.

Another thought occurred to Sally. "You know Jim, with this way of identifying levels on the value chain and in buying patterns, we could also designate accounts according to what level St. George is on with them in the value chain, helping us to segment the market in terms of Commodity, Solutions, Business Solutions, and Strategic accounts.

"And if there are accounts where we are working at multiple value levels, I suggest that we identify them by the highest value chain level we are on with them. If we see the potential to move up a level, based upon the Value Potential Evaluator, we could express that as, say, a Solutions account with Business Solutions potential, for example. I'd prefer that to the Plus indication that we were thinking about earlier. It is a very clear way of expressing a world of information."

"I'm fine with that, Sally, I like it a lot," said Jim. "We will have to keep in mind that what we mean by the word Strategic is different from the more common, historically used tactical interpretation. Later I would like to talk with you both about the idea of restructuring the sales organization around such designations. An account manager would also be a value manager, in that arrangement, and play a different role at each level, even though he or she might have the same position and title at each level. In any event, we will need to talk later about new ways of identifying field roles and competencies, in order to be more consistent with these new levels of selling.

"I agree with you and Jim about the new designations for the color patterns," said Mary. "Let's ink it."

"Done."

Jim went on to talk about the currency and competency requirements for Solutions selling.

"From a currency point of view, to be effective at the Solutions level a salesperson needs to be at the low end of the Middle Management range. Now if a regional manager, like Mark for example, is involved with the field salesperson, perhaps that's not always true, in that an Operations level of currency, combined with good coaching where currency is being borrowed, could suffice. But, if the potential to move up to a Business Solutions account exists, I believe that it will require at least Middle Management currency.

"On the competency side, to successfully manage Solutions level sales situations or Commodity accounts with Solutions potential, a salesperson will need Commodity pipeline management skills and tactical proficiency, along with Stage II capabilities in the following Primary Characteristics:

- Political Acumen—discerning and professionally capitalizing on the political forces within an organization.
- Business Savvy—insight relative to business issues and trends along with their corresponding industry and customer implications.
- Executive Bondability—establishing a relationship and sustaining credibility with senior executives.
- Resource Optimization—maximizing the return on the investment of company resources.
- Product/Service Proficiency—understanding the functionality, features, and benefits of your products/services.
- Communication Effectiveness—the ability to express ideas and information clearly to create action."

Business Solutions Accounts

"To sell effectively at the Business Solutions level, or to develop a Solutions account with Business Solutions potential, requires a shift in sales focus and selling orientation. It is here that the food chain begins to stretch from Operations to the Executive levels of the customer's organization. No longer responding to an RFP, the salesperson is helping to shape the RFP, aligning it with the strengths of his or her company, products, and services.

"To some extent, it is winning the battle before it is fought, interacting with customer executives before Solutions or Commodity competitors ever see the sales cycle.

"It becomes more of an inside-out sales campaign. That means an increased investment in time and effort by the sales professionals involved, which comes at the expense of developing other accounts. That makes it essential to focus on the right accounts and win the majority of the sales that are pursued. The GLOS, or qualified opportunity-to-sale ratio here, should be rather tight, since it's an inside-out sales development effort. Mary, do you have any sense for our GLOS ratio, here at St. George?"

"Well, historically, I have been focused on what we are now referring to as Commodity and Solutions opportunities. I would say that between myself and the other salespeople I know, we are at about a thirty to forty percent GLOS rate at the opportunity-to-sale point, or a 3 : 1 ratio. On the newer Business Solutions opportunities, we would be lucky to reach a 5 : 1 GLOS ratio, maybe less. Actually, we have just begun to compete on that value chain level, so it's hard to say."

"That's the point I'm trying to make. First of all, we have never measured sales effectiveness, or tracked GLOS ratios here at St. George, and second, as we move up the value chain, whatever the current ratios are, they will probably get worse. I think that could be the case, big time. Sally, this is an area where we definitely will need your help. We must drive more sales and marketing accountability into our organizations. That means putting new metrics in place—well, new for us here at St. George, anyway. Perhaps that effort could become part of the task force, involving our finance group. Take Consolidated. Do we really know how much we spent in pursuing that business, only to lose it?"

"Not really," replied Sally. "No question about it, Jim, we need to understand what the margin potential is at every level of the value chain. If Mary agrees, I suggest we invite finance to participate in the task force project."

"Speaking for myself and other high performers in the sales organization, let me say that is music to my ears," said Mary. "It would certainly help us justify investing in the right accounts and, by the way, I would not be opposed at all to being compensated, in part, according to profitability over time with any Business Solutions and Strategic accounts I handle. I don't think we have ever kept track of cost of sales by account, but with Consolidated, I can tell you it cost six months of my time, and that's just for starters.

"But what is more disconcerting to me is the loss of future business, or the opportunity cost, at Consolidated over the next few years. It could reach millions of dollars in sales. Added to that is the additional opportunity cost of my not having pursued other sales while I was fully focused on the Consolidated account. And that hurt me in the wallet this year."

"I don't know what all that adds up to," said Jim, *"but it's my guess this area of sales operations is one of the most significant, least understood, and under-managed costs of doing business in many companies, not just at St. George."*

"We know that we will be seeing the need for more Business Solutions and Strategic account development efforts in the future," he added. "Without knowing those numbers, given that we must begin tracking account development costs and segmenting the market, and that we will have to estimate how many of these new-type account development efforts we will want to become involved in, our costs could eat us alive.

"On the other hand, if we don't get higher up on the value chain with acceptable GLOS ratios, we will soon find ourselves relegated to the low end of the market. And we don't even know, at this point, what acceptable GLOS ratios are in our industry."

"Well, all that is true," said Sally, "and it's a compelling argument to segment our market and reshape how we work at different levels of the value chain. The good news is that, as behind the market curve as we think we are at this point, we are still ahead of most of our competitors. That lead time should translate into significantly improved GLOS ratios once we have our sales methodologies properly aligned with the right buying patterns and the right accounts. I agree with you, we need to begin tracking our GLOS ratios immediately."

"If we then work with finance to develop the right way to track cost of sales, including opportunity cost, we can relate those back to our ratios and get a handle on the average direct and opportunity costs for lost sales. That is, we should assess the direct costs of sales in pursuing business ultimately lost, and the sales revenue that we don't receive as a result of that loss. It's a twofold hit," said

Mary. "After a year or two of tracking such data, that would really help us to evaluate what it might take to pursue various opportunities, especially at the upper Business Solutions and Strategic levels, where it can be very costly to bid and lose—not to mention your earlier point, Jim, about measuring revenue and profit per value chain level."

Qualifying Business Solutions Opportunities

"I agree with both of you. It has never been so critical as it is now, with the changes we are experiencing in the marketplace," Jim continued. "As with the Commodity and Solutions sales cycles, we qualify Business Solutions opportunities, although we expand the criteria to include the potential for repeat business or orders and to assess the competitive dimension of the sale—that is, objectively determining if we can win the business. We need to address both, because the longer Business Solution sales cycle, and the increased cost of sales, must be amortized over repeat business and justified by a reasonable expectation that we can win the business. We are not only trying to identify good business that we can win, we are working to find business that will help us develop an account, creating an asset for our company, in terms of repeat business potential. That produces a qualification criteria list like the following:

- Product or service fit.
- Funding availability.
- Decision timing.
- Customer competency.
- Customer resource availability.
- Potential for repeat business.
- Potential to build a strong support base, developing supporters and allies that are in the Power Base.

"The point here is to create a narrower and narrower gate, through which leads must flow in order to receive active sales attention and disbursement of resources, as you can see in Figure 8.5."

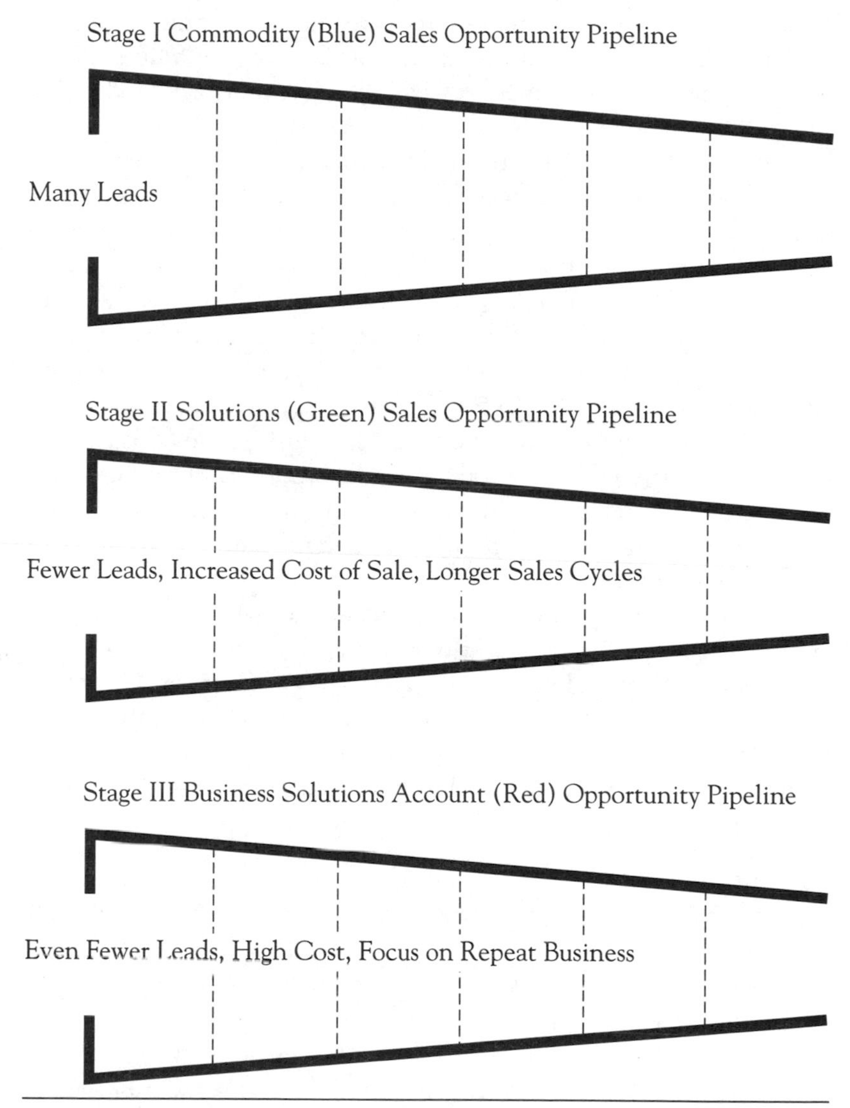

Figure 8.5 Comparative Opportunity Pipelines at Stages I, II, and III.

"At the Stage III Business Solutions level, competitive advantage is being generated from how the salesperson is managing the sales situation, in addition to the value of the business solution provided to the customer. That is evidenced by the result of 'pre-wiring' the RFP. In fact, nearly all activities associated with a Business Solutions sales campaign are intended to create competitive advantage.

That makes strategic formulation, FOX hunting, and alignment with the Power Base critical, as you can see in the Salesperson's Focus of the Stage III Sales to Customer Comparison Model (see Figure 8.6).

"That's not to discount the significance of value. In fact at this stage, the value proposed becomes more unique. It becomes real, as in measurable, and more multifaceted. It is at Stage III, the Business Solutions level, that you graduate from Value Statements to Value Propositions on the value chain, which extends the sales cycle into the Results Tracking Phase of the customer buying process. At this point, measurable results are recorded and reported back up to executive management, closing the buying process cycle. This not only helps ensure repeat business within the account, but also becomes the basis for producing case studies on results to support industry articles and other promotional activities. It also is not uncommon to include them with new customer proposals, as a credibility source.

"Value becomes more multifaceted at this Business Solutions level. You are providing operational value, business value, and political value to key individuals. In the latter, it is done by advancing their personal agendas. That creates a multilevel, mutualistic relationship, where both companies benefit. It also creates a value foundation to support mutual benefit in the future, which causes each company to become an asset to the other."

	Stage III	
Quality	**Sales**	**Customer**
Salesperson's Intent	To create repeat business	Capitalize on a business opportunity
Salesperson's Focus	On the competition	Supplier expertise and resources
Relationship with Customers	Mutual in nature	Strong mutual dependency
Value Chain Level	High middle-management focus, providing business solutions	Able to codevelop and create custom offerings to solve complex problems

Figure 8.6 Stage III Sales-to-Customer Comparison.

Business Solutions Personal Currency

"Personal currency becomes more important at this level, as too little will lead to excessive borrowing, beyond what might be practical, creating an inability to build and maintain the necessary support base, or incurring a problem with credibility in presenting a Value Proposition. For those reasons, the minimum level of currency to be congruent with a Business Solutions campaign, in my opinion, is high Middle Management to low Executive."

Business Solutions Competencies

"Just as the sales cycle, sales revenue potential, and cost of sales all increase here, so does the sales capability required in order to be successful. Tactical proficiency continues to be important, but begins to give way in priority to the following Primary Characteristics, some of which we have already defined as necessary to Stage I and II phases of selling:

- Political Acumen.
- Business Savvy.
- Executive Bondability.
- Product/Service Proficiency.
- Communication Effectiveness.
- Resource Optimization.

"Now, to achieve the kind of competency needed at this Stage III level, we must add the following Primary Characteristics:

- Change Agency—influencing and shaping an organization's strategic plans and direction.
- Competitive Adeptness—maximizing competitive advantage while disadvantaging competitors.
- Leadership Effectiveness—mobilizing others toward advancement of a common vision.
- Management Effectiveness—the ability to get things done through others.

"This list of Characteristics defines the scope of skills and knowledge needed to be successful at this stage. We can focus on them by using a Competency Map, structured on a Primary Characteristic macro plane (see Figure 8.7).

"You can see that even though the project is at the Business Solutions level, the proficiency required by the sales professional in Political Acumen, Executive Bondability, and Competitive Adeptness is Stage IV, as those proficiencies directly impact the salesperson's

Primary Characteristic	Stage I	Stage II	Stage III	Stage IV
Political Acumen				
Business Savvy				
Executive Bondability				
Change Agency				
Competitive Adeptness				
Resource Optimization				
Leadership Effectiveness				
Management Effectiveness				
Product/Service Proficiency				
Communication Effectiveness				

Figure 8.7 Business Solutions Level Competency Map.

ability to build a competitively strong customer support base. And yet, Product/Service Proficiency can be Stage II, because knowing more about products or services, while always useful, is not critical to Business Solutions success.

"So as we can see, the trends from Commodity to Solutions to Business Solutions are evident. The number of opportunities being pursued decreases, the cost of sales increases, the asset-building potential increases, the need to be more and more selective as to what opportunities are pursued increases, the value customers receive increases, the personal currency required increases, and the level of sales skills and knowledge necessary to be successful increases.

"All these trends, except one, continue to apply as we move to the highest level of the value chain, where the operative word is Strategic. Which trend do you believe does not hold true?"

"I'm not certain," Mary responded. "They would all seem to apply."

"You're right if we look at our business and how we have run it in the past, but if you consider the new, nontraditional opportunities we have to bring value to our customers, the answer changes. All those trends do apply, but so does something else—the opportunity to offset cost of sales with new, nontraditional services."

Strategic Accounts

"At the Strategic level, the sales cycle spans the full ten-phase customer buying cycle. While that makes it longer and more costly to pursue, it also opens up new opportunities."

"I don't follow. What opportunities are you talking about, Jim?" asked Mary.

"Well, when you conducted the sPlan at Alexander, what were you doing? You were planning, right? You were helping Alexander move up their value chain, and moving us up along with them. What I'm talking about is using our company's resident expertise to assist Business Solutions and Strategic accounts during the Corporate Planning and Forming Corporate Initiatives Phases of their business cycle. It means that for these types of accounts we operate more like a professional services firm—consultants, if you will.

"That not only brings us in at the beginning of the buying cycle, it means we also get paid for it.

"Take another example. Helping to move a customer up a notch or two on their value chain with their customers means that we will be providing nontraditional value to them, right?"

"Yes, that's right," agreed Mary.

"Well, do you suppose they will know how to measure the value that we are providing, never having done it before? Most companies don't measure customer impact as it relates to their traditional business, much less know how to measure nontraditional value provided to them or by them, high up on the value chain. That gives us the opportunity to assist customers in developing metrics to measure and analyze the nontraditional value that we are generating together, during the Tracking Results and Analyzing Results phases of the buying process.

"Moving to a Strategic level on the value chain gives us the opportunity to consult to the customer, for a fee, at both the front and back ends of the buying cycle.

"Now, I know that is new thinking, but let's look at what it does for us. It:

- Generates consulting fee income, thus offsetting our cost of sales, and
- Gets us in early in the cycle, where we can work down rather than up the food chain, moving from corporate down to departmental levels."

"Does the direction we go on the food chain make all that much difference?" Mary wanted to know.

"Yes, because that enables us more easily to connect corporate political issues with those at the departmental levels, providing valuable recognition for lower level managers with their senior executives," Jim explained. "Which in turn significantly strengthens our support base, involving key people at lower levels who might otherwise derail an initiative, even when it is sanctioned from above.

"Graphically, connecting these corporate and departmental political issues to build a stronger support base looks like Figure 8.8."

"You can see in this illustration that connecting corporate and departmental politics creates a backbone to the account development effort. This backbone is your support base, consisting of powerful

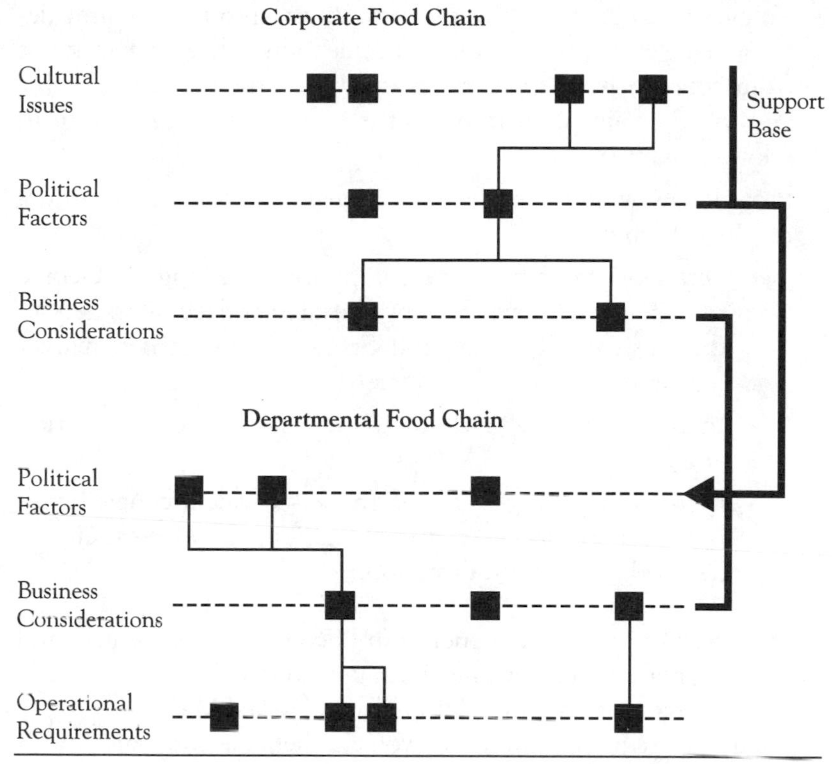

Figure 8.8 Downward Food Chain Process at Strategic Level.

supporters and allies. As we have said before, the language of politics is manifest in business, which is why connecting corporate and departmental business considerations becomes so important. *Whenever influence is flowing, so to should business value be flowing, the two always moving together down the same stream.*

"What we are talking about is creating association between key individuals at the departmental levels and those in corporate, recognizing that people are brought into the Power Base by association with powerful people. You know, we as suppliers can help individuals become recognized by their senior management, often far more effectively than they could themselves. Getting in early and being there for the full cycle also:

- Allows us to influence the vendor selection process, for all the right reasons, even including acquisitions that do not directly relate to our business.

- Enables us to build competitive immunity into the account development effort, by providing unique value, thus protecting us from competitive displacement and losing the account. At this level on the value chain, that is the one thing we don't want to allow to happen.
- Provides us with concrete case studies, based upon measured results, which can:
  - Differentiate us from the competition, helping St. George to become acknowledged by the marketplace as leaders in the Business Solutions and Strategic value chain market segments,
  - Increase our GLOS ratios in new account opportunities, and
  - Increase our margins as the increased value, coupled with increased competitive differentiation, drives elasticity of demand in the right direction.

"So as you can see, the benefits in becoming value-centric and moving higher up on the value chain are overwhelming."

"Then why isn't everyone doing it, Jim?" asked Mary.

"Sally, please jump in on this if you can help me out," said Jim. "I think it is mainly because of the organizational issues associated with doing it well, Mary. We have known for the last two years or more that there were good opportunities for us to do some consulting with customers.

"The problem was that we didn't have enough clarity of vision to assess what is required to be successful at it. We've addressed that now. Also, I think we've all seen companies that have tried it, and failed."

"Jim is right, Mary," said Sally. "In order to succeed at this, the sales and marketing functions have to be integrated, jointly identifying the Commodity, Solutions, Business Solutions, and Strategic market sectors. Then, the sales methodologies and marketing practices for each sector would have to be defined and put into operation, so that the company knows what types of consulting services might apply to which accounts, and further, how to sell them to those accounts. And remember something else: *In today's marketplace, when you go higher up on the value chain, you also go global.*

"That's another value chain trend. At the Commodity and Solutions levels, you can operate centrally, for the most part. At the

Business Solutions level, localization in different countries becomes an issue, as an additional level of customization, and for Strategic accounts, it becomes a requirement.

"For us, it would mean being able to service and support customer facilities all over the world, in the same way they are trying to support their customers all over the world. *Therefore, we're talking about integrating sales and marketing on a global scale, not just locally.*"

It had never occurred to Mary that an account like Alexander might want to implement her Value Proposition in other countries, but she knew they had numerous operations abroad. She wasn't aware of who in the St. George sales operation covered those facilities, or even if they had coverage at them. What she did know was that Alexander Drugs was expanding aggressively in a number of countries, in both Europe and Asia. *Hmmm, that is certainly something to think about, something I'll need to address in this sPlan.*

Jim picked up where Sally left off.

"In addition to the organizational implications of becoming value-centric, we'd have recruiting, hiring, compensation, and training issues to deal with, and that means integration of the Human Resources Department, too.

"The Competency Mapping piece will help us to identify what skills and knowledge are required to be successful in these new positions, for each level of the value chain, but that doesn't help us find the talent we need to fill them. In many instances it will be a development challenge for our existing sales professionals at St. George, but we will also need to hire new people from the outside to average up the quality of our overall salesforce.

"The good news is that we can work with human resources, using Competency Profiling and Mapping as a recruiting and selection engine, identifying, interviewing, and hiring our sales professionals based upon the Maps for each value level."

Sally smiled over at Mary. "I think you're beginning to see now what is ahead of you with this task force, Mary."

"I do, and you're not kidding, Sally. It's quite a project. But if we can just break this formidable challenge—this elephant of change, which would scare anyone away—down into manageable, bite-sized pieces, I believe we can sell it to senior management and make it work to St. George's advantage."

"So do I," agreed Sally. "Let's wrap the Strategic piece, Jim, and then we can talk some more about organizing the task force."

"Okay. Knowing which accounts are Strategic, unfortunately, is not an easy or quick assessment to make. It becomes more of a process, focusing on three areas:

1. The qualification criteria used for a Business Solutions opportunity, if a sales opportunity exists.
2. The Value Potential Evaluator, if you can identify a future opportunity.
3. The four key areas of alignment needed for implementation of an sPlan—Reward, Risk, Accountability, and Philosophy.

"I believe that alignment of those four key areas, and a strong Value Potential Evaluator score, are the most critical elements to the qualification of a Strategic account.

"It's not a determination you make based upon the amount of sales revenue being realized from an account, as that revenue reflects past, not future, value.

"In any event, these accounts are very few in number, which is fine, because like most companies, St. George would not have the organizational resources to handle very many of them. Comparing them to the others, in terms of our qualification graphic, better illustrates the point (see Figure 8.9)."

"At present," Jim acknowledged, "I can't name one St. George account that will come knocking at our door for this level Strategic value. Maybe it will happen some day in the future, but for now we need to create demand, or leads, for the opportunity to get to the

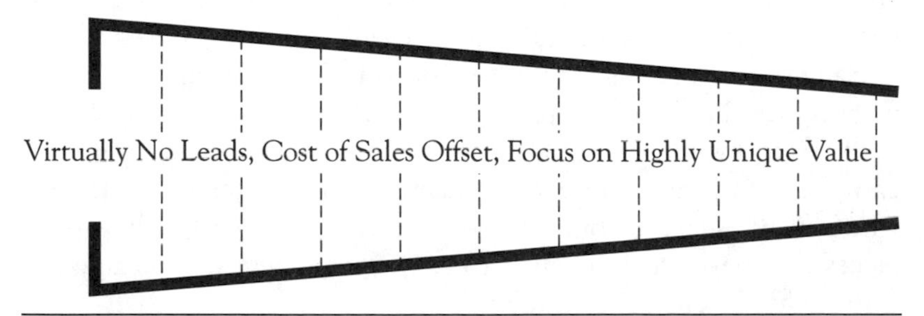

Figure 8.9 Stage IV Strategic Level Opportunity Pipeline.

point that we can provide Stage IV value. Let's take a look at it on the Sales to Customer Comparison Model (see Figure 8.10)."

"From this, you can discern another trend as we move from Commodity to Strategic business levels. The field of view is tightly focused on product at the Commodity level. At the Strategic end of the spectrum, it has broadened to encompass the customer's customers, and even the customer's competition.

"*As a result, there is generally no one sales methodology that can be applied to Strategic accounts.* This is a 'custom design' area. In fact, a company may be working at every level on the value chain with some accounts, implementing Commodity, Solutions, and Business Solutions sales methodologies with different departments. That means team selling, which is still another value chain trend: *The higher you go on the value chain, the more teamwork comes into play.*

"This is particularly true when you think about providing consulting services on a global basis. Organizing individual roles, especially on an international basis, and coordinating team activities can be a handful, which is why I believe an sPlan should be a prerequisite for every Strategic account. And, if it is an installed Strategic account, *i.e.* one where we are already doing business, I recommend we run the Valu-Driver, as we did with Alexander Drugs, so we're sure we know where St. George stands in the eyes of the customer, and can create alignment on that.

	Stage IV	
Quality	**Sales**	**Customer**
Salesperson's Intent	To become the dominant supplier	Create a new business opportunity
Salesperson's Focus	On the customer's customers and competition	Supplier strategic ability and commitment
Relationship with Customers	Symbiotic in nature	Business partners and advisors to each other
Value Chain Level	High executive focus, providing strategic direction and expertise	Receives insight into business issues and creativity in addressing them

Figure 8.10 Stage IV Sales-to-Customer Comparison.

"If the customer doesn't perceive that we are providing sufficient value, or if they perceive the level of value we're providing them to be different from our own perception of it, we'll fall flat on our faces proposing a Value Proposition or a Performance Bond."

Strategic Currency

"We've already covered a lot in this discussion, I know, but I would like to finish up with some discussion of what is required at this level of the value chain in terms of currency and sales capability. I'm sure you already recognize that from a currency point of view, an Executive Level is required."

"Absolutely," agreed Sally, "but unlike the other levels, borrowing currency is less appropriate at the Strategic level. If you cannot offer enough personal value and are obliged to borrow currency, the customer may just tune you out. *Keep in mind, Mary, the Strategic level of the value chain is not a forgiving one.*"

Mary nodded. "Yes, I certainly learned that with Consolidated Hospitals. I'm going to be very careful now with how we handle Alexander Drugs."

Strategic Competencies

"From a competency perspective," Jim continued, "the Strategic Map changes in two ways. First, you will see a different set of competency requirements, and second, these competencies are not required by any one individual. Strategic selling is team selling. *The Map at this level reflects what is required by the team in order to be successful.* Again, it is illustrated on a macro plane (see Figure 8.11)."

"From a personnel or staffing point of view, shifting to a Team Map here is a good tactic," said Sally. "I don't think we could ever hire enough strategically skilled and knowledgeable people to meet all the Map requirements for each Strategic account. In fact, it even builds a case for using teams at the Business Solutions level, thus reducing the need to find sales professionals who possess all the requisite skills and knowledge to penetrate and develop Business Solutions accounts. I even wonder how many of that type of sales professionals exist, if any."

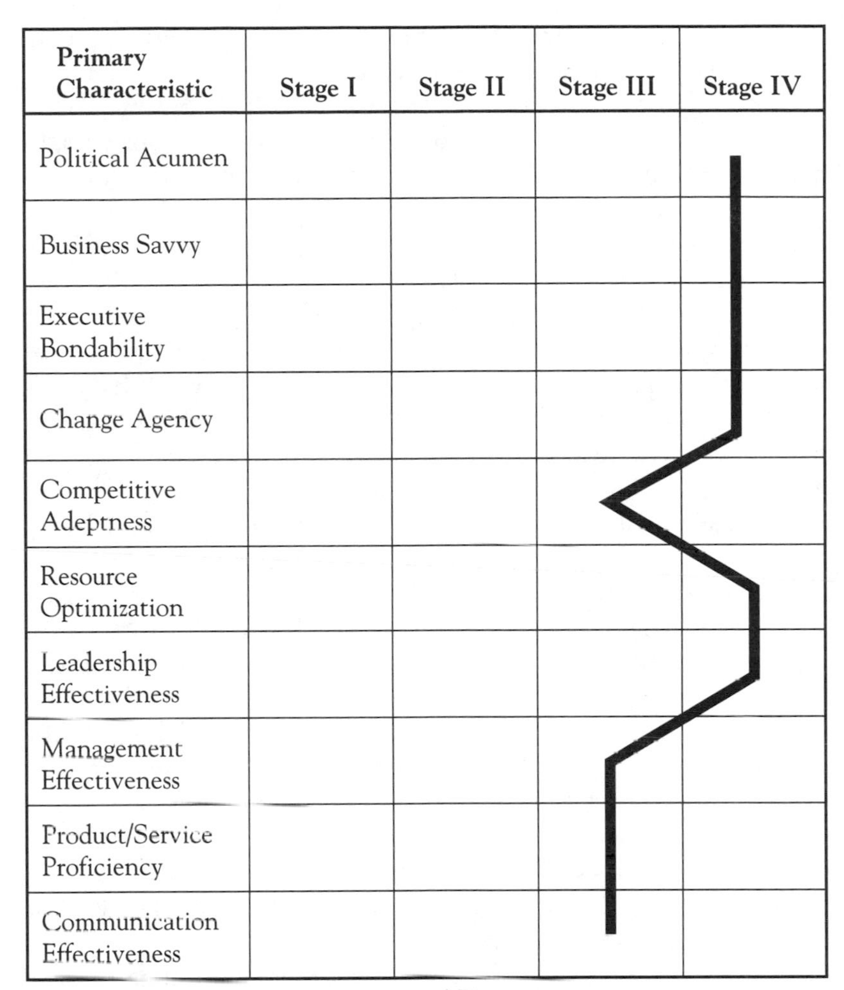

Figure 8.11 Strategic Level Team Competency Map.

"Well, I've been wondering how this would work," said Mary. "Do either of you have an idea?"

Sally was the first to speak up. "I view the Map as a composite requirement for the whole sales/marketing team. That is, if you took the Competency Profiles for each individual on the team, and added them together, you would create a composite. No one team member needs to fulfill all the requirements of the Team Map, but it does put a critical emphasis on hiring the right additional people to construct the best sales team."

"What kind of a Competency Map would be used in this case, in the recruiting process?" Mary wanted to know.

"The Team Map becomes an essential part of the hiring process at this level," said Jim. "As we interview prospective employees, or consider internal employees for the team, we compare the composite Profile for those individuals with the Strategic Team Map, checking off what required Primary Characteristics of the Team Map they can contribute to, or cover for us. We then look for other team members to fill the gaps between the composite of the people we have hired and the Map. Those gaps make up the hiring profile, which changes every time we hire a new team member. It's a dynamic, fluid process. Otherwise, to aspire to value chain management would require a cadre of one hundred percent superstars, and we know that's impossible."

"Notice that here Competitive Adeptness is at Stage III, not Stage IV. That's because at this level, competitive advantage comes less from out-selling the competition and more from providing strong and recognized customer value, which builds a symbiotic relationship between the supplier and the customer. Both supplier and customer become codependent, to the extent that to disengage would be costly and painful. In addition, Product/Service Proficiency moves to a Stage III, reflecting the team's need for increased expertise to support the creation and implementation of virtually unique strategic solutions."

"Well, I guess that tells us what life is like on the value chain. I suppose the bigger question is, what will life be like here at St. George if we adopt this philosophy?"

Sally meant the question to be light rather than reflective, but Mary took it to heart. It was at that very moment that she recognized what the role of the task force should be.

"When you first asked me to head up this project, I envisioned it as a collective effort, involving a number of people. Now I see it differently. We have seen what the three of us can do together, working as a team. We also know that Danilo is on board, and very supportive.

"I propose that for the moment we continue our discussions on this and lay out a complete course of action. Only when we are absolutely certain exactly where we are going with this, and how we can get there, should we begin to involve others in the formal task force. Otherwise, it will fail before it gets off the ground."

Sally and Jim knew where Mary was coming from, in the political sense. She meant that they needed to maintain control, but should allow others to give input and contribute without having a vote on the matter. "Others" in this instance meant sales, technical support, marketing, and human resources representatives.

Actually, Mary was not worried about them—it was Dick Chainy she wanted kept out of the loop for the moment.

"I think we should form the committee, interview people, run focus groups, build an action plan, and then report to top management, as in Dick Chainy, but only when the outcomes would be predetermined," she suggested.

Hmmm, very FOX-like, thought Sally. "I agree. We'll do it Mary's way."

CHAPTER

9

Integrating Sales and Marketing

Mary, Sally, and Jim proceeded to formulate an operational direction for the task force. Its charter was to automate sales and marketing practices in a value-centric manner, which was broad enough to allow them significant maneuvering room, yet focused enough to provide specific direction.

If all went well, that direction would enable them to build a value chain management integration blueprint, which would identify all the critical areas that the task force had to address in order to achieve full St. George integration.

Next, they identified the initial participants: Along with the three of them, they decided on their CIO Danilo Salenger, plus Mark Avery, and Jack Loggins, the vice president of finance at St. George, as the core group. They'd also add two others from marketing, to be chosen by Sally, and one additional participant from sales, whom Mary would choose. Bill Wilmington, the vice president of human resources, and Terry Freedland, from R&D, would also be included. The group would report, for executive oversight, to Dick Chainy.

That was the formal structure. However, the committee's informal organization had already been determined, with Sally as the FOX, Jim and Mary in the Power Base, Danilo one step outside the Base, and then the others. Like everything that happens politically within a company, that informal power structure simply coalesced, without discussion. The task force chairperson would be Mary. She would devote almost full time to the effort, the only exception being the time she'd be required to devote to the Alexander Drugs sPlan account. It would have been too disruptive to the Alexander development effort to assign another salesperson, and no one knew the Alexander sPlan like Mary. In any event, she planned to include customers on the task force, so her situation with Alexander would dovetail neatly with that, to create a stronger, yet managed, customer perspective and influence on the process. After all, becoming more value-centric meant first becoming more customer-centric. In that way the process itself would be truly customer oriented.

Approach to Market

The task force kicked off with focus groups and individual interviews involving people throughout the company. Mary opened each session by presenting the committee's charter, and giving an overview of value chain management, focusing heavily on customer buying patterns and the sales methodologies that map into those patterns. She explained that it was the task force's initial intent to determine how to automate these sales methodologies, along with the marketing practices that complement them, actually integrating sales and marketing.

By the second meeting, they realized they'd have to modify that approach, as it became clear that focusing on the methodologies alone would not work. Bill Wilmington pointed out that they were putting the cart before the horse by going first to automation, for with the wrong people in the right positions, automation was academic, and with the wrong people in the wrong positions, automation would become a nightmare.

What was missing, they decided, was a clear definition of St. George's Approach to Market.

First, they needed to determine how best to reorganize the salesforce into groups, each of which would focus on a particular market segment. In that way, the sales organization would be aligned with its marketplace, and functioning with the right salespeople, in the right positions, implementing the right sales methodologies.

To consult on what that new structure might be, Sally, Jim, and Mary decided to meet off-site, at Jim's house, on a Saturday morning. Their intent was to develop the Approach to Market concept, refine it, and have it ready to present at the next task force meeting. In that way, they would be ahead of the task force, maintaining a leadership role. At the same time, others on the committee would be working on assignments from the last meeting, and would present their results then, too.

It promised to be a warm and sunny fall day as the three of them got straight to work in Jim's study at seven o'clock that Saturday morning.

"Okay, we're in agreement, I believe, that St. George should segment our markets in terms of Commodity, Solutions, Business Solutions, and Strategic accounts, along the lines of geographical and industry boundaries," Jim began. "We already have a good handle on the latter two, since we know where all our accounts are located, and what they do."

"What about sales revenue to St. George? Should that be a part of the segment characterizations?" Mary asked.

"I have wondered about that, too," said Sally. "I think it's probably best not to include it, and for this reason: Historically, we have prioritized accounts by revenue realized, as it was the best indicator we had then of account significance, but today a customer might look relatively small in annual sales revenues, but have the potential in some way to become big in a hurry. Or, we may have an account where, if we notched up our position on the value chain a level or two, sales revenue would significantly increase. Therefore, revenue alone is not as reliable an indicator as it used to be."

"I agree," said Jim. "I feel it's critical that we set up a way to track revenues and margins by segment. Jack Loggins and his people in finance, and of course Danilo in information systems, will be a big help to us in setting that up, but let's not make revenue a determining factor for what accounts belong in a particular segment."

They all agreed with that. They began to work through the process of identifying the Commodity accounts, which they believed would be the simplest and largest group of St. George customers to identify, and it was. Once they had that list constructed, there remained only to run a Value Potential Evaluator on each, to determine which accounts on that Commodity list might have Solutions or perhaps even Business Solutions potential. Jim decided to assign the Value Potential Evaluator task to his regional managers, who were closer to many of the accounts. Besides, he reasoned, it would give them additional experience in doing Value Potential Evaluators on all customers, something that up to now they had not routinely done, even informally.

Next, they went to accounts they could class as Solutions customers—so few they could be counted on both hands, and a few fingers would still be left over. A bit discouraged by how small that number was, the team nevertheless pressed onward, moving up into the Business Solutions category. There, they identified even fewer accounts, less than a handful. When they reached the very top of the value chain, they could not identify a single Strategic account at St. George.

The bright sun that had helped get their day off to an optimistic start seemed suddenly to dim, bringing clouds of dismay to the meeting. Although they'd already guessed that St. George was out of alignment with its marketplace, none of them had estimated how severe that misalignment was. Now the evidence stared them in the face.

Mary was the first to speak. "I know this doesn't look good for us and that as a company we appear to have fallen asleep at the switch. However, most of our competition is in the same market misalignment boat along with us. As long as we are aware of our situation, and have come to that realization ahead of the competition, we have a good shot at working all this out without losing significant market position.

"Also, just because we can't identify higher value chain level accounts now does not mean that they don't exist. Many of our accounts might have significant potential, ready to be capitalized on, even if we're not yet there. The lesson here, I believe, is that we need to mobilize the regional managers to do the Value Potential Evaluator on the Commodity accounts, and run a value chain level assessment on *all* of our accounts."

"You're right, Mary," said Jim. "We can set up a meeting next week to brief them on the task force, which we had planned to do anyway, and at that time secure their help on this other business. What do you think, Sally?"

"I like that idea," Sally acknowledged. "You know, when we sit back and look at our accounts by revenue, you see all these high revenue-generating customers, and that naturally engenders feelings of security and comfort in our managers. Now I'm really concerned—I think we have been resting on our laurels too long, contemplating the nice trees in the foreground, and missing the forest, which is about to swallow us up."

"Yes, now is certainly the time to take action," said Jim, "and speaking of action, let's look at a possible salesforce structure that would include four suborganizations, or sales departments, that align with the value chain (see Figure 9.1)."

"Now, I'm not at all certain these are the best departmental designations, but you can see where I'm going with this. It would enable us to create Competency Maps for our TSU representatives, CSU account managers, BSU account managers, and SADU account executives. Those Maps would reflect what is required, in terms of job-related skills and knowledge, to be successful in each position, implementing the sales methodology appropriate to each value chain level.

"It's my vision that each sales unit would have its own manager, with a corresponding Competency Map for that position, and the unit managers would report to geographically related regional managers. With that structure, it would probably make sense to reduce the number of sales regions down to three for our domestic operations. In that way, our salesforce will become properly aligned with the marketplace.

"Now, taking that a step further, and thinking about the discussions that we had with Danilo to formulate a technology strategy, I believe doing this will enable him, working with Bill Wilmington for

Value Chain Level	Sales Department
Commodity	Territorial Sales Unit (TSU)
Solutions	Customer Solutions Unit (CSU)
Business Solutions	Business Solutions Unit (BSU)
Strategic	Strategic Account Development Unit (SADU)

Figure 9.1 Sample Approach to Market Structure of Sales Force.

the HR piece, and maybe with Terry's input, too, on our products and services in the pipeline, to build a technology blueprint using information-level and insight-level value technology components."

Sally sat forward eagerly. "Yes, remember what we said back in that meeting? *'In short, this will put technology, selling, and customer buying into the right value-centric relationship to one another.'* Jim, I think you have done it."

Achieving Sales and Marketing Alignment

"Thanks Sally, but there are still two major pieces to be addressed. We've touched on them, but not in detail. Now that we see how we can align our sales and technology efforts with our customers on a value platform, we need to figure out how to align marketing with sales, and then how to align human resources with both sales and marketing, not to mention the role that technology should play in all that. Poor Danilo is going to be blown away! I think we better include him in our next meeting, if you agree, Sally."

"Absolutely. We know we need to involve him in this process as early as possible. He'll have budgeting problems, as well as resource allocation issues to sort out. Mary, we'll need to provide Danilo a little ammunition, or at least some positive justification to support his request for an increase in his budget. Do you have any update on the Alexander Drugs project that might help us on that?"

"Not at the moment, but I am scheduled to meet with them Monday morning. The first phase of the sPlan is being implemented as we speak. The question now is whether or not we will get the green light from them to proceed with the Value Proposition. They have been modifying the numbers to what they believe will be a more accurate scheme. Our side will then review what they have done, and if it looks good, we'll move immediately to close the deal."

"Well," said Sally, "that sounds very promising. To hit your point on marketing, Jim, I believe we need to go back to the Four-Stage Sales Model and compare it to the four stages of marketing, then try to be more specific as to how marketing can support sales methodology in the field. To do that, I would like us to spend some time today building a combined Sales/Marketing Four-Stage Model (see Figure 9.2)."

Quality	Company Function	Stage I	Stage II	Stage III	Stage IV
Intent	Sales	To be considered	To make a sale	To create repeat business	To become the dominant supplier
	Marketing	Provide product or service information	Position solutions relative to customer needs	Position business solutions relative to competition	Position all offerings relative to value chain levels
Focus	Sales	On the product or service	On the customer	On the competition	On the customer's customers and competition
	Marketing	Feature advantage	Benefit advantage	Competitive advantage	Customer advantage
Sales Relationship to Customers	Sales	Casual in nature	Trust-based	Mutual in nature	Symbiotic in nature
Sales/Marketing Relationship	Marketing	Disconnected	Informally supportive of each other	Collaborative and teamwork-oriented	Partnership oriented
Value to Customers	Sales	Low operations focus, providing product or service options	Low middle-management focus, providing applications solutions	High middle-management focus, providing business solutions	High executive focus, providing strategic direction and expertise
Marketing Value to Sales	Marketing	Product presentation assistance, lead generation	Solutions packaging	Market positioning, direct sales support	Equips sales to provide strategic leadership to customers

Figure 9.2 Sales/Marketing Four-Stage Model.

Together they created the marketing equivalent of the Four-Stage Sales Model, which showed how the various Stages of the marketing role compared to sales, forming a cumulative progression up the Stages.

Mary was particularly interested in the comparison, as she knew marketing had a lot to offer sales, which was one of the reasons she'd been drawn to consult Sally early in the process with Alexander Drugs. She now knew that Alexander was a Solutions account, with the potential to become a Business Solutions customer for St. George. To capitalize on that potential, and eventually realize it, would require strong marketing support from Sally's group. That had been the purpose of their meeting, to define what "support" actually meant. Mary knew it could be done, unlike the Consolidated Hospitals situation, where her entire sales campaign was operating on the wrong level of the value chain.

Mary was feeling strongly confident now about what they could achieve with Alexander, but next week would really tell the story on that. She also liked Jim's thinking on restructuring the sales organization. Now that she was no longer constantly on the defensive about corporate politics, she began to see it as Sally and Jim viewed it—something to recognize, to manage, and in addition, an opportunity to move up in an organization. There would be a number of new positions generated by realignment, and if all went well with the task force, her personal currency would rise, and her value to St. George should be recognized and rewarded.

Mary realized with a start that Sally and Jim were staring at her. She had totally tuned out, but snapped back quickly.

"Sorry, I was off on a mental tangent. Sally, what does this sales-to-marketing comparison mean to us strategically?"

"Well, first of all, it shows us that marketing will be out of alignment with Jim's new sales organization. We match up to the CBUs okay, and to some extent to the SBUs, but when we get to the Business Solutions Units and the Strategic Account Development Units, we are not even in the game. *It also tells me that at this moment, marketing is out of alignment with a number of our accounts, too, and that can create some as yet unknown level of competitive exposure for St. George—and that disturbs me.*

"We haven't identified who those customers are, but we do know from this that they will continue to grow in number. What it tells me is that we need to move marketing to a Stage III as quickly as possible, and progress to Stage IV in the near future.

"*Competition is forcing our customers to move up their value chains, so we have to keep pace if we hope to remain competitive.* I only wish I could define what 'keep pace' means, but we definitely know what failure to keep pace will mean. According to the Model, there are two critical aspects of value that we need to be providing to sales right away—market positioning, and direct sales support.

"If we use the worksheet we developed earlier to define buying patterns, and modify it to illustrate the Commodity, Solutions, Business Solutions, and Strategic sales cycles, that will enable us to identify specific Stage III marketing activities that are needed to produce value for the salesforce (see Figure 9.3)."

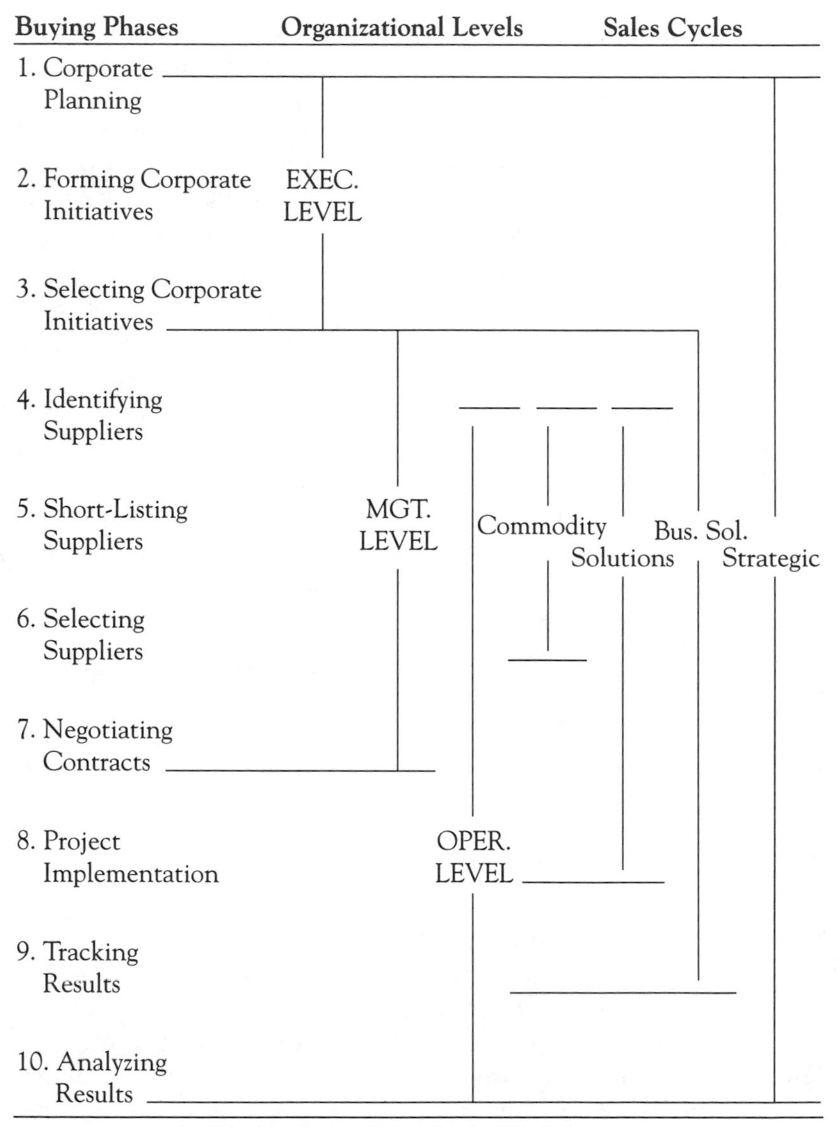

Figure 9.3 Sales Cycle Worksheet.

Marketing-to-Sales Cycle Alignment

"You can see that Business Solutions selling spans from #3, Selecting Corporate Initiatives, to #9, Tracking Results," Sally continued. "That creates a well-defined sales cycle, that marketing can map into quite nicely. It also is one that can be preceded by certain pre-sales cycle marketing activities, and followed by other post-sales cycle marketing activities. In that way, marketing's involvement consists of a front-end sales cycle and back-end role, to construct a Stage III Business Solutions Marketing Cycle. It looks like Figure 9.4.

"Now, we can organize specific marketing activities that characterize this marketing cycle, according to the Pre-Sales Cycle, Sales Cycle, and Post-Sales Cycle phases, creating a one-to-one marketing-to-sales alignment. In the Pre-Sales phase, we have three marketing activities that are key to alignment."

PRESALES CYCLE

A. *Geometric Product Development*

"Here, we are building the design concept for new offerings, incorporating input from every appropriate angle; i.e. sales, customers, R&D, manufacturing, professional services, finance, and marketing. With marketing at the core, each of these groups provides a perspective that, when weighed and put in balance with one another, will result in the creation of a value-centric product or service."

B. *Market Pre-Conditioning*

"This marketing activity is intended to increase customer receptiveness to a new offering. When that is achieved, salespeople are

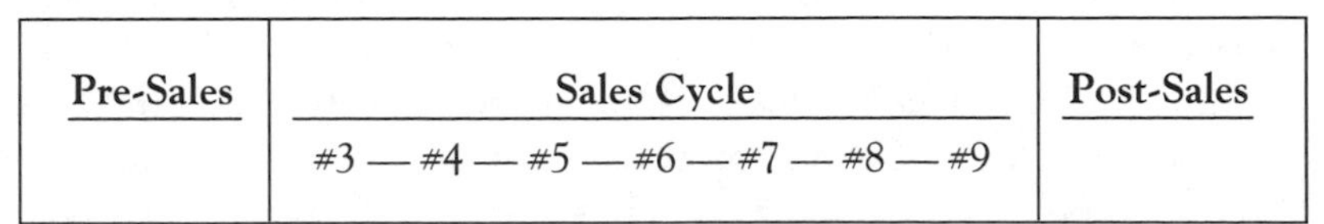

Figure 9.4 Business Solutions Marketing Cycle Template.

called in by customers early in the sales cycle or even before the sales cycle begins. This is particularly important for new, leading-edge or nontraditional offerings where the marketplace will have to learn about the offering and the value it can represent. From a sales perspective, that would mean an educational process would be required with accounts, which would in turn mean a longer sales cycle. Preconditioning can help shorten that cycle, by educating customers early to the value opportunity that the offering will represent. Sometimes, this can be accomplished through advertising or other promotional activities. It can also be achieved by leveraging competition. When you leverage competition," Sally explained, "your company times its new product or service announcement to follow that of the competition. In that way, you 'draft' on the competitor in front of you by letting them consume their resources to do the spade work and educate the customers. To mitigate loss of market share and protect salespeople from losing business to the competitor, marketing must also equip the field with an early Statement of Direction, identifying when your company's offering will be available, what it will look like, what value it will provide to customers and what customer investment will be required to realize that value."

"The intent here is to contain the competition and capitalize on them, as a preconditioning vehicle to shorten sales cycles, thereby reducing cost of sales, and enabling us to grow market share."

C. *Value Chain Notch Up*

"This implies entering an account one value chain level above where that customer is currently operating. Running the Value Potential Evaluator will tell you whether or not there is an opportunity to notch up. To do that requires that sales brings a higher-level perspective to the customer's business. The presentation of that perspective should be developed by marketing.

"Basically, it would consist of packaging industry trends and other information that would allow the salesperson to develop and share insight with the customer as to how those trends will be likely to impact their present business practices," explained Sally. "It would put forth the value of proactively modifying those practices, with your help, to gain competitive advantage, increase market share, or achieve some other expression of business value.

"These marketing activities should be in place," she cautioned, "before a Business Solutions sales cycle ever begins, if you are to optimize sales results. And, from a Strategic sales cycle perspective, they are mandatory (see Figure 9.5)."

"Once a Business Solutions sales cycle is initiated, there are a number of additional marketing activities that will improve sales performance, by providing the field with the following sales cycle marketing activities."

SALES CYCLE

D. Market Qualification

"Sales cycles begin with salespeople qualifying accounts to determine if it is appropriate to pursue particular sales opportunities. At a higher level, it is the job of marketing to qualify specific market segments (remembering that value chain level identification is a part of segmentation), based upon the position of the product or service within those markets. This positioning is based primarily upon

1. Customer value perception,
2. Competitive differentiation, and
3. The required customer investment.

"As a result, some markets will be more receptive than others, and some will not be receptive at all. Equipping the salesforce with this information will save precious time in establishing a critical mass of successful installed base for a new offering. It becomes less likely that salespeople will waste time pursuing the wrong accounts, *i.e.* accounts that will not buy, or accounts where the cost of sales

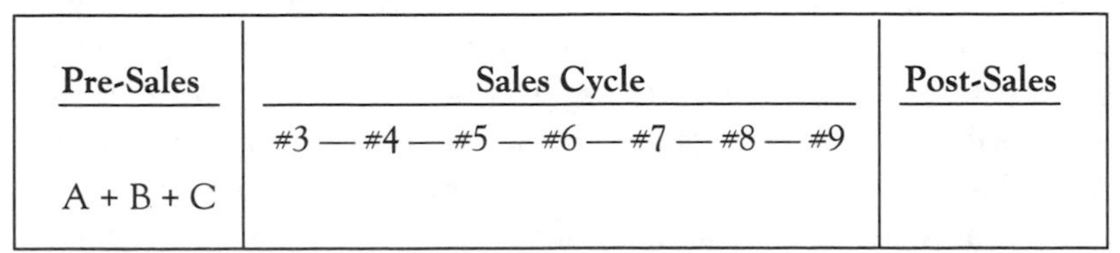

Figure 9.5 Pre-Sales Business Solutions Marketing Cycle.

would be too high. Instead, they will be diverted, first by market segment qualification and then by account qualification, to accounts where a higher probability of success exists."

E. Value Templates

"Building powerful Value Propositions for Business Solutions accounts or Value Statements for Solutions customers is the heart of a sales campaign. That means equipping the sales organization with the ability to build highly compelling and engaging expressions of customer value. In order to accomplish that and provide a means to continuously improve these expressions, it is critical that marketing build Value Templates for Statements and Propositions on a per market segment basis. Salespeople can then select the appropriate template and apply and modify it to suit a particular sales situation."

F. Competitive Profile

"Tracking competitive information, in terms of new offerings, organizational changes, and more, is essential, in order to understand what level of a customer's value chain competitors are targeting, and in what industries. Therefore, placing a competitive overlay on market segmentation efforts can be invaluable for our company's salespeople, enabling them to determine where the competition's sales efforts will most likely be concentrated before they present themselves in accounts, putting our own salespeople at competitive risk. Evaluating competitive threat potential at the market segment level is something that only marketing can do effectively."

G. Competitive Strategy Analysis

"If providing customer value is the heart of a sales campaign, then its soul is formulating a good competitive sales strategy. Tracking and analyzing the classes of strategy that competitors are employing within specific market segments is critical to assisting salespeople in anticipating competitive thrusts. It is not practical to expect that every salesperson will have strategic formulation ability, in fact, most don't have it. This means that marketing, insight-level technology, and the sales managers who have capability in that area, must take up the slack. This is not a training issue. *To strategize effectively, a person needs to be able to make the intangible tangible: To*

think in the abstract, to see the unseen, and to distill the essential elements that give rise to strategy, which is the quintessential expression of true competitive insight."

H. Tactical Assemblage

"At the tactical level, salespeople need to be able to manage competitive sales cycles effectively. That often requires that they be proficient in dealing with objections, both when they surface, and proactively, before the customer voices a concern. Often, the most difficult issues or objections to handle are those engendered or seeded by the competition. They may relate to St. George as a company, or to our sales proposal, as perceived deficiencies in our products or services. This creates an opportunity for marketing to identify and catalog from a customer viewpoint the strengths and weaknesses of doing business with St. George. Then they can develop, with the help of sales, an approach to addressing each issue, enabling salespeople to be more confident in heading off objections, or in dealing directly with them. When salespeople are able to be proactive in unearthing a weakness, and can present a solution *before* the competition alerts the customer, they not only defuse the issue, they strengthen their own credibility with the customer. Therefore, marketing should equip the salesforce with tactical offense tools, operating on a per offering basis, and sometimes on a per competitor basis.

"These marketing activities, or inputs to sales, map into a sales campaign, creating marketing cycle alignment that looks like Figure 9.6.

"Of all the marketing assistance that can be provided to a sales organization, perhaps the most significant is creating post-sales alignment. This is where results are measured and analyzed and true supplier credibility is established, and it is also where the first

Pre-Sales	Sales Cycle	Post-Sales
	#3 — #4 — #5 — #6 — #7 — #8 — #9	
A + B + C	D + E + F + G + H	

Figure 9.6 Pre-Sales and Sales Business Solutions Marketing Cycle.

steps of the next sales situations begin. Post-sales alignment is achieved when marketing provides the following."

POST-SALES CYCLE

I. Results Metrics

"Many companies have no way to measure in a valid and reliable manner the value impact that a supplier has committed to provide, particularly if the value promised is nontraditional in nature. Marketing is in the best position to handle that. When a company embarks upon the development of a new offering, marketing should first produce a design concept that includes the value they intend to provide to customers. Designing and building metrics is simply an extension of that process. That's not to say that sales, or those in a professional services group, could not do the job, but it's unlikely that any such effort will be effectively leveraged or replicated within the organization, or that the company will build expertise, as it would with a centralized effort. While that places the metrics responsibility with marketing, it doesn't mean that others should not be involved. In fact, sales can play a key role in helping to test a new offering.

"Early in the new product or service design process, when marketing and sales first identify intended customer value, it is time for them to self-test their thinking," said Sally. "If they cannot design metrics to effectively quantify and measure projected value (Value Propositions) for new offerings that will reside at higher levels of the value chain, and clearly describe value (Value Statements) for lower value chain offerings, then the value of those offerings is not real, and, therefore, the offerings are not real, in the sense of added value to the marketplace.

"Quantifying value creates early accountability, in which some marketing organizations elect to involve certain customers, thereby establishing or introducing a form of customer accountability into the process, as well."

J. Results Analysis

"This is the phase where value provided is analyzed, where marketing takes the results information provided by metrics and works to build insight into the significance of that information. Those insights can then be distilled and packaged into executive abstracts for the customer's top management, enabling salespeople to conduct customer briefings on results, and can also be pumped into industry articles and customer case studies, to assist in Market Preconditioning (see B). A careful Results Analysis can also provide important feedback to the product or service design process, enabling marketing and R&D to compare value results to value intended."

K. Win/Loss Tracking Analysis

"History does repeat itself. Identifying competitive trends, as part of the Competitive Strategy Analysis (see G), requires that competitive information be effectively captured and retained. Additionally, the internal political and business exposure issues, that salespeople take into account in reporting reasons for sales losses, need to be carefully analyzed and managed. Companies should consolidate and track win/loss information on a per market segment and per product or service basis, creating a matrix. In that way, a company can view its strategies, its competitors' strategies, and its product positioning from a value chain point of view, within specific market segments. It provides insight into sales and marketing effectiveness, and if customers are selectively and carefully involved in the process, it could actually advance certain account development efforts.

"Now," said Sally, "with the addition of these post-sales marketing activities, we are able to complete the Business Solutions Marketing Cycle chart (see Figure 9.7)."

"Incidentally, if we were to look at the marketing activities necessary to align with a Strategic sales cycle, they would be the

Pre-Sales	Sales Cycle	Post-Sales
	#3 — #4 — #5 — #6 — #7 — #8 — #9	
A + B + C	D + E + F + G + H	I + J + K

Figure 9.7 Complete Business Solutions Marketing Cycle.

same as for a Business Solutions opportunity. The difference resides with the level of currency of the marketing people involved in supporting the sales effort. At the Strategic level, an individual must have currency measured at the High end of the Executive range. Otherwise, there will be insufficient value and credibility to support participation in the Corporate Planning, Forming Corporate Initiatives, and Selecting Corporate Initiatives Phases of the customer buying process. Going downstream, however, to a Solutions or Commodity level is simply a matter of reduced marketing activities."

With the Marketing Cycle defined, Jim, Sally, and Mary were then able to pinpoint exactly in which areas the St. George marketing group was out of alignment with the new sales structure that Jim was proposing. In fact, it provided a degree of resolution beyond what they needed to make that determination.

In reviewing marketing's historical role at St. George, Sally realized they were doing bits and pieces of a few of the activities, but a lot more was needed to align marketing with the higher value chain level sales campaigns that represented much of the new opportunity in today's marketplace. The good news was that they now knew what had to be done, and with Danilo's help, they felt they could capitalize on technology to create and maintain a much more effective sales and marketing alignment.

With that, the meeting ended on a positive note. They all hoped this was the beginning of a pleasant weekend for all of them, and a new era at St. George.

Emerging Internal Opposition

The timing could not have been better. Mary's meeting with Alexander Drugs brought her to a new personal high. The sPlan and her Value Proposition were accepted by Alexander Drugs senior management after only minor modification. That meant a significant order was in the offing for Mary, and it constituted the first successful value chain exercise for St. George.

The following Thursday, Mary was scheduled to brief Dick Chainy on the progress of her task force. She would now be able to present not only what they were doing, but also, using the Alexander Drugs success, she could cite the positive potential of becoming more value-centric. Mary planned to ask Jim and Sally to participate, too. She figured the briefing would take about an hour, including time for questions.

Tuesday morning, when Mary checked her e-mail at the office, there was a message from Dick Chainy. As part of the upcoming briefing, he requested that a detailed budget be presented to him. He wanted figures for the automation effort, including projected costs, and time frames for restructuring sales and marketing practices. He also wanted a breakout of costs for the task force itself. Mary took stock. It was short notice for them to produce such an extensive budget breakdown, to be sure, but the COO's request was not an unreasonable one. She accepted it as a positive sign. *Perhaps Dick has more interest in this project than we've given him credit for,* she thought. Mary felt that addressing the budget now would also give her the opportunity to make senior management aware of the need to allocate adequate funding for these projects.

She decided to ask Sally, Jim, and Danilo to incorporate their budget estimates into their individual presentations, following her overview. Then she'd give the roll-up figures and the task force estimates. It would push the meeting time well into another hour, but would be well worth the time.

By Wednesday afternoon, everyone was ready. Danilo's technology blueprint and detailed budget reflected a lot of work on his part, and demonstrated his command of what had to be accomplished. Mary was very impressed, and it was also reaffirming for Sally, who had recommended Danilo to Dr. Tullis. Then, late Wednesday night, Mary received a phone call from Sally.

"I have some bad news for you, Mary. I'm not going to be at tomorrow's meeting, so you or Jim will have to present my piece of it. I have to fly to Denver—a family emergency."

"Oh, Sally, I'm so sorry to hear that! Is there anything I can do to help?"

"Not really, except cover for me tomorrow. My sister Judy, in Denver, has gotten a rather disturbing medical report. She's my only family, and I have to go to her and see what this is all about. I'm leaving first thing in the morning and should be gone only a few days."

"I know how upset you must be, Sally. Don't worry about anything here, just take care of your sister. Jim and I will manage at the meeting."

"Well, if you have a few minutes now, let's go over the points I feel are most important for you to make on behalf of marketing. Sorry, but I just don't have anyone in my department familiar enough with what we've been developing to step in for me."

After spending nearly an hour on the phone with Sally, Mary felt reasonably prepared to present Sally's marketing piece, and her estimated budget. She would give her own overview, move into the marketing presentation, then turn to Jim and Danilo for their pieces. *It should work,* she decided.

The next morning, the meeting opened, and Mary thought Dick seemed affable and receptive. She began with her overview, pitching the positive developments with Alexander Drugs as a concrete example of success of the process. Dick listened closely and appeared interested, asking questions periodically. When she presented the marketing and task force operating budgets, they gave rise to a number of questions. Dick seemed merely to be looking for clarification on the various pieces.

It wasn't until Jim got up and began to talk about restructuring the sales organization that Dick showed any open resistance. His questions became more pointed, and at times he made statements that were judgmental or critical, bordering on being hostile. Jim handled him well, not reacting to obviously baited questions, but Mary and Danilo could tell that Jim was becoming very frustrated. Dick's attitude began to reveal what he was thinking—that for St. George, becoming value-centric really meant becoming salesforce-centric. He saw the team moving more control of the business to the salesforce, calling it "providing customer value." *They're empire building,* was his unspoken position.

Chainy didn't dispute the need to provide customers with more value, but he was convinced in his own mind that a personal agenda of enhancing their own careers, at the expense of what had fueled St. George's growth in the past, had to be behind the task force's concept. He had quickly shifted the whole affair into the arena of internal politics, and projected his own personal values, and the way he operated in business, onto the team. This, coupled with his mistrust for salespeople, made him extremely negative.

Mary saw what was happening, and her previous experience with Dr. Tullis kicked in, warning her to take control. Politely noting that they'd better move along if they wanted to finish, she got Danilo up, and he skillfully refocused Dick onto other issues. The mood, however, remained tense and uncomfortable. The COO consulted his notes, recapped what had been presented, and told them bluntly, "In my opinion, you'll have to scale this project back considerably, to save money. You should be prepared to go forward on a much smaller scale, and that will be one of my recommendations."

Hearing that, Jim was reminded of how St. George management had responded back when they had initially attempted to automate the sales organization. The issue then had been one of time, and acceptance of the new automated system. When sales complained that using it would be too time-consuming, at the direct expense of face-to-face selling time, management had responded by insisting that the new system would increase sales efficiency by giving the salespeople *more* time. They had learned only after considerable expense, and a system failure, that their response had been way off base. Jim sighed. He knew in his gut that Chainy was somehow going to sabotage this initiative. It was time to fight fire with fire. He spoke up.

"I understand your concern about the budget, Dick, but I also believe you will find that this initiative will be self-funding, with the increased volume of business and increased margins it can produce for St. George. Alexander Drugs is just one example of how we are able to target and procure business that never existed before, by pursuing higher value chain levels. It is incremental revenue."

"I accept that, Jim. I'm sure you will have the opportunity to prove that theory by starting small. If it is 'self-funding,' then it will generate enough capital to fully fund this operation later. That eliminates the need to allocate the full amount of funding you just presented. That is, unless any of you doubt the statement Jim just made."

No one spoke. Jim realized he had put his own foot squarely into his mouth. Chainy was a master chess player. Jim had set himself up, and in one move, Dick had been able to kill additional funding and use Jim's own logic to support it! Chainy brought the meeting to a close, but asked Jim to stay a few minutes.

Mary was concerned about how the meeting had ended, not so much because of Dick's lack of interest in the task force, as she believed that with Jim and Sally and Danilo solidly behind it they would make it work one way or another, but because of how she had observed Chainy operating. She hadn't realized he had such a strong intellect. He could grab something in mid-air, twist it to his advantage, and immediately capitalize on it. In a lighter vein, she mused that maybe Dick should have been a politician. Or even better, an attorney. In any event, he would be a difficult and wily opponent.

When they were alone, Dick asked Jim point blank about the cost of the task force. "How will Mary Gagan be able to cover all her accounts and chair the committee at the same time?"

"She won't," replied Jim. "With the exception of Alexander Drugs, she will not cover any customer accounts. In fact, she won't be in the field salesforce during the year she's heading up the task force, Dick. Oh, her compensation will continue to come out of my budget, but she'll be reporting to Sally Loxner in marketing."

"I see." Dick thanked Jim for his input and left.

That night, Jim called Sally in Denver. He had promised he'd report to her about how the meeting had gone. He played back Dick's comments and behavior almost word for word, and openly expressed his frustration at how the meeting had gone and at what he'd done to give Dick ammunition against them.

Although she was disappointed, Sally was not surprised. She had recognized Jim's tactical blunder, but chose not to dwell on it. "I think the budget is not the real issue with Dick, it's the task force itself, and, more specifically, Mary. Dick has a thing about sales people running anything in the company, and we know that."

In discussing it further, they decided to shift Mary's compensation over to Sally's budget, which meant that Sally would run over budget for the year. That was not a good thing at St. George, but Sally felt that she could risk it, and that it would be unwise to attempt to increase her budget to cover Mary's compensation, which could lead to another confrontation with Dick.

"I'll just look to cut somewhere else to make up for it," she said, "and if that doesn't work, I'll let Robert know soon enough that I'll be over budget this year, and by approximately how much, so he'll be expecting that." She had always made it a rule that Dr. Tullis never be taken by surprise by anything that might concern him or cause him a problem with the Board.

At the end of the conversation, Sally agreed to call Mary, to be certain that she was not too discouraged. "If all goes well with Judy's surgery, Jim, I should be back in Chicago by the middle of next week."

The next executive briefing was only a month away, and Jim and Sally knew that the team had a lot to accomplish before then, if they were to create enough momentum to keep the task force project alive at St. George. They also knew from long experience that Dick Chainy could be a formidable adversary, and it was obvious from his comments to Jim that day that he had become just that—an open opponent to their plan to bring any kind of major change to current business practices at St. George Pharmaceuticals.

CHAPTER

10

Integrating Sales and Human Resources

When Sally returned to Chicago three days later, Jim and Mary wasted no time in getting together with her. They all found it difficult to remain focused on the direction of the task force, given the negative vibes Jim had received in his post-meeting session with Dick, but they knew that moving to the next step was critical to completing the design of the newly restructured sales organization.

"Let's just press forward on it," Sally recommended. "We need to have our blueprint completed, if we ever hope to sell it to Dick Chainy and Dr. Tullis. Let's ask Danilo and Bill Wilmington to join us tomorrow."

Their intent was to determine how to create alignment between the human resources group and sales, exploring how to build a Human Resources (HR) infrastructure to support Jim's new Commodity, Solutions, Business Solutions, and Strategic sales departments. If they could make that work, the next step would be to create the same realignment for marketing. After he was briefed on the structure they proposed, Bill Wilmington, the director of human resources at St. George, took the lead in the discussion.

"First, I would like to say how pleased I am to be part of this effort. For years, HR has been viewed by many in the corporate world as little more than a compliance organization. To use your lexicon, Jim, we have been a Stage I company function, very much focused on hiring, salary administration, and developing HR policies and procedures. I believe that we can change that, positioning HR as a resource to sales, marketing, and St. George's customers. My goal is to establish that value, with you and senior St. George management, so that at some point we are participating at the Executive levels of the buying process, helping to influence corporate planning and the formation and selection of corporate initiatives.

"Like the sales and marketing organizations, we will always have Stage I responsibilities, but this new initiative can also move us into higher-level roles, even a Stage IV role, providing strategic as well as operational value to the company.

"Let's focus on the three main areas of human resources, since all of them would be affected by your new plan:

1. Recruiting and selection,
2. Performance management, involving evaluation, coaching and development, and
3. Compensation."

Mary studied Bill closely as he spoke. He was clearly a mission-driven individual, with strong convictions. After the meeting with Chainy, it was clear that they would all need to be mission-driven, and that Mary would need strong allies like Bill Wilmington. She knew that building allies begins with belief in a common mission. Bill obviously believed in this project, and was a good man to have on her team. She was glad they had invited him to participate.

Recruiting and Selection

"Recruiting and selection," said Bill, "generally consists of several activities in sequence. The process begins with the advertising of openings, then resume or background screening, followed by a telephone interview to establish that there is interest on both sides. If so, we schedule an initial interview with HR.

"If that goes well, follow-up interviews are conducted with all appropriate people in the hiring purview for that candidate, which can vary according to the position and level of responsibility. The hiring manager, to whom the candidate will report, actually makes the employment-offer decision, with my department organizing and coordinating the whole process from start to finish.

"We advertise opportunities internally and externally, we place ads, go to college campuses to recruit, and on occasion engage search firms, to get resumes and candidates flowing into the pipeline. Those resumes or candidates are then screened for the appropriate educational background, work experience, and other factors that might indicate that a candidate has the capabilities required in a particular search. Once resumes are reviewed for basic bona fide employment qualifications, we begin the personal interview process."

"That's not too much different from what we do in sales, with a pipeline of leads that hopefully will become customers," Jim commented.

"Exactly, and just as you track the numbers of sales opportunities that move through the various phases of that pipeline, we do the same. For example, we might receive two hundred responses for a single position. Depending on the level of the position, we'd probably screen out at least one hundred and eighty-five and set up maybe fifteen initial interviews. We'd continue with eight final rounds and make one, two, or three or, in the case of outstanding college grads for whom we are competing with other major corporations, four offers of employment eventually to fill one position."

"Really?" said Mary. "I never thought of recruitment in terms of those levels of numbers, or that much preliminary activity, Bill."

"The traditional approach to hiring is a game of numbers, just like your Commodity Approach to Market. And, just as the GLOS ratio in sales helps you quantify sales effectiveness, we have a similar measure. Ours in HR might be termed a CISE ratio: Candidates to Interviews to Selection to Employment.

"Our cost of hire is like your cost of sales: A high ratio between Interviews, Selection, and Employment drives up hiring costs, especially if the candidates are being flown in from some distant city. Costs mount up pretty quickly, and they become non-recoverable, as you know, if the candidate doesn't get an employment offer, or gets one and turns us down in favor of someone else. That's why the initial screening process is so critical.

"After our last meeting, I put together a process that I think you would consider a Stage III approach, which is consistent with your goal, Sally, to create a Stage III marketing capability. I would like to overview briefly the four stages of recruiting and selection, based on your Four-Stage Model, from an HR point of view, to see if you agree with me.

"At a Stage I, we are really filling requisitions. At a Stage II our intent is to fill positions successfully, as expressed in traditional terms, that is, a typical job description identifying role and responsibilities. At a Stage III we are moving to a structured, reliable, and repeatable approach to matching Competency Profiles to Maps. When we move into Stage IV, we are anticipating tomorrow's needs and Competency Maps, along with building strong teams through composite profiling and mapping. Does that reflect your thinking?"

"It definitely fits our working model," Sally responded. "Now, how do you envision it in actual operation, Bill?"

"Well, first we'd start with a different kind of resume screening process, identifying background experience that is consistent with Primary Characteristics we need."

"Question, Bill," said Jim. "How do we know what kind of experience listed on a resume would signal the presence of these Primary Characteristics, or sales-related qualities we need? Forgive me if that's a stupid question, but we're all pretty new at this."

"Not at all, Jim. The answer is, we don't know yet, either. It will be a learning process for all of us to be able to spot those qualities, but what we do know is that the process can be self-correcting.

"If we take a closed-loop approach, constantly going back every time we hire or don't hire a person, to review what that individual's background looked like in terms of their resume, we will eventually fine-tune the initial screening template to become very accurate. In fact, we can even backup a step further and evaluate our recruiting sources, or review how our internal and external advertising is written, to be certain that we are cultivating the most fertile soil available to us.

"In the initial HR interview, we verify and explore what has been stated on the person's employment application. If there are no anomalies detected that would eliminate him or her from further consideration for the position, the candidate advances to the interview phase. Here, selected people interview the individual. For your proposed core competency requirements, we'd have to develop a more structured interview guide, which provides specific questions that correlate to the four stages of observable behaviors for each core competency. The interviewers will each be provided with different sets of questions that correspond to different competencies. When a response to each question is given by the candidate, the interviewer then moves into a proof statement mode, that we can refer to as the STORY. Here, S is for situation, T for task, and O for opportunity, requiring the candidate to identify the context within which the competency was employed. Then, they go to R and Y, role and yield. What role did the individual play, and what were the outcomes or yield?

"Since each interviewer will have different questions, at the completion of the interviews we will be able to compare responses and construct a Competency Profile for the candidate, then compare it to the appropriate Competency Map. Depending upon those results, and other factors that we take into consideration during the interviewing process, such as observing candidate attributes, we'll recommend whether or not the person move into the simulation phase.

"As a rule, we will recommend that every candidate who successfully completes the structured interview go to that next phase, as even a good structured interview process can be fooled. You know that a skilled sales professional will project any image he or she feels you want to see. Therefore, we need to move all candidates into a simulation center to verify the results of the interview. Now, that protracts the hiring process and increases our expense per candidate, but the cost of a bad sales hire, particularly the opportunity cost to St. George, is so high that, given the limited number of people who complete the structured interview phase, it's well worth it to double-check.

"The same people who conducted the structured interviews will run the simulation, or SIM Center, where case studies and role-playing exercises emulate the customer environment. The candidate's performance score will be four-stage based, so that we can compare the SIM Center results to the Competency Profile constructed earlier on the candidate, and spot any deficiencies or anomalies.

In keeping with what I said before, we also compare the SIM results back to the individual's resume, employment application, and initial interview results, to look for trends or anomalies. The four tools (see Figure 10.1) which we will need to build to support implementation of the process are:

1. Resume/Application Screening Template—identifies what to look for in evaluating candidate resumes/applications.
2. Initial Interview Guide—typical first-pass evaluation of the individual by HR.
3. Structured Interview Guide—specific questions, organized per observable behavior for each core competency, along with provisions to record STORY proof responses.
4. Simulation Center Guide—operating manual to administer case studies and role plays, with the scope and direction of exercises determined by the results of the Structured Interviews.

"Clearly, there is a lot more work to be done, but you see the direction that I am proposing," Bill concluded.

"Nice work, Bill," said Jim. "I can see you've done a lot of thinking about this new process. From my point of view, it appears to be a very sound approach, and certainly value-centric, when you use the Competency Profiles and Maps as a foundation."

The others nodded agreement. Mary felt Bill's contribution was on target, but couldn't help thinking about the informal side of the process, that is, from the candidate's point of view. It only underscored the importance of working for a FOX or, at a minimum, someone who is in the Power Base.

Yet, how many people, she wondered, *go through the hiring process focused only on the visible, i.e. the organizational structure, roles,*

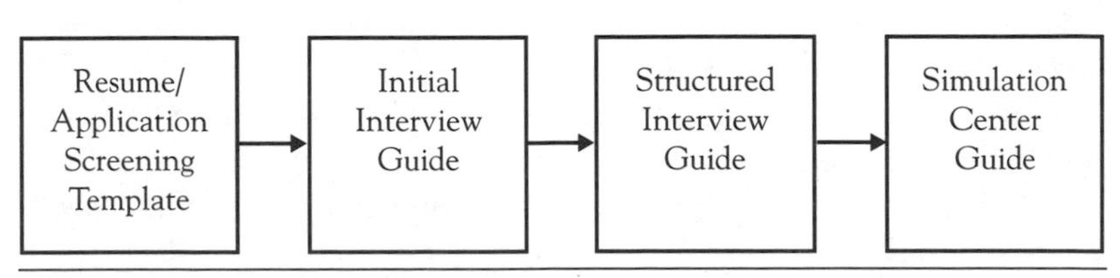

Figure 10.1 Selection/Interview Tools for Competency Profile Hiring.

responsibilities, and maybe now, to St. George's credit, Competency Profiles and Maps?

Her recent experience in coming to grips with corporate politics enabled Mary to see the unseen, and to appreciate its significance.

From now on, she vowed, *if I ever find myself looking for a new position, I'm going to search out, and try to interview with, a FOX in the organization. If an association with a FOX is not possible, I won't go any further in the hiring process with that company.*

The group was just about to move into a discussion of performance management, when Jim's assistant interrupted them.

"Excuse me for a few minutes, folks, this is something I need to address right away," said Jim, apologetically. "Please continue the discussion. I'll catch up when I return."

While Jim was gone, the team turned to a discussion of how they would go about building the interview tools and templates Bill had described.

However, when Jim returned, they could tell immediately that something was seriously amiss.

"A major competitor has just announced an important breakthrough in the management of depressive disorders, introducing a new drug," said Jim. "This is aimed squarely at St. George's primary market."

He further explained that the offering was positioned at a Solutions level, coupling the drug with disease prevention and diagnosis programs, which signaled that the competitor was moving up the marketing value chain.

"In fact, it could be argued that they are at a Business Solutions level," said Jim, ruefully. "This is a blow to St. George."

"Yes, I can see that, but you know, Jim, looking at it from the task force team's perspective, it just might help us," said Mary.

"Mary is right, Jim," agreed Sally, "in that this move by a competitor certainly reinforces what we are saying and doing. On the downside, it also suggests that we are behind the eight ball, in the area of R&D. And that's not good news. Jim, what is Dick saying or doing about this, do we know?"

Mary sensed Sally's concern. Dick had always been a vociferous supporter of Research & Development over other aspects of business at St. George. *How might this affect budgeting for the task force,* she wondered?

"Dick is meeting with Dr. Tullis right now to address this new development, and that's all I know," said Jim.

The group decided to conclude their meeting for now, and pick it up later in the week. In that way they could more effectively factor in this new development. And in truth, no one could concentrate on HR issues in the face of this new bombshell.

Dick Chainy and Dr. Tullis spent the rest of that day, and subsequent days, in meetings with the head of R&D.

Mary was surprised when Dick requested that the next task force executive briefing meeting be moved up, instead of postponed. He moved it forward to early the following week. Mary believed that the value of the committee's work had become apparent in light of the new competitive threat that had emerged. Jim wasn't as optimistic as Mary. He had a distinct sense of foreboding.

The team organized its current blueprint, and briefed Chainy. Sally was present and Dick listened, asking very few questions, then brought the session to a close, thanking them for their input. Afterward, none of them could say whether or not it had gone well, but Sally knew that the meeting's significance was not in what they had said, or in the questions Dick had asked, but in what was not said.

She decided that maybe she'd better try to catch up with Dr. Tullis. She got an appointment to drop by his office around six thirty, when most people had gone for the day. Dr. Tullis was open with Sally about the fact that Dick Chainy was seriously questioning the prudence, at this critical juncture, of allocating funds to restructuring and automating the sales and marketing functions.

"Understand, Sally, Dick isn't attacking the validity of your project, merely the timing. He believes that the company's capital would be better spent on R&D at the moment, to protect our product foundation. And I'll be honest with you, Sally—I tend to agree with him on that. I'm afraid you'd have to come up with a pretty compelling argument for funding such an expensive reorganization project as you've proposed, at this particular time at St. George."

"Well, I think that when you've examined our ultimate goals, especially in light of what our competitor has just done, you'll see that they dovetail with your concern that St. George remain competitive in the marketplace," said Sally.

"I don't doubt that your task force project is very worthwhile, Sally. Nor do I mean to dismiss its importance to St. George. So you can be sure Dick and I will examine it in great depth before making a decision one way or another. But I'm sure you also understand that right now, we have the Directors and, with our stock declining, our shareholders to worry about."

"I do understand, Robert. I'd just hate to see this project trashed, since I'm convinced it's germane to your long-term goals for St. George, and will eventually realize enough additional revenue to be self-funding." Sally left that meeting very discouraged.

The next day, when Sally recounted the highlights to the rest of the team, Mary said, "Dick Chainy is implementing an INDIRECT strategy with Dr. Tullis, changing the focus from the merit of the project to its timing, which he considers inappropriate. I'll bet he was even somewhat complimentary about what we're doing, and sketched out our progress to Dr. Tullis, from his standpoint, as a result of that meeting he just held with us."

Sally didn't like Dick personally, but she was not foolish enough to underestimate his political ability, nor his power. As she mentally dissected her conversation with Robert, looking for clues she might have missed, she realized that not only was the CEO favorably considering the reallocation of funds to R&D as Dick had proposed, but a Board of Directors meeting had probably been scheduled to discuss the competitive situation and determine what they could do to keep the company's stock from sliding any further.

Sally knew that Robert Tullis would be forced to take some kind of action to appease the Board and stockholders, and to counteract this announcement by the competition. She feared their task force would be one of the targets.

Several days later, they met again. Sally did not share all the insights she had gained from her meeting with Dr. Tullis, but she was firmly convinced that the group had to move quickly, making as much progress as possible, if it was to prove the value to St. George of its continued operation. She felt she could probably influence Robert Tullis, if she could give him the ammunition and all the right reasons for continuing the project. But Sally also knew she was no match in competition with the Board for the CEO's loyalty and direction of purpose. She didn't know whether or not Dick had supporters on the Board or who they might be. Clearly, timing for this restructuring was not in their favor. But Sally didn't say that. Instead she said, "We need to press on, and have some concrete results I can show to Dr. Tullis and Dick Chainy fairly soon. So I suggest we continue with the HR segment today. Bill, why don't you update us on what you've come up with so far?"

Performance Management

Bill began with Performance Management. "What we are talking about here is coaching and development of the salesforce. First, I would like to list a few performance management qualities that need to be present for any process to be successful."

1. Accountability—*There must be accountability, not just at the salesperson's level, but all the way up to top management.*

"Using Competency Profiles and Maps to determine what the individual coaching and development focus should be is excellent, but if the managers are not held accountable, all the way up the organizational chain, for closing the Profile-to-Map gaps of their employees, the process will break down. In some cases, it's because the sales managers don't have the core competencies themselves to do the coaching, nor to recognize the Primary Characteristics needed in new hires. In other instances, it's a time problem, or maybe a management style issue, where an individual is simply not a hands-on manager. *That's why vertical cascading of accountability is so crucial.*"

2. Management Competency—*I feel our biggest challenge here at St. George will be management competency, given what is required to be successful in today's marketplace.*

"Jim, you would be the best judge of that, but I suggest we develop Competency Maps for every level of sales management, to determine what kind of a developmental challenge is ahead of us."

"I agree, Bill, and would personally look forward to participating in such an effort. What else do you see as a critical quality that must be present?"

3. Clearly Stated Expectations—*If the field does not understand, operationally, what is expected of them by management, accountability falls apart.*

"It is very similar to something you said earlier, Danilo, when you were talking about behaviors complementing technology. With expectations and accountability in place, coaching and development effectiveness becomes a function of process. Incidentally, you'll note that I always say coaching and development. The reason for that is that a sales manager must compensate, in real time, for an identified competency weakness that a salesperson might have, so as to not compromise current sales efforts. In parallel, the manager must effect that same salesperson's development over time, not only to eliminate that weakness, but also to remain current with changing sales methodologies.

"The manager may employ formal training of a classroom or seminar type, do intensive personal coaching, team the salesperson up with others for hands-on On-the-Job Training (OJT), or even reassign accounts, but both pieces—coaching and development—ultimately must be addressed. The process consists of several components:

- Installing Sales Performance Metrics. Just as you described with Alexander Drugs, Mary, when you worked with them to develop an approach to measuring the impact of your Value Proposition. We need to develop metrics that measure the extent to which salespeople implement the Commodity, Solutions, Business Solutions, and Strategic sales methodologies—and how well.
- Installing Sales Management Metrics. Taking accountability north means having the ability to measure how well managers are coaching and developing their people. But, unlike the Sales Performance Metrics, which are top-down, these are three-hundred-sixty-degree tools, or loop-based, involving an assessment by the manager's subordinates, peers, and senior managers.

"In fact, Jim, just as you have defined four specific sales methodologies, you could also define the specific sales management responsibilities that relate to those methodologies. For example, reviewing and approving Value Statements or Propositions, participating in customer FOX hunting activities, or doing win/loss reviews, just to mention a few. Another component in the process is:

- Closing Competency Profile to Map Gaps. For the first time in St. George's history, we will be able to articulate what is required to be successful in a particular sales position, based upon value chain management. Closing those gaps as quickly as possible will be key and an area in which to focus our sales training efforts.

"There is a lot more I could say about performance management," Bill concluded, "but I believe you can see the direction that I'm proposing."

The meeting continued with discussion about what the measurement criteria might look like for both the salesforce and the sales managers, in order to configure the measurement metrics. Everyone felt good about the team's progress that day, even though it made them realize there was still a lot more work to be done on this.

They were optimistic, though, because they knew that soon they would be able to provide senior management with a blueprint for sales and marketing integration, complete with HR infrastructure and automation plans to support it. On that high note, they closed the meeting, agreeing to get together the following week.

What none of them knew, however, was that Dick was busy behind the scenes, building a cost reduction plan to assist Robert Tullis and the Board of Directors in dealing with the problem of St. George's stock, which had declined considerably since the competitor's big announcement. The Board had tasked the CEO and COO, in no uncertain terms, with finding a way to keep their earnings per share within an acceptable range.

Two days later, Robert asked to meet with Sally. "I know that you and the task force have made good progress in this area of value chain management, Sally, and I agree that it is key to our future, and could even fund itself. But I'm afraid that at the moment I must address what is key to our present, and in that respect, I have some bad news for you. In the interest of preserving margins, we are going to put all existing initiatives on hold, except R&D projects. I'm sorry, but that includes your task force project, at least for the time being. In addition, we're going to implement some other, very stringent cost-cutting measures. We'll task all departments with finding a way to cut costs by at least ten percent. At the same time, we are planning to beef up R&D. We are very close to several positive developments there that will positively impact our stock and our competitive position in the near term. Perhaps when the dust settles from all that, we will be able to consider reinstating the task force."

Tullis went over to his desk and picked up a folder, which he handed to Sally. "This is a copy of a draft plan that Dick has put together, addressing all the necessary actions. You know I respect your opinion Sally, and I'm sorry to have to disappoint you for the moment on this task force thing, but I would be interested in your views on that plan before I present it to the Board."

"Thank you, Robert. I can appreciate your position. Look, what about just scaling back the committee's operations? We have made so much progress that's beneficial to St. George, I'd hate to see it completely stalled, even briefly."

"Well, Sally, all I can say is, if you feel that strongly about it, and if you and Jim can pull enough cost out of marketing, in addition to the ten percent cut I just told you about, to offset what is required to keep the project going, I'll be happy to look at it again. But understand, I'm making no promises."

"I understand. Are you putting a freeze on hiring?"

"Absolutely, for the moment," he responded.

Sally could see that Robert Tullis was not happy about the actions that were being taken, but she was certain that in his mind, he had no choice. She was also sure that Dick Chainy had colored Robert's thinking. Otherwise, Robert would have signaled Sally about the cost reduction effort earlier, before it was an accomplished fact. Well, at least she had been given an opportunity to see the plan before it was formally announced.

The next day, Sally met with Jim, Bill, and Danilo. She briefed them on her meeting with Dr. Tullis, and gave them the bad news. She also provided each of them a copy of Dick's cost-reduction plan.

"This is a case of déjà vu, like going back in time," Jim commented, "when the microscope of commerce was trained on nothing but cost reduction."

"Well, that's true enough, but so is this," said Sally. "If we don't find a way around this, we can forget about St. George becoming a value-centric company, at least any time soon. I suggest you take the plan home and see what each of you can come up with in response to it," said Sally. "By the way, no one is aware that you have copies of the cost reduction plan. It's clearly a sensitive document, but Dr. Tullis did not ask me to keep it in confidence, so I'm comfortable giving you copies. However, if word of this gets out, it could significantly damage morale, so I'm counting on your confidence."

"You've got it. What about the next task force meeting? It's scheduled for early next week," Bill reminded her. "Should we cancel it?"

"No," said Sally. "We'll stay the course and go forward with the meeting, since nothing has been announced yet. I have to fly to Denver again tomorrow, but I should be back here in time for the meeting."

Working with Alexander and the task force was keeping Mary very busy, but she was looking forward to their next meeting. Bill had said he'd address the compensation aspect of their HR-to-sales alignment plan. That would be the final piece of the puzzle, and they would then be able to get started on building the complete integration blueprint to present to top management.

Mary was concerned about Sally, who was flying back and forth to Denver every other weekend, and seemed rather distracted lately. Her sister Judy was apparently doing better following her cancer surgery, but still needed Sally's help and encouragement. It was nice to see families that looked after one another, but Mary was worried about Sally and the toll this was taking on her.

I'll be glad when things settle down for her, and we get past this serious blip the competition's new drug has created and continue moving forward on the task force blueprint, she thought.

Value-Centric Compensation

Sally had not returned from Denver when the next meeting occurred. Apparently, her sister had developed some new and very serious complications, and Sally decided to take a two-week leave and remain in Denver. Everyone was disappointed that she could not attend, but fully understood. Bill began by addressing the final element of the human resources process, compensation.

"I won't talk about benefits," said Bill, "since those are company-standard, except for top management packages. Today we'll just look at the compensation aspect, since that relates directly to our goal of becoming more value-centric.

"As I see it, there are three principal components to the new compensation system we're proposing, all of which are performance-management driven."

1. Base Salary—*We're proposing that a salesperson's base pay be a function of the relationship between the individual's Competency Profile and the Competency Map for the person's position.*

"Now, I know that's very different from what we do currently, but it would enable us to compensate for value to St. George, not just follow industry norms. Incidentally, keep in mind that those norms will reflect yesterday's thinking and value chain levels, so we need to be careful with them. To achieve this goal of setting salary to value, we would establish three compensation bands, or salary ranges. The individual's Competency Profile would be quantified to create a point score, which could then be compared to the Map point score. Establishing three ranges, based upon whether the Profile score was below, met, or exceeded Map requirements, would indicate the appropriate salary ranges, which would then be compared to industry averages, particularly at the entry levels for new hires.

"In that way, if people we hire invest in themselves, developing their capabilities, and it is evident in observable behaviors, their base pay will increase on an annual basis.

"However, I will caution you that we'll have to develop a way to track our ranges carefully against industry averages, even if those do reflect traditional thinking. Understand that if our system is too innovative or complex for applicants to comprehend, or our base falls below industry average, we won't be able to attract applicants of the caliber we seek."

"What about existing salespeople whom the new system might overcompensate, as compared to the new base?" asked Jim.

"Good point, and I'm sure that will happen," said Bill. "We're thinking of giving everyone a twenty-four-month grace period to improve their Competency Profile and meet Map requirements, in order to maintain their current base salary. How does that resonate with you?"

"Sounds reasonable," said Jim. "Include it in the proposal, and we'll support it."

"Okay, will do," said Bill. "Now, the second principal component is:

2. Variable or Performance Compensation—*Today, our commission structure is based upon quota performance. In the future, I believe, it needs to be based upon both sales and how those sales were achieved, that is, the Sales Performance Metrics.*

"Jim, this will be your call, of course, but I would recommend you consider basing fifty percent of pay on quota attainment, and fifty percent on Performance Metrics. That means if a salesperson is not effectively implementing the appropriate sales methodologies, they put fifty percent of their commission at risk. It also means that the quota setting process needs to be a solid system to address several elements—exigencies of the market, a salesperson's performance potential, and improvement of our corporate position or share—not just an informal negotiation between salesperson and manager."

"Now, whatever gave you the idea we have an informal system, Bill?" asked Mary, smiling. "We do have a process. Jim takes everyone's sales quota from last year and increases it ten percent."

"Very funny," Jim replied, but he was smiling, too. "I'll admit there's certainly room for improvement in how we work that piece of our budget system, Bill. We'll definitely work on the quota setting piece to include the elements you just mentioned."

"Well, you're not alone, Jim, if that's any consolation," said Bill. "Most of corporate America is in the same boat, but that's because the value chain management concept is so new. Soon value-centric thinking will prevail everywhere, not because we are so smart, but because the market will demand it. Again, there is much more to be discussed here, but I think you can see how the compensation system can be integrated with competency work and sales methodology metrics.

"*That should enable us to draw a line from each sales-compensation dollar paid to the competencies, or skills and knowledge, required by specific Maps, to the sales methodologies being implemented, to sales realized by working effectively with customer buying patterns that reflect the customer's value chain.*"

"I challenge you to say that three times fast, Bill," said Danilo. "Anyway, believe it or not, I'm beginning to see how technology can overlay that progression, and help define it. What is the third component?"

3. Recognition—*The power of recognition is underestimated. Without it, value does little to advance a person's career.*

"When we design the new value-centric compensation system, I propose that we include an integrated recognition program, one that goes hand in hand with compensation. If the right people don't see the good work being done, the individual doing that work will never build the corporate associations critical to moving into the company's Power Base, not to mention the psychological importance and organizational productivity impact of recognizing good work. But, having said that, I will need input from all of you on how to approach it."

"I wholeheartedly agree with that idea, Bill," said Jim. "As a suggestion, let's all think about how we can implement that effectively, and bring our ideas back to the next meeting."

A Blueprint for Value Chain Management

The task force still had a long way to go, but even so, they had succeeded in operationally defining value chain management. Consistent with Sally's earlier thinking, they now had an integration blueprint that identified all the critical components that needed to work together in order to create a value-centric organization. After the meeting, Mary sketched out the Blueprint.

Her intent was to show, on one side of one piece of paper, the critical initiatives that were necessary to develop their Approach to Market, Front-end Structure, and Front-end Infrastructure. These initiatives move basically from left to right, graphically showing what would be required to create proper alignment, and from bottom to top, illustrating their relationship to the Approach to Market, Front-end Structure, and Front-end Infrastructure.

In this way, they created a diagram (Figure 10.2) or road map, that enabled them to see precisely what elements contributed to achieving alignment between customer, sales, marketing, human resources, and technology. It was a very simple block diagram, but

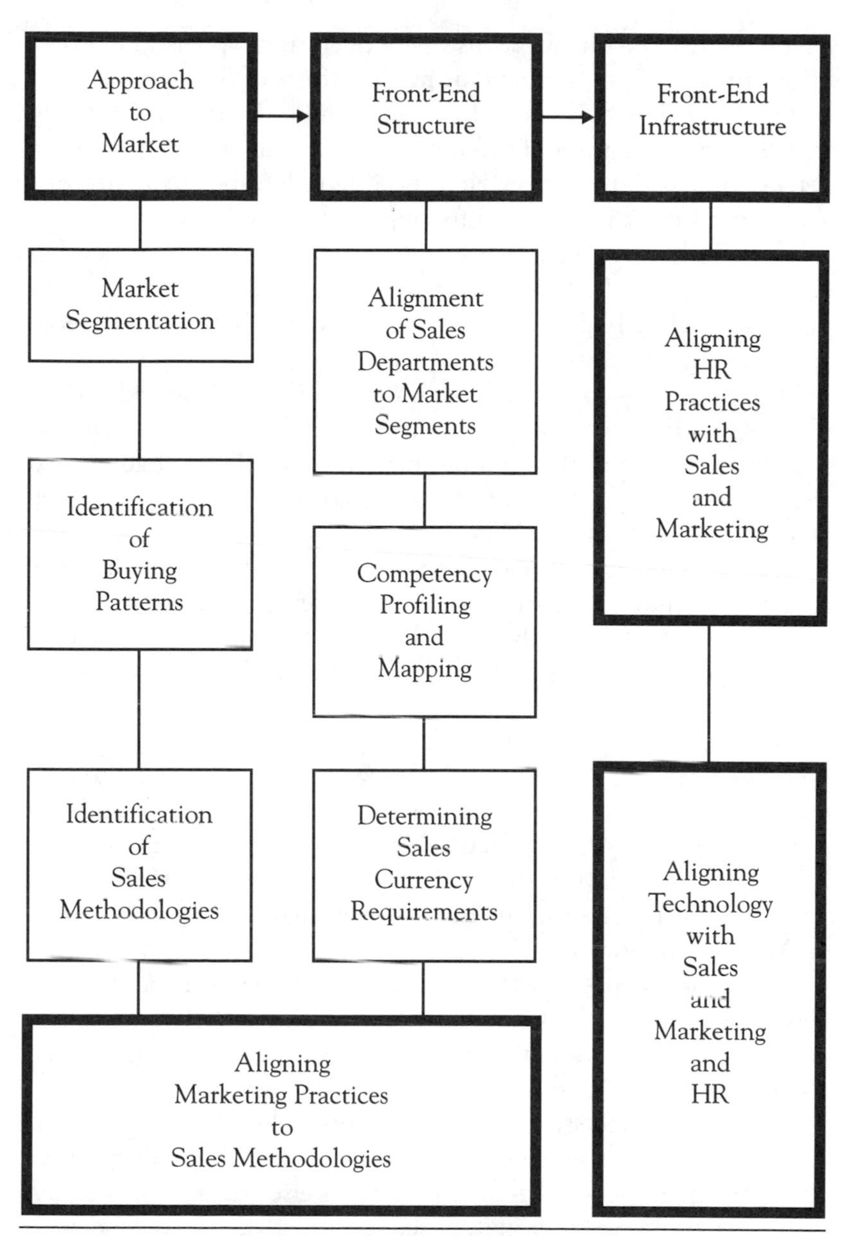

Figure 10.2 Value Chain Management Integration Blueprint.

effective in laying out the areas where operational plans would then be put in place, compartmentalizing the efforts of the task force.

The next day, Sally called Jim, Bill, and Danilo, individually, from Denver. She wanted to know if they'd come up with their ten percent reductions, and what they might be able to contribute above that from their budgets to support the task force.

They all had suggestions as to how they could save money, but even so, they could not come up with enough reductions to save the task force. They had decided not to tell Mary that it was in jeopardy, since they still had hopes of saving it.

However, Sally couldn't shake the feeling that Dick had not yet played his full hand. *How far will he go,* she wondered? Her calls to Robert had not shed any light on that, although Robert had made it clear to her that he intended to go ahead with the cost-reduction plan at St. George, so she'd better plan accordingly.

The timing couldn't have been worse for Sally. She hadn't told anyone, but Judy's condition was steadily deteriorating. After talking with the doctors, Sally knew she had no choice except to leave St. George and move to Denver, to oversee full-time care for her sister.

By the time she returned to Chicago, the cost-reduction measures had been announced at St. George, and Sally arrived to find everyone in a state of concern. She realized with a sinking heart that while they'd all been focused on preserving the task force and the work it was doing, they hadn't even stopped to think about what impact Tullis' cost-cutting and the hiring freeze might have on Mary's situation.

Now, Sally realized, with the task force project on hold, and a freeze on hiring in the field, Mary had no place to go to in the organization. Sally wouldn't be able to hire her into marketing, either. Mary's current position at St. George would simply evaporate.

Dick Chainy had struck them all a telling blow. Not only was the effort to empower the sales organization dead, he had taken out its chairperson. It clearly signaled to anyone else in the organization who might oppose him the consequences of doing so, and with Sally out of the picture to boot, no one could stand up for Mary to Robert Tullis, or anyone else for that matter.

In one of the most wrenching scenes they might ever contemplate, Sally and Jim called Mary in and gave her the bad news—not only that Sally was leaving St. George, effective immediately, but that Mary's position as head of the task force had also been eliminated by this latest move. She was given two weeks' notice.

"In the next two weeks, Jim will try to figure out some way to retain you at St. George," said Sally reassuringly. "But if he can't manage that, and there's anything we can do to help you in any way to find a new position, you know we're both behind you one hundred percent. As soon as I'm settled in with a new company in Denver, I'm going to see if there's a way to bring you on board there."

Throughout the following week, Mary stumbled through her days like the living dead. Twice, she passed Dick Chainy in the hallway, and he never even acknowledged her presence. Being treated as if she were invisible at her company after all those years was a painful blow to Mary's self esteem. Every time she passed Sally's empty office, despair welled up inside her. Everything had blown up in her face in the space of two days! What a macabre joke. She had seized the moment, and finally taken on the corporate political specter that had created so many casualties in her life. And like her father and Jo, she had lost everything because of it.

Deep down, Mary knew that she had done the right thing. Given another chance, she'd do it again. No one could have predicted all these terrible coincidences. Who could have known when they began the task force that the competition would launch a new product, or that Sally's sister would become seriously ill, or that Dr. Tullis would impose a hiring freeze on the whole company? Those were the imponderables of business and life that couldn't be anticipated.

Jim, Bill, and Danilo were very sympathetic to Mary, but they were thrown into survival mode themselves. They had families, and they had to be careful now, with Dick wielding so much power. He might as well have displayed Mary's head on a pike at the corporate entrance, as his personal trophy.

In the days that followed, Mary needed a lot of support, but with the exception of Jo, Jim, Danilo, Sally, and a few other friends, little was forthcoming. She was amazed at how easily and quickly her colleagues had written her off. The thought of having become a supernumerary brought about a sick feeling, one that seemed to get worse with each passing day.

One night, early in her final week, trying to get a grip, she began to toy with the idea of moving to New York and looking for a sales position there. She picked up the phone and dialed Jo.

"Hello Jo, it's me again. Hope I'm not bothering you, I just needed to talk to someone."

"Please, don't be bashful about calling. I'm always here for you, Mary."

"Thanks, Jo, I know that. It's just that, well, I know you have your own problems and I'm afraid I haven't been much help to you."

"Never mind that, we will both get through this. Only God knows why all this has happened to us, but I haven't lost faith in Him."

"You think He has a purpose in this for us?"

"Without doubt. We'll understand it eventually. You know, at times like this, when I find myself under heavy duress, I always think about my father. When something bad happened to us, he would quote Romans 5:3–4. ' . . . *suffering produces perseverance; perseverance, character; and character, hope.*' And you know, the connection between character and hope is not a speculative one. Think of character as personal currency, providing you good reason for hope. Somehow, Mary, we're going to come out ahead from all this, and be stronger people for having experienced it. Now tell me, have you made any plans yet?"

"Thanks for sharing that quotation with me, Jo, and for giving me such encouragement. You don't know what it means to me right now. In fact, my future plans are why I called you. What do you think about me coming to New York and looking for a sales position there? With all that's happened, I feel I need more than a career change—maybe I just need to get out of Chicago, away from all this."

"I think coming to New York is a wonderful idea! I'll help you set up interviews and anything else you need. Plan to stay with me. My apartment is plenty big enough, and I can't think of a better roommate—it will be like our old days together at school in Chicago."

After talking to Jo, Mary's morale rose considerably. She felt she had a new direction, and the opportunity to be near her friend Jo again was the first good thing that had happened to her since this awful mess began. *Could it have been only a week ago?* Mary felt like she'd lived a month since Sally and Jim told her that her career at St. George was over.

She was packing her office belongings the next day when she received notice that there would be an announcement later in the day to all St. George employees, by Robert Tullis himself. That was unusual. Mary continued working on her office, and had just about loaded the last box into her car, when she realized it was time for Dr. Tullis to speak. Even though she was technically no longer a St. George employee, she decided to attend, more out of curiosity than anything else.

The background buzz of speculation was almost deafening as Mary walked into the company auditorium. No one really knew what to expect. Then Dr. Tullis came out, cleared his throat, and without preamble, began his announcement.

"I am here today to inform you that St. George Pharmaceuticals has signed an agreement to be acquired by Consolidated Hospitals. As some of you already know, Consolidated has been aggressively acquiring companies to build a continuum of care, diversifying into every major area of the health care market. Consolidated will soon be our new parent company, enabling us to broaden our market focus in ways not otherwise possible. St. George will continue its operations as a stand-alone company, and no major changes in day-to-day operations, or substantial staff reductions, are anticipated.

"I'd like now to introduce the man who will be in charge of the transition team for St. George: Mr. Bill Stensland, senior vice president at what will soon be known as Consolidated Health Care."

Mary sat in shock, watching her friend Bill Stensland step to the microphone. *Did I hear right,* she thought? *Is this possible?*

Two days later, Mary was seated in Dr. Tullis's office, trying not to look as stupefied as she felt. She didn't even have an office any more, and here she was, meeting with the CEO of the company. Then Bill Stensland came in.

"Mary, I asked Robert to invite you here today because I wanted to speak to you personally. I know what has happened to the task force you were heading up, and I am sure you also understand now what the circumstances were that unfortunately eliminated your position at St. George. However, Dr. Tullis and I are prepared to immediately rectify that. I know you are upset over what happened to you, but I hope you will be patient and hear me out on what we propose to do."

"Certainly I will, Bill, but I guess I need to know first, does this proposal concern giving me a job here at St. George again?"

"Yes. You still have a fine career ahead of you here, if you'll stay with us."

Bill then reviewed for Robert Tullis his view of the sales situation that Mary was engaged in at Consolidated before they acquired her competitor. He spoke with admiration about her professionalism, integrity, and commitment to deliver value. Mary listened, taking everything in. Inside she didn't know how she felt, or what to believe. Her whole internal value system had been shaken, and restructured, in the past couple of months. *What is going on here?* Then their words began to sink in.

"We are reinstating you as an employee of St. George, Mary," said Dr. Tullis, "effective immediately. In fact, I am pleased to offer you Sally's former position, as director of marketing. I think you'll be happy to know that your first order of business will be to crank that task force back up."

Mary sat silent for a moment. Then she said, slowly, "I don't know, Dr. Tullis, a great deal has happened to me, to all of us, very quickly, as I'm sure you're aware. So it's difficult to absorb it all, and give an immediate answer." She took a deep breath, and looked straight at both of them. "I appreciate your consideration of me, and certainly the promotion to director of marketing is appealing, to say the least. But I do have some concerns about returning to St. George, and one is that there might be strong upper-management resistance to the committee's ideas for restructuring in some areas. So I'm not sure I'd want to continue with it."

"Well, you certainly get to the point, Mary," smiled Dr. Tullis, "but that's one of the things I like about you. Incidentally, have you heard that Dick Chainy has decided to retire? No of course you wouldn't have, it hasn't been announced yet."

Hearing that, Mary felt a wave of relief, and began to reconsider her situation.

"That does put things in a different light for me, of course," said Mary candidly. "Um . . . what about Jim Watkins? Will he be staying with St. George?"

"You mean the Jim Watkins who has agreed to replace Dick Chainy as chief operations officer at St. George? Yes. Mark Avery will move into Jim's old position as vice president of sales."

Bill Stensland stepped in to add something he felt would help secure Mary's decision to return to St. George as marketing director.

"Becoming value-centric, to use your phrase, is why this acquisition is taking place, Mary," Bill explained. "When your work with the task force is completed at St. George, we will want to roll out the initiative across all our companies."

"Does that mean you intend to make more acquisitions, Bill?"

"Well, we're certainly looking in all directions." Her question puzzled him. "Why do you ask?"

"I have a good friend in New York, Josephine Stiller, who is an expert at corporate acquisitions. She handled a lot of them for Newman International Banking, and is looking for a new position. Just wondering if you might need some additional talent at Consolidated, perhaps taking value chain management into account in the identification and valuation of companies. . . . "

"That's a good thought. Ask her to contact me," said Bill. "We're always on the lookout for talented people. And speaking of that, can we discuss your new position at St. George, and answer any lingering questions you might have?"

Fifteen minutes later, they had covered a lot of ground. Not only was Mary on the threshold of making her decision to move into Sally's director of marketing position at St. George, she had lined up a meeting between Jo Stiller and Bill Stensland for next week. Bill said that Consolidated could probably use someone with Jo's skills at their new corporate headquarters in New York.

Overwhelmed, Mary broke out in a huge smile. "I accept," she said. "Even before I see the package. I trust you, Bill. And you, too, Dr. Tullis."

As she stood to shake hands with both men, Mary felt that this was one of the happiest days of her life, and not just because her career had been saved, and the dark side of politics—the specter—defeated. Today a lot of her doubts had been resolved. What had happened today meant that for her, and for her father, and everyone else who believed in doing things the right way, for the good of the company and of people in general, there could be reward and recognition. And that meant there was still a lot of integrity, and good, in the corporate world.

Also, it never hurts to have a FOX or two on your side, she reminded herself. She couldn't wait to call Sally in Denver tonight, give her the good news, and thank her for what must have been a very strong recommendation to both Tullis and Stensland.

She was also anxious to share this wonderful news with her son and daughter. Arlene would be ecstatic that she wouldn't have to move and leave her friends, and Harry would be happy to know he didn't have to quit school and get a job.

And then she'd call Jo. With Consolidated Health Care so heavily into acquisitions these days, and Mary's knowledge of Bill, she knew he and Jo would have a good meeting. Once again, her life and Jo's might track together, as friends and professional colleagues.

Back home again, Mary got out her calendar and circled today's date. A defining moment, she wanted to highlight it, remember it as the day that everything good had coalesced in her life. A new career door had been opened for her, too. Her company was now ready to make the necessary changes to become a value-centric organization—an industry leader in the concept of value chain management.

This book is dedicated to a very special person.
In loving memory of my mother, Mary Gagan Holden.

ABOUT THE AUTHOR

Jim Holden's background includes more than two decades of experience as a sales executive and as a consultant on sales methodology and practices for major corporations.

A 1972 graduate of Northeastern University in Boston, Jim received his Bachelor's Degree of Electrical Engineering (BSEE) *cum laude*, and was also honored with membership in Phi Kappa Phi, the National Interdisciplinary Honor Society, and Tau Beta Pi, the National Engineering Honor Society. He began his sales career in 1974 as assistant to the vice president of sales at Teradyne, a Boston based high technology company. He then moved into a position as senior sales engineer for Teradyne, working in the Chicago area. By 1977, he was vice president of sales at Aegis, an independent rep firm in Chicago.

It was at about that time that Holden began to intellectualize the selling process, particularly its informal political dimension, something that has been a mystery to most sales professionals for more than half a century.

In 1979, he struck out on his own and founded Holden Corporation, now an internationally recognized leader in the field of sales effectiveness, focusing on the development and integration of sales, marketing, and human resources within the global high technology marketplace, as well as in other industries. By 1990, Holden Corporation had established itself as the first company to model sales effectiveness with their four stage approach, and his success as an entrepreneur was recognized that year by Ernst & Young, Merrill Lynch, and *Inc*. magazine with the award of the Regional Entrepreneur of the Year for the Service Industry. That same year, Jim published what has become a definitive work on how to engage and defeat competition, recognizing the informal political structure of a company, and utilizing that knowledge to achieve success and higher sales margins: *Power Base Selling: Secrets of an Ivy League Street Fighter* (John Wiley & Sons, New York), a work that is still in print. He also has authored numerous articles on all aspects of sales and marketing.

He was a founder of the First National Bank of Roselle, where he chaired the Marketing Committee, and is currently a director of Harris Bank, Elk Grove, Illinois, in addition to several other high tech, early development-stage companies.

An avid sportsman and climber, Jim has scaled Mount Kilimanjaro in Africa and Mount Rainier in Washington on several occasions.

Jim and his wife Chris currently reside in the greater Chicago area, where they are active in their community as well as their business interests. The Holdens were founders of the Partnership to End Homelessness in Chicago, a program developed with the Community Emergency Shelter Organization. They are also patrons of the Chicago Zoo and other charities. Jim is also a founder of the Fitness Ministry at Willow Creek Community Church.

For more information, contact:

Holden Corporation
2800 W. Higgins Rd., Suite 235
Hoffman Estates, IL 60195
Tel: (847) 310-9294
Fax: (847) 310-9962
Web site: www.holdencorp.com

efox.com
2500 W. Higgins Rd., Suite 715
Hoffman Estates, IL 60195
Tel: (847) 755-9713
Fax: (847) 755-9716
Web site: www.efox.com

Index